CHICAGO PUBLIC LIBRARY

CHICAGO PUBLIC LIBRARY
WOODSON REGIONAL
9525 S. HALSTED ST   60628

FORM 19

CHICAGO PUBLIC LIBRARY
WOODSON REGIONAL
9525 S. HALSTED ST   60628

BENJAMIN H. HILL
SECESSION AND
RECONSTRUCTION

BENJAMIN H. HILL

SECESSION AND RECONSTRUCTION

HAYWOOD J. PEARCE, JR., PH.D.
Professor of History, Brenau College

NEGRO UNIVERSITIES PRESS
NEW YORK

Originally published in 1928
by the University of Chicago Press

Reprinted from a copy in the collections
of the Brooklyn Public Library

Reprinted 1969 by
Negro Universities Press
A DIVISION OF GREENWOOD PRESS, INC.
NEW YORK

SBN 8371-2727-0

PRINTED IN UNITED STATES OF AMERICA

TO MY FATHER
WHOSE GENEROSITY
MADE THIS STUDY POSSIBLE

PREFACE

The life and work of Benjamin Harvey Hill in secession and reconstruction has never been the subject of a critical study. Indeed, the only life of Hill is the admittedly slender sketch of the father by the son, Benjamin Harvey Hill, Jr., published in 1891. This sketch possesses the limitations which always attach to such filial works. Alexander Stephens, Robert Toombs, Howell Cobb, Joseph E. Brown, even Linton Stephens, have been the subject of biographies of more or less merit. The purpose of this study is to supply the deficiency in the case of Hill, who, in the opinion of many, was quite as significant a force in Georgia, the South, and the nation as any of the others named.

Some manuscript has been used, but the chief sources employed in the study have been the printed speeches, letters, and writings of Hill; the published letters of his contemporaries from a variety of sources, chiefly the press of the day and from Professor Phillips' collection of the *Correspondence of Toombs, Stephens and Cobb;* and official documents, state and national, where they bore on the work of Hill. In addition, certain local Georgia studies, biographies, and memoirs of prominent characters of the period, state and national, and standard secondary histories of a broader scope, have been consulted. Fortunately Hill was a prolific writer of public letters and addresses, most of which are preserved in the files of old newspapers. These have been sought out.

I am indebted to many persons for invaluable assistance in prosecuting my investigations. I desire to acknowledge personal indebtedness to Mrs. Caroline Holt McConnell, of Lithonia, Georgia, the granddaughter of Hill, for access to private material and for generous co-operation; to Miss Sallie Eugenia Brown, of Atlanta, the daughter of Georgia's Civil War governor, for access to the very remarkable and voluminous *Brown Scrap Books* and for many other courtesies; to Mr. Wymberly De Renne, of Wormsloe, near Savannah, for access to the Davis manuscript in his remarkable private library; to Judge Eve, the ordinary of Richmond County, Augusta, for assistance in using the valuable files of the Augusta papers which are preserved, complete, in his office; to Mr. James Gilbert, of Columbus, Georgia, for the use of his complete files of the Columbus papers in the offices of the Gilbert Printing Company; to the editors of the *Savannah Morning News* for use of their files; to Mr. Sam Small, the genial and veteran newspaper writer of Atlanta and Washington, and the former private secretary of Hill, for advice and counsel; to Mr. H. H. Cabaniss of the *Atlanta Journal,* to ex-Senator Hoke Smith, and to Judge George Hillyer, all of Atlanta, for valuable suggestions; and, finally, to Professor Ulrich B. Phillips, of the University of Michigan, for kind suggestions by letter, and to the writer's teacher, Professor William E. Dodd, of the University of Chicago.

HAYWOOD J. PEARCE, JR.

GAINESVILLE, GEORGIA
JUNE, 1928

TABLE OF CONTENTS

CHAPTER	PAGE
I. Hill's Entrance into Political Life	1
II. The Fillmore-Buchanan Canvass	12
III. Gubernatorial Race against Joe Brown	22
IV. Secession	32
V. Champion of the Davis Administration	55
VI. Reluctant Surrender	86
VII. Coming of Congressional Reconstruction	113
VIII. The Fight against the Reconstruction Acts	142
IX. Continued Resistance—The Greeley Campaign	172
X. Hill's Change of 1870	201
XI. The State-Road Lease and the Delano Banquet	216
XII. Political Proscription	239
XIII. In the House—Southern Champion	265
XIV. Conclusions	301
Bibliography	310
Index	319

CHAPTER I

HILL'S ENTRANCE INTO POLITICAL LIFE

Benjamin Harvey Hill, popularly known in Georgia as "Ben Hill," entered public life in 1851 at the age of twenty-eight when the state and nation were but recently committed to the great compromise measures designed to end sectional agitation on the slave question. In fact, a desire to secure the perpetuity of this settlement moved Hill to accept an unsolicited election to the lower house of the Georgia general assembly in 1851.[1] At this time Hill began a lifetime of devotion to the twin objects of his affections, the Constitution of 1787, and the union of the American States—a lifetime, however, which was destined to be prematurely cut off in 1882 at the age of fifty-nine. Its close found him a nationally known figure representing the state of Georgia in the United States Senate.

When Hill entered public life, the acute phase of sectional hostility, bred of the Mexican War and its legacies, had just ended. The Compromise Measures of 1850, popularly ascribed to Clay, had been adopted in Congress. In December of 1850 the people of Georgia, in constitutional convention at Milledgeville, had adopted a series of resolutions which came to be known as the "Georgia Platform."[2]

[1] B. H. Hill, Jr., *Senator Benjamin H. Hill, His Life, Speeches and Writings*, p. 17. (Referred to hereafter as "Hill, *Life of Hill*.")

[2] *Journal of the State Convention of December, 1850*, pp. 18-19. The resolutions are also given in R. M. Johnson and W. H. Browne, *Life of A. H. Stephens*, p. 259.

BENJAMIN H. HILL

The Georgia Platform set forth, in substance, that the state of Georgia, while not approving unreservedly the Compromise Measures, was yet willing to accept the settlement as a basis for remaining in the Union, but that in the event of any further encroachment by the federal power upon her reserved rights as a state, Georgia would consult her own interests. The plain implication was that secession would follow further "encroachment."

It is generally conceded that Georgia's acceptance of the Compromise Measures, represented in the Georgia Platform, put an end, for the time, to disunion and resistance talk in the south.[3] Within the state the Georgia Platform occasioned a new party alignment. The compromise settlement had been favored by practically all the Georgia Whigs, and by a large portion of the Democrats, especially in the northern counties, accustomed to follow Howell Cobb, who, burying past political animosities, had labored tirelessly with Toombs and Alexander Stephens to effect the settlement.[4]

The Platform adopted, the Cobb-Toombs-Stephens following, representing a fusion of Democrats with the main body of the Whigs, proposed to maintain the fruits of the Union victory by constituting themselves into a new political party, which they denominated the "Constitutional Union party."[5] This party, calling on all the friends

[3] U. B. Phillips, *Georgia and State Rights*, p. 165. Phillips also quotes Von Holst, *Constitutional History of the United States*, IV, 6, to the same effect.

[4] Phillips, *op. cit.*, pp. 165–66.

[5] *Milledgeville Federal Union*, January 21, 1851; also Phillips (ed.), *Toombs, Stephens, Cobb Correspondence, American Historical Association Report, 1911*, II, 221 n. (referred to hereafter as *"Toombs, Stephens, Cobb Correspondence"*).

of the Union for adherence, entered the gubernatorial canvass of 1851 with Howell Cobb for standard-bearer and with the Georgia Platform as its enunciation of principle. Against this ticket the irreconcilables of the state, calling themselves the "Southern Rights party," and composed largely of former Democrats, ran ex-Governor McDonald, a former colleague of Cobb. The result gave a decided majority to Cobb and Union sentiment.[6]

Hill had accepted election to the Georgia general assembly when the outcome of the Cobb-McDonald gubernatorial struggle was still in doubt. He was warm in his advocacy of the compromise settlement. He had been appointed a member of the Executive Committee of the new Constitutional Union party.[7] He entered the General Assembly in November, 1851, determined to labor in the interest of peace between the sections.

Hill, though young and virtually an unknown figure in state politics at this time, immediately assumed a leading rôle in the General Assembly in the session of 1851–52. His reputation as a lawyer had preceded him, and he was forthwith appointed to two of the most important house committees, the Judiciary Committee and the Committee on Public Education.[8]

Following the success of Cobb and Union sentiment in the state, and the acceptance by both parties in the nation of the Compromise Measures, the session of the Georgia

[6] Phillips, *Georgia and State Rights,* p. 166; Herbert Fielder, *Life and Times of Joseph E. Brown,* p. 73.

[7] Phillips (ed.), *Toombs, Stephens, Cobb Correspondence,* letter of John B. Lamar to Howell Cobb, p. 316.

[8] *House Journal,* 1851–52, p. 57.

Assembly in the winter of 1851–52 was fairly quiet. About the only subject of more than local interest that came up was a bill "to prohibit the importation or introduction hereafter of any negro slave or slaves into this state for the purpose of hire, sale or traffic."[9] This bill was introduced on the second day of the session, November 6, 1851, and engrossed a good part of the attention of the Assembly from that date to its final passage by the house in an amended form on January 19, 1852. Hill had presented the bill as it came out of the Judiciary Committee of the house on November 20, 1851, and led the two months' fight to its successful passage.[10]

At the conclusion of his first and only term in the lower house of the General Assembly, thinking that the sectional agitation in the nation was definitely ended by the Compromise Measures, and having a large and lucrative law practice in his own section of the state, which required his attention, Hill declined to stand for re-election, and retired to private life.[11]

In the meanwhile the party alignments in Georgia were shifting again. The essential incompatibility of the Whig and Democratic wings of the short-lived Constitutional Union party in Georgia had manifested itself. In August, 1852, the Executive Committee of the newly formed party decided to disband the organization. This decision was

[9] *Ibid.*, p. 8.

[10] *Ibid.*, p. 298. The bill finally passed the house 82–29. The *House Journal* (pp. 8–298) abounds in references to the various stages and votes on the bill. The Act as passed is found in *Georgia Laws*, 1851–52, No. 163, pp. 263–67.

[11] *House Journal*, 1851–52, p. 17.

ENTRANCE INTO POLITICAL LIFE

announced in a public address from Macon, advancing various reasons for the action, none of which seem very plausible.[12]

In the gubernatorial election of 1853 most of the Whigs, following the lead of Toombs and Stephens, split from the Cobb wing, which dropped back into the old Democratic organization. The Whig group calling themselves the "Union party" put a state ticket in the field, headed by Charles J. Jenkins; but the Democratic candidate, Hershel V. Johnson, defeated by Cobb in 1851, was elected by a safe majority.[13]

In Georgia, then, the two old parties faced each other in 1854, when the Kansas-Nebraska debate precipitated the final stage of the irreconcilable sectional struggle. Neither of the parties, it is true, was in a normal or healthy condition. The Democratic party had been but recently divided against itself within the state. The Whigs had been alarmed since 1848 at the course of their northern brethren on the slavery question. From a national view the great Whig party had steadily disintegrated since the Mexican War; but the southern Whigs clung to the name, and yet looked for, or pretended to look for, relief and support from the northern wing of the party. Such an expectancy or pretended expectancy, however, had not prevented the Georgia Whigs, led by Toombs and Stephens, from bolting the Scott ticket in 1852 and from voting for the deceased

[12] These reasons are recounted in a letter from John B. Lamar to Howell Cobb from Macon, Georgia, August 10, 1852. See Phillips (ed.), *Toombs, Stephens, Cobb Correspondence*, p. 316. Ben Hill was a member of this Executive Committee.

[13] Fielder, p. 78; Phillips, *Georgia and State Rights*, pp. 168–69.

Daniel Webster on a sort of Georgia Independent Whig ticket.[14] This election of 1852 marked the final stand of Georgia Whiggery in a presidential contest—or, for that matter, the final independent stand of the National Whig party.[15]

With the convulsion of 1854 the Whig party in Georgia abandoned its name and national organization; the bulk of its membership followed Toombs and Stephens into the Democratic party; a minority of the party, conspicuous among whom was Hill, assumed a rather impotent rôle as the opposition party within the state, at times known as "Know-Nothings," again as "Americans," and finally in 1860 followed Bell and Everett under the revived name of "Constitutional Unionists," in the futile endeavor to prevent the sectional parties from wrecking the Union.

However, in 1852 when Hill retired from the Georgia Assembly, this series of events, the imminent break-up of the Whig party, the sectionalization of the Democratic party, and the birth of the Republican party, was not anticipated by any except extremists, North and South. Men were rejoicing at "the business man's peace" which had set in with the election of Franklin Pierce. It is now known that these years were but the proverbial calm before the storm. In the repeated assurances of individuals, of national parties, of state legislatures, and Congressional resolutions, that the Compromise was indeed final, the impression is somehow derived that men were whistling to keep up their courage. They did protest too much. And Frank-

---

[14] Johnson and Browne, p. 268; Phillips, *Georgia and State Rights*, p. 168; Pleasant A. Stovall, *Robert Toombs*, pp. 100 ff.

[15] J. F. Rhodes, *History of the United States*, I, 285.

ENTRANCE INTO POLITICAL LIFE

lin Pierce had been inaugurated scarcely fifty days when he "was closeted with Stephen A. Douglas, Chairman of the Senate Committee on Territories, and some other members of Congress in lending the executive approval to a measure which was destined not only to disturb the country's repose but to head it straight toward civil war."[16]

Hill always asserted that the repeal of the Missouri Compromise, as embodied in the Kansas-Nebraska Act of 1854, drew him into public life. "The repeal of the Missouri Compromise fell on my ears like a fire ball [sic] at night and called me into politics. From that day to this [1868] I have been fighting the progress of the revolution then clearly begun."[17]

Hill affected to see in the passage of the Kansas-Nebraska Act through a coalition of Douglas supporters and the southern congressmen, Democratic and Whig, an act of bad faith, a mere "reopening of sectional agitation."[18] "Take care my fellow citizens," he writes, "that in endeavoring to carry slavery where nature's laws prohibit its entrance, and where your solemn faith is pledged it shall not go, you do not lose the right to hold slaves at all."[19]

The nature of this study does not seem to call for a discussion of the fateful Kansas-Nebraska Act; the incidents of its passage are common knowledge. Suffice it to

[16] D. S. Muzzey, *The United States of America*, I, 483.

[17] From letter to *New York Herald*, October 8, 1868, in the *Brown Scrap Books*. Hill evidently means bell for "ball," and doubtless has in mind the well-known remark attributed to Jefferson that the Missouri Compromise debate fell on his ears like an "alarum bell in the night."

[18] *Columbus Sun*, February 25, 1856.

[19] Hill, *Life of Hill*, p. 18.

say that the fateful legislation brought an end to the peace which had precariously sat upon the land since the Compromise Measures of 1850. The train of events leading from the passage of the Act in 1854 to the secession of South Carolina in 1860 is one of the most clearly established sequences in American history, if it is not one of the best understood.

Georgia and the South acclaimed the Act and Douglas, its manipulator, with enthusiasm, though there were a few skeptics.[20] In the debates over the legislation Toombs and Stephens, coming to despair of aid from the northern Whigs, made their long deferred decision to cast in their lot with the Democratic party, which they had vigorously, and not always considerately, fought for more than a decade. They took the majority of Georgia Whigs with them.[21]

Hill did not approve the Kansas-Nebraska legislation and could not, therefore, go into the Georgia Democratic party. In this situation he found himself forced into a fellowship which was not entirely congenial, but which he could not avoid unless he should act independent of all parties. A fragment of the old Whig party with a miscellany of other elements was becoming articulate in Georgia about the time of the passage of the Kansas-Nebraska Act. This was the strange political phenomenon of Know-Nothingism, or Americanism. The movement was short lived and almost amorphous. Religious proscription, racial prejudice, especially against foreigners, a hankering after secret

[20] A. H. Stephens, *Constitutional View of the War Between the States*, II, 254–58; Phillips, *Georgia and State Rights*, p. 173.

[21] I. W. Avery, *History of Georgia*, p. 25; Johnson and Browne, pp. 276–77; Phillips, *Georgia and State Rights*, pp. 172–78.

ENTRANCE INTO POLITICAL LIFE

and fantastic ritualism, in varying proportion, made up the appeal of this semipolitical party. In Georgia any opponent of the Democratic party was forced into affiliation, more or less intimate, with this group.[22]

Hill is usually accounted a Know-Nothing, or American, from 1854 to 1860, and it is true he derived the large part of his support from this party during these years. He was, however, opposed to the ritualistic and secret features of the party, and especially to the religious proscription which it advocated.[23] He therefore declined a nomination of the party for Congress in 1855 and presented himself as an independent candidate before the people of the Fourth District against Judge Warner, the regular Democratic nominee.[24] He made the canvass on the single issue of opposition to the continued agitation of the slavery question and the desirability of the maintenance of the Union. Slavery he regarded, then and later, as secondary in importance to the preservation of the Union. The Fourth District, in which Hill lived, had always given a substantial Democratic majority; and Hill drew state-wide attention when he cut the Democratic majority of Judge Warner down to twenty-four votes.[25]

It was during the congressional race against Judge Warner that Hill gained the sobriquet "Our Ben" which

[22] For the rise and spread of the Know-Nothing movement in the nation, see Rhodes, II, 6–13. For the activity of the party in Georgia, 1854–55, see Avery, pp. 26–27; Fielder, pp. 79–80; Stovall, pp. 121–28; Phillips, *Georgia and State Rights*, pp. 178–79.

[23] Hill, *Life of Hill*, p. 18.

[24] *Ibid.*

[25] *Ibid.*

followed him, among his supporters, throughout his life. The late Senator A. O. Bacon of Georgia, then a young lawyer and aspiring politician, gives the circumstances of the christening:

> A big American rally was held at Newnan, Georgia. There was a great crowd assembled to hear Mr. Hill speak. One of the spectators drew a cartoon which was mounted on white linen and hung from a pole. It represented a big Shanghai rooster all tattered and torn and overthrown, while a trimmed Georgia game cock fluttered over him in triumph. The Shanghai represented Judge Warner while the native game cock represented Mr. Hill. Underneath the picture were these lines:
>
> When Shanghais meet our native birds, they are sure to get a licking
> Old Hiram Shanghai tried Our Ben and there he lies a kicking.[26]

This was Hill's first experience on the hustings where he was later to gain so much fame. Heretofore known only as a brilliant young lawyer, his eloquence in conducting his congressional campaign brought him recognition as one of the most powerful orators in the state. "The admiration of his party for him arose almost to idolatry," says the Georgia historian Fielder.[27]

Hill's influence with the Know-Nothing, or American, party in the state was now great. Although deprecating certain features of the party, he was left no choice. He attended the Georgia State Convention of the American party in Milledgeville in December, 1855, and took a prominent part in its deliberations.[28] He was selected by the Convention to represent the Fourth District of Georgia as

---

[26] *Ibid.*, p. 18.

[27] Fielder, p. 81.

[28] *Milledgeville Federal Union*, December 25, 1855.

a delegate to the National Convention of the party to meet in Philadelphia in 1856.[29]

It was probably Hill's influence which caused the Georgia State Council of the American party to abolish secrecy in connection with the party. In April, 1856, this Council in Macon passed resolutions abolishing all obligations of secrecy and recommending an open organization to the National party.[30] Hill now entered enthusiastically into the work of the party and soon made two state-wide campaigns under its banner.

[29] *Columbus Sun*, December 24, 1855. This was the convention which nominated Fillmore, for whom Hill made an active canvass, as will appear in the text. I have not been able to ascertain whether Hill went to the convention.

[30] *Columbus Sun*, April 24, 1856.

CHAPTER II
THE FILLMORE-BUCHANAN CANVASS

Before 1856 Hill had never appeared in a state-wide political contest. The mass of the Georgia people had had no knowledge of his somewhat local activity within the Fourth Congressional District or within the councils of the American party. It was in the presidential contest of 1856 that he became an outstanding figure in state politics and dared to beard the redoubtable Toombs and Stephens in their own strongholds. At this time Hill was only thirty-three years of age and had never held political office except the one term in the lower house of the General Assembly, while Toombs and Stephens had represented Georgia in Congress for more than a decade and were the unchallenged political dictators for a large following in the state.[1]

On February 22, 1856, in Philadelphia the American party had nominated ex-President Millard Fillmore and announced a platform.[2] Besides a generous sprinkling of pious platitudes about the nature and duties of government, the platform condemned "the present reckless administration" (that of Pierce), advocated the complete separation of Church and State, opposed the enfranchisement of foreigners until after twenty-one years' residence in this country, reasserted the inviolability of the "reserved

---

[1] Stovall, pp. 144-45.

[2] *Columbus Sun*, February 25, 1856. The platform was widely published in the state press.

rights" of the states, condemned the "reopening of sectional agitation by the repeal of the Missouri Compromise," and attacked the "vacillating course" of the Pierce administration on the Kansas question.

In Georgia the party centered its attack on the Kansas-Nebraska Act and its implications. Resolutions adopted at an American mass meeting in Columbus on July 20, 1856, embody the pith of the American contentions as echoed by Hill and others over the state. After indorsing the previous record of Fillmore, the resolutions proceed:

> Repudiating any responsibility for the squatter sovereignty and Alien Suffrage heresies that have received the sanction of the present administration and been approved by the candidates and platforms of our opponents, we adhere to the principles of the Utah and New Mexico territorial bills, approved by President Fillmore, as establishing and embodying the true Territorial policy of the government. By those acts the principles of the Missouri Compromise were first repudiated, the odious Wilmot proviso defeated, and the government returned to the constitutional doctrine of non-intervention. . . . .
>
> We deprecate further sectional agitation whether by attacks upon the Compromise Acts of 1850 at the south, or by a crusade at the north for the admission of Kansas with the Bogus Topeka Constitution, or for the restoration of the Missouri Compromise line.

The resolutions conclude with an endorsement of Fillmore as the candidate upon whom truly conservative and national men may unite.[3]

In early July, Hill was nominated as elector on the Fillmore ticket by the American State Convention at Macon; and on July 20 he addressed an American Fillmore ratification meeting in Columbus.[4] From this time until the election in November he strenuously canvassed the state in the interest of Fillmore.

[3] *Ibid.*, July 23, 1856.   [4] *Ibid.*, July 10, 1856.

BENJAMIN H. HILL

The Democratic party had nominated Buchanan and approved the Kansas-Nebraska Act in the Cincinnati Convention in June.[5] The Georgia Democracy ratified this action, and the resultant contest between Fillmore and Buchanan was a heated one.[6]

Hill bore the brunt of the campaigning for Fillmore; and his activity led him into collision with Toombs, Alexander Stephens, and the latter's talented, if less well-known brother, Linton Stephens.[7] The Fillmore strength in the South gave the Democrats much concern. Buchanan wrote to Howell Cobb on July 22, 1856: "I think we have more to apprehend from Fillmore in the south than any other cause."[8] Especially did the Georgia Democracy fear the outcome in the Eighth Congressional District. Thomas W. Thomas, an ardent Democratic politician in that district, reveals this fear. Writing to Alexander Stephens, he says: ". . . . but the great fight is in the 8th. . . . . This district is not safe unless you put in strong."[9]

Henry W. Hilliard has given an account of a mass meeting addressed by himself and Hill in Atlanta in August, 1856. Speaking of Hill's address on the Fillmore

---

[5] Rhodes, II, pp. 127-28.

[6] Of course Fremont, the Republican candidate, had no following in Georgia and need not be counted.

[7] *Milledgeville Federal Union*, August 5, 1856; also James D. Waddell, *Biographical Sketch of Linton Stephens*, pp. 124-25.

[8] Phillips (ed.), *Toombs, Stephens, Cobb Correspondence*, p. 377. Cobb replied to Buchanan, endeavoring to alleviate his fears but admitting that if Fillmore had any chance of election in the nation at large, he would be dangerous in the South (*ibid.*, p. 378).

[9] *Ibid.*, p. 381; also see letters of Stephens to Thomas, p. 371, and of Toombs to Stephens, p. 380.

candidacy, he says: "His magnificent speech brought out from time to time enthusiastic cheers; and as I listened to him I comprehended the wealth, power and grandeur of this great statesman. His speech was remarkable for its great beauty—ornate, comprehensive, eloquent and powerful."[10]

But it was in the clashes with Alexander Stephens and Toombs that Hill established himself as a brilliant debater and a power in Georgia politics, paving the way to his gubernatorial nomination on the American ticket for 1857.

On October 22 he met Stephens at Lexington, Oglethorpe County, in the latter's own political stronghold; and on the next day invaded the home of the imperious Toombs at Washington, Wilkes County.[11] Stovall writes: "There was a charm in the very audacity of this young Georgian. The man who would beard 'the Douglas in his hall' was a curiosity to the people, for since the leadership of Toombs was established in 1844, no one, probably, had assumed to cross swords with him before his home people."[12] As much might be said of Stephens, for, while differing from Toombs in every physical respect—and in nearly every other respect, for that matter—he yet resembled Toombs in his power over his constituency.

As has been pointed out, Stephens and Toombs were

[10] Henry W. Hilliard, *Politics and Pen Pictures*, p. 275. For Hill's debates in his campaign with William L. Yancey of Alabama, see *Columbus Sun*, October 2, 1856; and with Linton Stephens, see Phillips (ed.), *Toombs, Stephens, Cobb Correspondence*, letter of Thomas W. Thomas to A. H. Stephens, September 5, 1856, p. 381.

[11] Stovall, p. 144; Hill, *Life of Hill*, p. 19; J. C. Reed, "Reminiscences of Ben Hill," *South Atlantic Quarterly*, V (April 1906), 135 ff.

[12] Stovall, p. 144.

new converts to the Democratic party and, like most converts, were abounding in zeal. Stephens at any time was not very patient of opposition, was disposed to be oracular in his utterances; and long political power, combined with poor health, had not promoted political civility. Especially did it nettle him to be faced by a young upstart, as he must have regarded Hill, who neither asked nor gave quarter. The consequence was that he lost his temper, and with it the debate.[13] From this meeting at Lexington in 1856 dated a hostility which never abated on Stephens' part. It flared up fitfully in after years, though at one period particularly,

[13] If it be thought that this characterization of Stephens is unfair, the writer will rest the case upon one piece of evidence, though there would be no difficulty in producing more. In the voluminous correspondence between Alexander Stephens and Linton Stephens, between whom existed an unusually warm affection, there is a letter, written by the younger Stephens in a playful spirit, but which none the less clearly reveals the foibles of the Georgia statesman. In 1844 Alexander had registered a vote in Congress, the intent of which was to lower the "great Whig tariff of 1842." Linton, writing to his brother, twits him on this apostasy to the Whig principle, and in a vein of playful irony reveals his real knowledge of Stephens' methods. He writes:

"The next stump speech I hear you make I shouldn't be surprised to find something after the following:

" 'FELLOW CITIZENS: I always said the tariff of '42 was not a perfect measure; it is beyond human ability to attain perfection in anything, much less in adjusting the difficult subject of the tariff, and the burthens of government press equally on every nerve (you are fond of medical figures) of this vast and extended people. Our fathers themselves (then you'll wax eloquent) foresaw the necessity of making changes in the constitution itself. . . . . I have been governed by these views (very explicit) in casting my vote which is now arraigned before the bar of your judgment and as a faithful servant I lay my work before you and commit my fate to the decision of an honest constituency. The duty on iron wern't right "nohow". I always told you *just the same.*' " (From a letter written December 24, 1844, in Waddell, pp. 74-75.)

THE FILLMORE-BUCHANAN CANVASS 17

in the fight against secession, Stephens and Hill were found fighting shoulder to shoulder.

Stephens was the more touchy in this contest because his own consistency in opposing Fillmore, whom he had indorsed in 1848, had not gone unchallenged.[14] And as a lifelong Whig, now fighting in the camp of the Democracy against a party composed, in large part, of his former colleagues, his position was peculiarly assailable. Hill did not fail to press home this advantage; and from the bitterness it engendered came a challenge from Stephens to Hill.[15]

The debate at Lexington seems to have degenerated into a contest in personal ridicule and a wrangle over Stephens' consistency. Hill scored Stephens for his desertion of the Whig party, but particularly for his intemperate abuse of his former Whig colleagues now supporting the American ticket. These men, Hill pointed out, had formerly been Stephens' best friends, by whose suffrage he had been sustained; and it little became Stephens to visit upon them such vituperation. A contemporary writing of the Lexington tilt gives the following conclusions:

> That the Little Hero as Stephens was called, had been completely discomfited by the young Ben Hill. Most of the auditors agreed that while Stephens maintained himself in the argument, his personal thrusts and severe criticism of his adversary and the latter's party were most befittingly chastised. Especially did all agree that Stephens's ridicule had been turned decisively against him.[16]

[14] Phillips (ed.), *Toombs, Stephens, Cobb Correspondence*, letter of Thomas W. Thomas to Stephens, September 5, 1856, pp. 380–81.

[15] Letter of Stephens to Hill dated November 29, 1856, printed in Hill, *Life of Hill*, p. 24.

[16] Reed, p. 135. The account in the text is taken from Reed's account and from the correspondence between Hill and Stephens referred to in note 18, this chapter.

Although this debate at Lexington had been planned as the first of a series of joint discussions, it proved so acrimonious that the discussions were not renewed.[17]

An aftermath of the Lexington encounter, as before stated, was a challenge to a duel extended by Stephens to Hill. In this communication Stephens demanded in the most approved form "that satisfaction which is usual between gentlemen on such occasions." This cavalier step had come about after an exchange of letters had failed to satisfy Stephens' "due regard to his honor as a gentleman and integrity as a man."[18]

In a communication rather notable for its force and dignity, Hill declined to meet Stephens under the code. He wrote:

> If the invitation to mortal combat is extended as a mere formal occasion to exchange a few harmless shots and then have an adjustment I can only say I never engage in farces nor make feigned issues.

---

[17] It is hard to place exact responsibility for the discontinuance of the discussions. The question enters into the epistolary controversy preceding the challenge. B. H. Hill, Jr., in his sketch of his father, claims that Stephens was so "utterly routed at Lexington" that he refused to meet Hill again. It is very probable that the acrimony between the two men was so great that there was a sort of mutual suspension of forensic relations.

[18] The entire correspondence regarding the challenge, embracing six letters, is printed in Hill's *Life of Hill*, pp. 20-30. There are also three letters from Stephens to Thomas W. Thomas, giving the Stephens version of the affair in Phillips (ed.), *Toombs, Stephens, Cobb Correspondence*, pp. 384, 386-89.

However picturesque, this personal controversy is too complicated to be unraveled in this study, as its importance does not justify the space it would take up. A dispassionate reading of the entire correspondence leaves the impression that Stephens' wounded vanity drove him to force a quarrel which Hill endeavored to avoid. This is also the opinion of Reed, p. 137.

THE FILLMORE-BUCHANAN CANVASS 19

If I could be made conscious that I had done you injustice, I should deem it a duty to repair it, and should not wait to be shot at. If you did me injustice I met the occasion with the remedy, and it does seem made a shot which produced a wider if not deeper sore than any within the power of powder or ball to produce.[19]

Hill demonstrated real moral courage in thus refusing satisfaction under a code which had not lost its force in Georgia and which a man, jealous of his honor, disregarded at his peril. It has been remarked that Hill's action at this juncture marked an end of dueling among public men in the South.[20] When the entire bellicose correspondence was published in the state press, Hill's conduct in this affair added greatly to the prestige which he had won at Lexington.[21]

Happily, the debate with Toombs at Washington, Wilkes County, was not attended by quite such acrimonious results, although from accounts of contemporaries each speaker went after the other with gloves off. The news of Hill's discomfiture of Stephens at Lexington the day before had spread rapidly, and people flocked to Washington by thousands to hear the new tribune. "A large part of the audience which had cheered Ben Hill in Oglethorpe [Lexington] followed him to Wilkes."[22]

[19] Hill, *Life of Hill*, p. 25.   [20] Reed, p. 137.

[21] *Ibid*. It should be said that Stephens was given to challenging. He challenged Hershel V. Johnson at one time, and the latter refused, saying that he "could not fight the man who had taught him to pray." Reed says that in 1861 T. R. R. Cobb said of Stephens who was fighting secession: "The only prominent support that Stephens has is that of two men, each one of whom he has tried to shoot."

[22] Stovall, p. 145; Reed, p. 136. Mr. Reed had not been present at Lexington but hurried to Washington on the twenty-third to hear the "new wonder."

Hill opened the discussion with the charge that Toombs was a turncoat and had gone back on the principles of a lifetime. "Toombs sat back with his fine features lit with scorn. .... He seemed to repel with a look the impudence of this fearless young statesman. .... A keen observer of this dramatic byplay declares that the pose of these two men reminded him of Landseer's picture of Dignity and Impudence."[23] At the close of his first speech, Hill sharply commented on Toombs's domineering manner but exclaimed: "It will be useless for Mr. Toombs to try to intimidate me. God has made me insensible to fear."[24]

Aside from personalities and the sharp give-and-take of repartee, the argument of the debate dealt with the Kansas-Nebraska Act. Hill declared the Act embodied principles of squatter sovereignty and alien suffrage and was not identical, as Stephens and Toombs had alleged, with the Utah and New Mexico bills. The Kansas bill he characterized as a swindle and a cheat, surrendering the dearest rights of the South. Toombs in reply maintained the Kansas-Nebraska Act was but a reiteration of the Compromise Measures of 1850, and branded any opponents of the Kansas bill as enemies of the South.[25]

Respecting these two great debates, common opinion held that while Hill had flayed Stephens at Lexington, he did no more than hold his own with Toombs at Washington.[26] But this was a great feat for a newcomer and established Hill as the uncontested leader of the American party

---

[23] Stovall, p. 146.

[24] Reed, p. 136.

[25] Stovall, pp. 147–50.   [26] Reed, p. 137.

THE FILLMORE-BUCHANAN CANVASS

in Georgia and as a force to be reckoned with by the Democracy.

In the contest of 1856, Hill again met with defeat. Buchanan carried the state by a majority of 14,000 votes.[27] It was to be Hill's fate to lead hopeless minorities up to and including the Civil War period.

In this year, 1856, Hill was elected a trustee of the University of Georgia, or Franklin College, as it was then called. He was a graduate of this institution and continued to take a lively interest in its welfare up to the time of his death.[28]

[27] Phillips, *Georgia and State Rights*, p. 179.
[28] *Columbus Sun*, August 19, 1856.

CHAPTER III

GUBERNATORIAL RACE AGAINST JOE BROWN

The gubernatorial struggle of 1857 in Georgia initiated a long and dramatic rivalry between Hill and Joseph E. Brown, heretofore an unknown figure in Georgia.[1] This rivalry, at times marked by excessive bitterness, only came to an end when Brown became Hill's colleague in the United States Senate in 1880, two years before the latter's death.[2]

Hill's campaign of 1856 in the interest of Fillmore had marked him as the logical candidate for the American gubernatorial nomination in 1857, and the party convention extended him this nomination by acclamation at Macon on July 8.[3] The defeat of 1856 had almost destroyed the American party in Georgia, and the convention could have entertained little hope of success in the canvass.[4] It is indeed probable that the older Whigs in the state did not desire the nomination and that only the youthful enthusiasm of Hill could have approached the prospect with any optimism. Nevertheless, the party represented "a large

---

[1] Avery, p. 39.

[2] *Memorial Addresses on the Life and Character of Benjamin H. Hill*, delivered in the Senate and House of Representatives, 47th Congress, 2d Session, address of Senator Brown, pp. 13-14.

[3] *Columbus Sun*, July 10, 1857; *Savannah Morning News*, July 10, 1857. Mr. Phillips thinks that Hill was nominated partly because of the dearth of other talented men among the Georgia Know-Nothings; see his *Life of Toombs*, p. 171.

[4] Phillips, *Georgia and State Rights*, p. 180.

THE GUBERNATORIAL RACE

volume of public intelligence and were determined to make a fight."[5]

The platform of the party adopted at Macon opposed squatter sovereignty, indorsed the Georgia Platform of 1850, condemned further agitation of slavery, attacked the Democratic policies in Kansas, and declared that the Dred Scott Decision (just handed down) was but a judicial indorsement of the position taken by the Georgia American party.[6] It will be noted that these issues are all national rather than state issues, and indeed the entire campaign reflected the national agitation and concerned itself little with local Georgia policies.

Hill accepted the nomination in a public letter to the Executive Committee of the American party, dated July 20, 1857.[7] The unanimous tender of the nomination with the accompanying sentiments constrained him to accept, he writes, against personal and private objections. The campaign will be conducted as a rebuke against the startling outrages in Kansas.

The people of the South, Hill continues, have hitherto unanimously favored non-intervention in the territories, and this great principle is being wantonly violated in Kan-

[5] Fielder, p. 86. Cf. Avery, p. 41. Avery thinks that Hill's nomination "created a sensation and his party exulted in his certain triumph over his unknown competitor Brown." Perhaps there was a momentary feeling of this sort, but Brown soon emerged from the obscurity which surrounded him at the time of his nomination.

[6] *Milledgeville Federal Union*, July 14, 1857; *Columbus Sun*, July 11, 1857; *Savannah Morning News*, July 10, 1857.

[7] The printed letter is found in the *Brown Scrap Books*. Unfortunately the clipping, as seldom happens in these books, does not give the paper and date.

sas. At great length Hill maintains that Governor Walker in Kansas had "intervened," had "dictated," had "threatened the Kansas convention and voters." The entire course of Walker is represented as a high-handed one of bribing and conciliating "black Republicans," while discouraging southern immigration. Such a course, Hill concludes, is certainly "intervention."[8]

The nomination of Joe Brown on the Democratic ticket to oppose Hill came about as the result of a long deadlock in the Democratic convention in Augusta.[9] When the convention met, Brown was practically unknown outside of his own section of the state. He was a resident of the mountain section of northwest Georgia, known as the Cherokee section. He had served inconspicuously in the General Assembly of the state and as an elector on the Pierce ticket. He had made a good record as a Superior Court judge since 1855.[10] He was, and continued to be, "a representative of a horny handed constituency."[11]

[8] Thomas W. Thomas writes to A. H. Stephens, January 12, 1857, that if Buchanan admits Kansas as a free state, "the cause of southern rights is dead .... we [Democrats] have led the people to believe otherwise; if their [Know-Nothing] predictions are fulfilled and history should write the verdict against us, we go down, and such knaves as Ben Hill and Co. will rule during the present generation. Mark this prediction." (See, Phillips [ed.], *Toombs, Stephens, Cobb Correspondence*, p. 392.) The situation also called forth from Stephens a long letter of explanation and apology, to the people of the Eighth Congressional District. Originally published in the *Augusta Constitutionalist*, August 18, 1857; reproduced in Phillips (ed.), *Toombs, Stephens, Cobb Correspondence*, pp. 409-20.

[9] Avery, pp. 30-37, gives the entire story; see also *Milledgeville Federal Union*, June 30, 1857.

[10] Avery, pp. 16-17, 21-23, 26-30; Fielder, pp. 102-7.

[11] Phillips, *Georgia and State Rights*, p. 181.

THE GUBERNATORIAL RACE

The Georgia Democratic party, divided for years into Southern Rights and Union factions, found itself hopelessly entangled in its nominating convention in 1857 between conspicuous leaders of each faction.[12] After nineteen ballots without a nomination, a committee was appointed to solve the tangle; and the committee reported the name of Joseph E. Brown of Cherokee. The nomination was then made unanimous.[13]

Immediately the American press of the state rang with the query: Who is Joe Brown?[14] The cue had been taken from Toombs, who, when handed a letter announcing the nomination of Brown on the Democratic ticket, while traveling in Texas in 1857, is reported to have said: "And who in the devil is Joe Brown?"[15]

The Democratic party did not draft a platform, feeling that its past record was sufficiently indicative of the party's position on all vital issues;[16] but its convention adopted resolutions condemning the inaugural address of Governor Walker in Kansas and designating his course in recommending the admission of Kansas as a free state "a gross departure from the principles of non-intervention and neutrality established by the Kansas bill."[17]

Hill and Brown were both young and apparently eager

[12] *North East Georgian*, July 29, 1857, in the *Brown Scrap Books*.

[13] Avery, p. 37.

[14] *Atlanta Weekly Intelligencer*, July 8, 1857, in *Brown Scrap Books*, contains a digest of this criticism.

[15] Stovall, p. 154.

[16] Phillips, *Georgia and State Rights*, p. 180.

[17] Avery, p. 38.

for the fray. A stumping tour of the state at once began.[18] In the beginning the Democratic leaders were very nervous about Brown's ability to meet Hill on the stump. Toombs, who had hurried home from Texas to bolster up the Democratic cause, wrote Stephens on August 15 from Washington (Georgia): "The Know Nothings here open vigorously with a very reputable ticket, and are quite fierce against both of us. You must let nothing but Providential cause prevent your being at Bulah" (Wilkes County).[19] Toombs had previously written Stephens on August 4, regarding a summons which the Democrats had made on him to meet Hill at Lexington: "I did not like the employment of fighting skunks nohow, but supposed there was a necessity in this district at least."[20]

Early in the campaign, Hill and Brown had met at Glen Spring near Athens, and Hill was reported to have worsted his opponent. Howell Cobb had written to Toombs, as a result, begging him to take charge of the campaign, as Cobb "doubted the ability of Judge Brown to handle Hill of Troup."[21] Toombs consequently summoned Brown to Washington for a conference and soon thereafter started with him in a speaking tour of south Georgia. Toombs, however, was soon convinced of the ability of Brown to take care of himself, and returned home, leaving Brown to stand unassisted "before the luminous oratory of Ben Hill."[22] This concern of the great Georgia triumvirate,

---

[18] *Columbus Sun,* July 29, 1857.
[19] Phillips (ed.), *Toombs, Stephens, Cobb Correspondence,* p. 420.
[20] *Ibid.,* p. 409.
[21] Stovall, p. 155.
[22] *Ibid.,* pp. 157–58; Avery, pp. 39–40.

THE GUBERNATORIAL RACE

Toombs, Stephens, and Cobb, is sufficient evidence that Hill had become a power to reckon with in Georgia, although he was at this time only thirty-four years of age.

The consensus of opinion on the campaign, as reported by contemporaries, seems to be that Hill proved the more brilliant and eloquent but that Brown was the more logical, prudent, and convincing.[23] The Democratic press affected to slur at the stump eloquence of Hill, calling him the "Ajax of the Mountains" and contrasting his "clap trap eloquence" with the good, hard common sense and practical manner of Brown. Hill they represented as "the young Hercules whose arguments always have a powerful effect on the women and children."[24]

The American press replied in equally partisan vein. One editor delivered himself of this passionate effusion: "Hill and Brown—the mountain and the mole-hill—the giant and the pigmy—the lion and the weasel—these men have just closed a tour of the state; can it be possible that the people of Georgia will hesitate which of the two to choose."[25]

A favorite device of political debaters at this period was to spring interrogatories on an opponent, at one of these joint debates, in an endeavor to trap him into a damaging statement. An illustration of one of these interrogatory exchanges may serve to throw some light on the character of the campaign and the issues. At Franklin,

[23] *Columbus Sun*, October 7, 1857; *Savannah Georgian* (undated) in *Brown Scrap Books;* Avery, pp. 44-45; Fielder, p. 88.

[24] *Savannah Georgian* (undated), *Brown Scrap Books.*

[25] *Savannah Republican,* reproduced in the *Columbus Sun,* October 7, 1857.

Heard County, in August, occurred this exchange between Hill and Brown:

HILL TO BROWN:

1. Do you approve of Buchanan recalling Walker from Kansas, as advocated in the Democratic platform of Georgia?

Answer: Yes—and of the entire platform.

2. Buchanan having failed to recall Walker, do you approve of his failure?

Answer: I will not condemn Buchanan unheard—give him time. If then he fails, I will not hesitate to condemn.

3. How long will you wait?

Answer: A reasonable time in the circumstances.

4. Do you sustain Buchanan's administration?

Answer: I do.

BROWN TO HILL:

1. Do you stand on the Democratic platform of the Cincinnati convention?

Answer: I do not.

2. Do you approve the Know Nothing platform of Philadelphia, 1855?

Answer: I do.

3. Do you still pretermit any expression of opinion as to power of Congress to establish or prohibit slavery in any territory?

Answer: I do not pretermit, but deny the power exists in Congress.

4. Do you still feel disgust at the wild hunt for offices?

Answer: I do, and especially for the wild hunt of those nominating my honorable opponent.

5. Do you approve of your State Convention and platform?

Answer: I do with all my heart.

6. Then what modification do you advocate in naturalization laws? How many years should be required?

Answer: A foreigner should remain in this country 21 years before naturalization.

THE GUBERNATORIAL RACE 29

7. Do you believe with Mr. Fillmore that all the evils of the country have come from the repeal of the Missouri Compromise?
Answer: Not *all* the evils.

8. Do you approve of the course of your nominating convention in having failed to condemn the course of Walker in Kansas?
Answer: I approve of the Convention and it did condemn Walker.[26]

One of the most interesting colloquies between Brown and Hill occurred at Lexington, where, the year before, Hill had met Stephens with such bellicose results. The debate here largely resolved itself, according to the account of an auditor, into an effort on Hill's part to embarrass Brown by forcing an answer, which, however made, would inevitably have alienated one wing of the Georgia Democracy.[27]

Hill pushed the question: "If Mr. Buchanan does not recall Walker will you regard your election as an endorsement or as a condemnation of the administration?" Now the Georgia Democracy was divided on this very point, and Brown was too shrewd to commit himself. He merely warned Hill against interfering in a quarrel which did not belong to him, and told a story of how a traveler once

[26] This interrogatory is found in the *Augusta Constitutionalist*, August 7, 1857. I have merely given an abstract of the questions and answers, not preserving the phraseology in every case. Taken from the *Brown Scrap Books*.

At Carrollton, Carroll County, Hill met Brown in an interesting debate. On this occasion each candidate was attended by a supporter, the debate being a four-cornered affair. A long account of the Carrollton debate is found in the *Atlanta Daily Examiner*, August 6, 1857, in the *Brown Scrap Books*.

[27] Reed, pp. 137–38. Mr. Reed's account is the basis for that given in the text.

sought to save a wife from being beaten by her husband, and of how husband and wife then turned with one accord upon the stranger. Hill turned this story to good account in his rebuttal:

> The Judge has made me understand this affair. Mr. Buchanan whom I thought a batchelor, has a wife—a southern wife. Kansas according to the Judge is the wife, and her husband is whipping her so mercilessly that 'bleeding Kansas' is a proverb all over the country, and when we, the American party, offer to help the wronged wife, the broomstick is to be given to us.

In his last rebuttal and the concluding minute of the debate, Brown pretended to answer Hill's question, "in his most ringing nasal twang": "I will tell you how I will regard my election. I will regard my election as an endorsement of my fidelity to the Democratic party—and a condemnation of Mr. Hill himself."

The only local issue entering into the campaign concerned the disposition of the state railroad, at that time a liability to the state.[28] Hill favored the immediate sale of the road, and accused Brown of desiring that the State should retain the operation of the road, even at a loss, that he (Brown) might make political capital of its management. Brown denied this charge and in a letter to a supporter, which was made public, gave the four conditions upon which he would consent to the sale of the road.[29] The road was not sold, and Brown was making it pay the state substantial returns when the Civil War came.[30]

The election returns, at the end of the canvass, gave

[28] Avery, p. 45.
[29] Published in *Savannah Morning News*, September 18, 1857.
[30] Avery, pp. 71–72.

THE GUBERNATORIAL RACE

Brown about 10,000 majority over Hill, the exact vote being Brown, 56,568, and Hill, 46,826.[31] Brown had registered a sweeping victory, and with him six out of eight Democratic Congressmen were elected.[32] This election overwhelmed the American, or Know-Nothing, party in Georgia. Some remnants of the party were to support Bell and Everett on the Constitutional Union ticket in 1860, but the party as such possessed no organization and put no ticket into the field after 1857.[33]

The responsibility for this crushing defeat cannot be attributed to Hill. Unquestionably he made a race as good as or better than any man in the party could have done. The American party at this time was artificial in its composition and fast disappearing in the nation. The tide to the solidification of the southern people in the Democratic party was flowing too strongly for Hill or any other man to arrest it as late as 1857. Hill had again given his best to the leadership of one more ineffectual minority struggle.

[31] *Milledgeville Federal Union,* October 20, 1857.
[32] Avery, p. 46.
[33] *Ibid.*

CHAPTER IV
SECESSION

Hill took no active part in public affairs from his defeat in 1857 until 1859, when he was elected to the state senate as a strong Unionist.[1] At this time secession propaganda, anticipating the election of a Republican president in 1860, was assuming alarming proportions; and Hill went to the senate with the avowed purpose of stemming the tide toward disunion.[2] His first service was in moderating the tone of the utterances of the General Assembly in the session of 1859. In the committee assignments he drew the very important Committee on the State of the Republic.[3] Considering the then existing parlous times, this was perhaps the most important committee of the senate.

The John Brown raid had just occurred, and exciting rumors were abroad regarding the complicity in Brown's schemes of certain officials high in the United States government.[4] It was quite the custom at this period for the state legislatures to devote much of their time to the discussion of federal relations. Resolutions, petitions, memorials, as the student of the period knows, emanated from the various state legislatures, in great profusion. Consequently, after the fashion of the times, the Georgia General

[1] Hill, *Life of Hill*, p. 36.   [2] *Ibid.*

[3] *Senate Journal*, 1859, pp. 7, 68. He was also appointed on the Judiciary Committee and one other committee, a minor one.

[4] See *Senate Journal*, 1859, pp. 121–23, for resolutions stating some of these rumors.

Assembly at once addressed itself to a consideration of the John Brown "conspiracy," assuming to point out the responsibility and obligations of the federal government in the premises. It was here that Hill could and did first assert himself in the cause of moderation and amity.[5]

On November 5 the following resolution, among others, was introduced into the senate:

Resolved: That the prompt and energetic action of Governor Wise of Virginia, and President Buchanan in suppressing the outbreak at Harper's Ferry, and in their efforts to capture the insurgents, evince a degree of manliness and patriotism honorable alike to themselves and worthy of our warm admiration as citizens of a Southern State.[6]

Hill, perceiving in the last sentence an invidious distinction, and wishing to avoid any utterance that might fan the flames of sectional animosity, moved to amend the resolution by striking out "citizens of a Southern State" and by inserting "the representatives of one of the States of this Confederacy." The amendment was agreed to and the resolution, as amended, was adopted.[7] Hill's position at this time was one of a broad nationalism. He believed extremists, North and South, were promoting unnecessarily the sectional quarrel, and solely for political and selfish purposes. He writes: "Bad, extreme men in both sections insult each other, and then both fight the Union which never harmed or insulted either."[8] The historian may differ with

[5] *Ibid.,* 1859, pp. 47-48.
[6] *Ibid.,* p. 47.
[7] *Ibid.,* p. 48.
[8] Letter of acceptance of his election as delegate to the Constitutional Convention of 1861, dated December 26, 1860; printed in Hill, *Life of Hill,* p. 40.

this inadequate view, but the sincerity and pertinacity with which Hill maintained such a broadly national attitude cannot be doubted.

Aside from his labors of moderation in the interest of a true national amity, Hill's work in the state senate in 1859 is of no large consequence.[9]

In the meanwhile, 1859 had witnessed an effort to revive and invigorate an opposition party to the almost unopposed Democratic party within the state. Hill had taken a leading part in this movement, but probably because he was indisposed to invite a second defeat in a gubernatorial race at this time, Warren Aiken had been named to make the race of 1859 against Brown.[10]

The Executive Committee of the almost defunct Know-Nothing, or American, party issued an address in the early summer of 1859, in effect dissolving the party, but denouncing the Democratic maladministration in state and nation and inviting all who opposed the Democratic party to join in an "opposition convention," to meet on the third Wednesday of July. Due to a misunderstanding regarding

---

[9] There was quite a tussle in this session over the management of the state railroad, in which certain policies of Governor Brown and his friend, the superintendent of the road, Lewis, were held up to criticism by Hill and others. See *Senate Journal*, 1859, pp. 329–35.

The Choice pardon struggle between Hill, urging the Assembly to pardon Choice, and Governor Brown, opposing and vetoing the pardon, occupied an importance in the public eye and press out of all proportion to its seeming importance. See *Columbus Sun*, November 19, and December 23, 1859.

Hill also introduced and championed some bills of local importance. See *Senate Journal*, 1859, pp. 51, 63, 77, 98, 258, 327.

[10] *Milledgeville Southern Recorder*, July 26, and August 16, 1859. Also see Avery, pp. 93–96.

the place of meeting, the "opposition convention" held in Macon in July was poorly attended and disappointing to its supporters, but the Macon gathering adopted a platform, indorsing the Federal Constitution and the Dred Scott Decision, denouncing squatter sovereignty as a delusion, condemning the further agitation of the slavery question, and censuring the extravagance and corruption of the Democratic administration. The body then adjourned, after calling a second "opposition convention" to meet in Atlanta on August 10.[11]

The second "opposition convention" came together at the appointed time and place during "a wet gloomy spell of weather that typified the spirits and prospects of the party it represented."[12] The platform of the Macon convention was ratified; and then Warren Aiken, as previously stated, was nominated to make the race against Brown.[13] Brown, however, had no difficulty in winning the election, securing a majority of 22,000 votes.[14]

The chief significance of this movement, into which Hill threw himself with his accustomed vigor and enthusiasm, is that it was designed to oppose secession and disunion. From the first, says Professor Phillips, "its promoters expected it to form part of a Constitutional Union party in 1860, appealing to men in all quarters of the country to quell the sectional wrangling."[15] And indeed such a move-

[11] Avery, pp. 93–96. [12] *Ibid.*, p. 94.

[13] *Milledgeville Southern Recorder*, August 16, 1859.

[14] Avery, p. 96.

[15] Phillips, *Life of Toombs*, p. 176, citing an editorial in the *Savannah Republican*, reprinted in the *Milledgeville Southern Recorder*. For Hill's part in this movement see *Milledgeville Southern Recorder*, August 9, 1859.

ment was well timed and fully necessary in the Georgia and the South of the winter of 1859–60. Events were moving rapidly toward a dissolution of the Union.

By the autumn of 1860 four national tickets were in the field for president, and there was little doubt where each of the candidates stood on the slavery and sectional issues. Lincoln, the Republican candidate, was avowedly against any extension of slavery in the territories; Douglas, representing one wing of the sundered Democracy, was explicitly for "squatter sovereignty"; Breckenridge, representing the extreme southern Democracy, proposed absolute non-intervention, by any authority, national or territorial, with slavery in a territory, before the territory should become a state. Only Bell and the Constitutional Union position could be considered equivocal and ambiguous, as he declared in general terms for the Constitution, the Union, and the enforcement of the laws.[16]

In Georgia a remnant of the American party had come together on May 2, 1860, at Milledgeville, as forecast in the gubernatorial struggle of 1859, and adopted resolutions declaring the right of property in slaves, the obligation of the Federal government to protect such property in the territories, and the unconstitutionality of the legislation in the free states against the federal Fugitive Slave Law of 1850. This group announced its affiliation with the National Constitutional Union party, which in Convention at Baltimore had nominated Bell and Everett but had failed to adopt a vigorous or unambiguous platform.[17]

[16] The position of these candidates is too well known for dispute or to require separate citation of authority.

[17] *Milledgeville Federal Union*, May 15, 1860. For the Constitutional Union Convention at Baltimore, see Rhodes, II, 410.

SECESSION

The presidential campaign produced in Georgia what Avery calls a "carnival of splendid speaking."[18] Manifestly only the Douglas, Breckenridge, and Bell parties put out electoral tickets in Georgia; and the three tickets brought out in the campaign the best talent that the state afforded. For Breckenridge, who eventually won the state: ex-Governor McDonald, Judge Henry R. Jackson, Toombs, Howell Cobb, the two Colquitts, Alfred and Walter H., Francis S. Bartow, and Henry L. Benning took the stump; for Douglas: Hershel V. Johnson, Hiram Warner, A. R. Wright, and the two Stephens, Alexander and Linton, campaigned; for Bell: Warren Aiken and Hill took the field.[19] Hill bore the brunt of the campaigning for the Bell and Everett ticket and "did it well."[20] An analysis of his speech at Macon on June 30, 1860, gives the gist of his argument.[21]

Hill defined the principle involved in the election as, "What power has the national government over slavery?" The election, he says, is in effect, a popular referendum on this subject. Hill's own answer to this question is that the national government has no power over the subject save that of protection; its sole function in the premises is to protect the slave-owner in his property rights. This is indisputably true, Hill avers, first, because it is the *law*, according to a Supreme Court decision; and second, because it is *right*, based on the fundamental duty and province of government itself, namely, that of protecting property. However, Hill declares that no special slave code is necessary or desired, since under the Constitution, slave prop-

[18] Avery, p. 128.
[19] *Ibid.*, p. 126.
[20] *Ibid.*, p. 128.
[21] Speech printed in Hill, *Life of Hill*, pp. 229–36.

erty is on the same basis as all other property, and rests, moreover, not on municipal law, but on natural and divine law.

Now to secure this principle, who should be supported in the pending election? Hill answers: first, not Mr. Lincoln, who asserts that the national government possesses the right to prohibit slave property in the territories; second, not Mr. Douglas, who says territorial legislatures may prohibit slavery, by non-action or hostile action; third, not Mr. Breckenridge, because he is a sectional or "rump" Democrat, whose platform on the subject is no better than Bell's and whose record is not so good, and whose election, moreover, is impossible. Therefore, by elimination, the decision goes to Mr. Bell who has already voted for the following propositions: (1) that the national government has no power over slavery in the territories; (2) that territorial legislatures have no power save that of protection; and (3) that the duty of government in the premises is only to protect property in slaves. Bell is therefore absolutely sound in record and in platform. A vote for Bell is a vote for the Constitution, for the Union, and for the laws.

This argument is recognized as the favorite constitutional argument of the pro-slavery southerner, and it is advanced by Hill in a severely logical and convincing way. Hill possessed in marked degree the power of close logic and convincing statement, if once the truth of his premises was granted.

As the campaign advanced, it became evident, as it should have been from the first, that with the National Democracy and the South so divided as between Douglas, Breckenridge, and Bell, Lincoln must inevitably win out.

SECESSION

Hill, in the spirit of his usual moderation, attempted vainly in Georgia to effect a fusion between the Breckenridge, Douglas, and Bell tickets.[22] In October he succeeded in carrying resolutions for such a fusion in a mass meeting in Atlanta of supporters of all the candidates; and he published an address to the people of Georgia, urging the plan.[23] His scheme was to propose an electoral ticket which should be pledged to neither of the candidates, specifically, but only to vote for that one "who should have the best chance to beat Lincoln."[24]

The scandalmongers and irreconcilables among the extreme Southern Rights faction immediately got busy and circulated damning rumors about Hill's proposal and his motives. His scheme was represented as a political intrigue, in which Hershel V. Johnson, who inclined to the plan, though he was running on the Douglas ticket, was to be elected United States Senator if Bell and Everett should secure Georgia's electoral vote; but if Douglas and Johnson should secure the vote of Georgia, Hill himself was to go to the United States Senate.[25] This, of course, was reducing what was later seen to be the only feasible plan of defeating Lincoln, to a mere bargain and sale transaction. The Breckenridge press especially lampooned the plan, affecting to see in it a trick to eliminate their candidate, who

---

[22] See letters of Linton Stephens to Alexander Stephens, July 13, 1860, and October 2, 1860, in Waddell, pp. 227, 236.

[23] *Columbus Weekly Sun,* October 30, 1860.

[24] Linton Stephens to Alexander Stephens, October 21, 1860, in Waddell, p. 236.

[25] See *Columbus Weekly Sun,* August 7, 1860, for article quoting the *Georgia Forester,* which professed to know the details of the trade.

they professed to believe would secure the election.[26] So bitter was the opposition of the Breckenridge party to the proposal that Varney H. Gaskill, a member of the Breckenridge Executive Committee in Atlanta, was removed from the Committee because he had expressed sentiments favorable to the plan of fusion.[27]

Subsequent events proved that some such arrangement as that proposed by Hill could alone have prevented the election of Lincoln. Georgia gave its vote to Breckenridge; but, as posterity has good reason to know, Lincoln secured a majority of the electoral college in the nation at large.[28]

The Georgia General Assembly was in session when Lincoln's election was confirmed. Immediately a spirited fight took place within the Assembly on the question of passing a resolution favoring immediate secession. Hill led the fight against the resolution in a debate abounding in personalities, and succeeded in defeating it. Later he was called upon in the senate to continue the fight, when a motion was made to reconsider the previous action. Again he was successful in preventing the passage of the resolution.[29]

[26] *Columbus Weekly Sun*, August 7, 1860; also same paper, October 30, 1860.

[27] *Ibid.*, October 30, 1860; also, Avery, p. 128.

[28] The popular vote in Georgia was: for Breckenridge and Lane, 51,893; for Douglas and Johnson, 11,580; for Bell and Everett, 42,855. Inasmuch as no candidate received a majority of this electoral vote, the election of the Georgia electors was thrown into the Georgia General Assembly, who named the Breckenridge slate (See Avery, pp. 129-31.) For Lincoln's electoral vote in the nation, see Rhodes, II, 456-57.

[29] Avery, pp. 138-39; see *Georgia Senate Journal*, 1860, pp. 63, 230-34, 284, 348-49, for Hill's fight against measures encouraging to secession.

SECESSION

In the meanwhile Governor Brown had sent a special message to the General Assembly on November 7 when the result of the national election was anticipated but had not been confirmed.[30] In this message, which bristled with acerbity, Governor Brown said, in part:

If it is ascertained that the Black Republicans have triumphed over us, I recommend the call of a Convention of the people of the state at an early day; and I will cordially unite with the General Assembly in any action, which in their judgment, may be necessary to the protection of the rights and preservation of the liberties of the people of Georgia against the further aggressions of an enemy which, when flushed with victory, will be insolent in the hour of triumph.

For the purpose of putting this state in a defensive condition as fast as possible, and preparing for an emergency which must be met sooner or later, I recommend that the sum of one million dollars be immediately appropriated as a military fund, for the ensueing year. . . . . Millions for defense, but not a cent for tribute should be the future motto of the southern states.

To every demand for further concession or compromise of our rights the reply ought to be, "The argument is exhausted," and we now "stand by our arms."[31]

The message further advised against a projected southern convention on the ground of the delay that would be entailed;[32] excoriated the anti-slavery northerners; expressed the opinion that the Constitution was a "compact," being wantonly violated in the North; and suggested that the

[30] *Milledgeville Federal Union*, November 13, 1860; also Fielder, pp. 168–69; *House Journal*, 1860, pp. 33–52, gives entire message.

[31] Fielder, pp. 168–69.

[32] Brown, in the message in question, had transmitted an invitation from the state of South Carolina addressed to all the southern states, to meet in a convention "to concert measures for united action," in the light of the emergency.

southern states make reprisal on the property in their borders, owned by citizens of the offending northern states.[33]

Thus it will be seen that Brown was in the forefront of the extremists against whom Hill was contending and, as chief executive of the state, was in a very strong position to influence public opinion. While pondering Governor Brown's message of November 7, the General Assembly invited certain prominent men in the state to appear before the Assembly and express their views on the posture of affairs.

On the twelfth of November, the young and ardent Thomas R. R. Cobb, the younger brother of Howell Cobb, appeared before the Assembly and urged immediate secession, using as a major and compelling argument, according to Stephens who heard him: "We can make better terms out of the Union than in it."[34]

On the thirteenth of November, Robert Toombs appeared and made a strong argument for secession.[35] On the fourteenth, Alexander Stephens replied to the speeches of Cobb and Toombs before the Assembly, in a masterful address, which drew the attention of Lincoln and of the nation.[36] Stephens pleaded for delay, for caution, and for moderation, insisting that southern rights might yet be secured within the Union.[37]

[33] *Federal Union,* November 13, 1860; *House Journal,* 1860, pp. 33–52.

[34] Avery, p. 130; Phillips, *Georgia and State Rights,* p. 194.

[35] Stephens, II, 321. For an account of an earlier speech in Macon, in which Cobb had advocated secession without awaiting the action of a convention, see Butler, *History of Macon, Georgia,* p. 235.

[36] Phillips, *Life of Toombs,* pp. 200–201.

[37] Stephens' speech is given in its entirety in Johnson and Brown, Appendix B., pp. 580–96; also found in Stephens, II, 279–300. The correspondence with Lincoln is found in Stephens, II, 265–70.

On the fifteenth of November, following Cobb, Toombs, and Stephens, Hill appeared before the Assembly and made an eloquent argument against immediate secession or any precipitate action. The speech is primarily a closely reasoned appeal for moderation and a plea that passion and prejudices be discarded in the face of the imminent crisis. The speech deserves some analysis.[38]

"What are our grievances?" asks Hill; and then he proceeds to enumerate them, outlining the discriminatory policies and propaganda of the Republican party and laying especial emphasis on the nugatory action of various free-state legislatures, affecting the fugitive slave laws. Hill represents the Republican party as the really disunionist party, and quotes from various abolitionists who damn the Union and Constitution because they permit slavery. The grievances, then, are plain, and agreed of all southern men.

The next question becomes, "Who shall inaugurate resistance, which all men agree must be made to these grievances, and who shall determine the mode, measure and time of this resistance?" Hill answers that all are agreed on that too—namely, the people in state convention shall exercise these prerogatives.

Now, agreed that a state convention shall inaugurate resistance to recognized grievances, what are the methods of resistance proposed? Here, Hill's argument must begin; the path of agreement stops. Two methods are proposed: the one, immediate secession; the other, "to exhaust certain remedies for these grievances in the Union with a view of preserving our rights and the Union with them." Hill

[38] Hill's speech is found most conveniently in Hill, *Life of Hill*, pp. 365–70.

can concede the wisdom of immediate secession only to those, an inconsiderable few, who "hold that the Constitution is wrong, and the Union bad *per se.*" Everything is to be gained by trying these remedies within the Union, and nothing is to be lost.

Moreover, Hill believes that redress of grievances is not so hopeless a prospect in the immediate future. Antislavery sentiment, Hill has apparently convinced himself, is weaker in 1860 than formerly. England, which had been formerly antislavery in its sentiment, is now, says Hill, the defender of slavery in the South; and he expects to see a similar change of sentiment in the North from a similar cause, namely, an economic one, the want of southern cotton by northern mills.

But suppose, for the sake of argument, redress of grievances within the Union is impossible, surely it is worth the effort; and all are agreed, admits Hill, that if such redress fails, then secession must come.

But what are the remedies, then, which are proposed within the Union? First, the demand must be made by all the southern states that the laws protecting slavery and requiring the rendering up of fugitive slaves must be enforced. This demand can be made as an ultimatum, if need be. If necessary, let the federal government enact a force bill against any recalcitrant northern state, refusing obedience, as was done in the case of South Carolina in 1833. Let the wrangling about slavery cease, and the entire machinery of government, if necessary, be put behind the enforcement of existing laws.

And Lincoln himself must come to this view. His only strength is in the law; he is bound by oath to carry out the law. A southern president had once coerced a southern state; now let a northern president coerce a northern state, if it comes to that.[39]

Hill insists that such a resolute attitude has never been taken by the southern states, and he pleads that the Union be not abandoned to its enemies without making this effort to save it. Moreover, he asks: "Is this Union a good? If so why should we surrender its blessings because Massachusetts violates the laws of that Union? Drive Massachusetts to the duties of the Constitution or from its benefits. . . . . Let us defend the Union against its enemies—not abandon it to them."[40]

And what are the benefits of this latter policy? If it succeeds, American constitutional government and liberty, so lauded before the world, shall stand vindicated; and slavery agitation shall cease forever.

But if it fails, there are yet advantages over the alternative course of immediate secession. Time will have been given to get ready for secession; and if war comes, this will prove invaluable. Moreover, the very failure of the earnest effort to redress grievances within the Union will unite the people of the state. In the third place, after the honest effort is made within the Union, its failure will result in the Union of all the southern states, an accomplishment not possible at present. Fourthly, this secession of all the southern states, if it comes about, can be accomplished peacefully, which is not probable of one state or a few states merely. And finally, this moderate course will secure

[39] Manifestly referring to Andrew Jackson's attitude toward South Carolina in 1833.

[40] Hill, *Life of Hill*, p. 247.

for us the good opinion of all mankind and of ourselves, says Hill, for our patience, our patriotism, and our forbearance.

Hill and Stephens, however, seem to have made but an indifferent impression on the General Assembly. By its acts in November and December, 1860, it demonstrated its essential sympathy with Brown, Toombs, and the Cobbs. The Assembly speedily appropriated one million dollars, as Brown had recommended; authorized the governor to accept not more than 10,000 troops for the various arms of the military service; and ordered a constitutional convention to meet on January 16, the elections for which were ordered to occur on January 2, 1861.[41] On December 19, the Assembly adopted resolutions setting forth the cause and justification of the previous warlike legislation and urging that should any or all of the southern states withdraw from the Union and resume sovereignty, such states should form a Southern Confederacy under the former Federal Constitution so altered and amended as to suit the new posture of affairs.[42]

On December 7 Governor Brown had issued a public letter which was virtually an answer to Stephens's speech of November 14 before the General Assembly. The letter was intemperate in its animadversions on the Republican party and program, and concluded with an urgent plea for immediate secession before Lincoln's inauguration, as the surest, safest, and most peaceful course remaining to the South.[43]

---

[41] *Acts of Georgia General Assembly*, 1860, pp. 26-49.

[42] *Ibid.*, p. 238.

[43] Letter found in *Milledgeville Federal Union*, December 11, 1860.

SECESSION

In the meanwhile, in the state at large, the people were expressing themselves in numerous memorials, adopted by mass meeting in county and municipality. For the most part, these memorials abounded in references to "southern rights," and the "legitimacy of secession"; and condemned so-called "Republican fanaticism." Occasionally, however, as in Upson County, these memorials were deprecatory of secession and counseled prudent co-operation of all the southern states.[44]

Public opinion expressed itself in other ways as well, in these days, as favoring immediate secession. Homespun clothing was worn to demonstrate independence of the North, and new organizations of cavalry and infantry militia sprang up spontaneously throughout the state.[45]

To oppose the drift toward immediate secession sentiment, Stephens took the lead in organizing the members of the General Assembly who were opposed to precipitate action. Fifty-two members joined him in adopting resolutions, advising the voters of the state in the coming election for members of the constitutional convention, to secure pledges from all candidates that they would support the movement for a southern convention, and adopt every possible remedy, before resorting to secession.[46] The members of this group were called "co-operationists," and they

[44] These memorials are found in *Confederate Records of the State of Georgia*, I, 58–156. The Upson County memorial is quoted in Phillips, *Life of Toombs*, p. 213. Also see memorial of Dougherty County in Avery, p. 136.

[45] *Milledgeville Federal Union*, December 11, 1860; also, Phillips, *Georgia and State Rights*, p. 196.

[46] *Milledgeville Southern Recorder*, December 25, 1860.

made some impression on public opinion. With them was aligned Hill.[47]

It is very probable that the action of Howell Cobb and Robert Toombs did more to stimulate immediate secession sentiment in the state than any other factor. On December 6, Cobb, in an address to the people of Georgia announcing his resignation from Buchanan's cabinet, averred that

> the Union formed by our fathers, which was one of equality, justice and fraternity would be supplanted on the 4th of March by a Union of sectionalism and hatred—the one worthy of the support and devotion of free men, the other only possible at the cost of southern honor, safety and independence.[48]

This was followed up on December 23 by Toombs's telegram to the *Savannah Morning News*, after the failure of the efforts to effect the Crittenden Compromise: "I tell you upon the faith of a true man that all further looking to the North for security for your constitutional rights in the Union ought to be abandoned. It is fraught with nothing but ruin to yourself and posterity."[49] And on January 1, 1861, Toombs sent the following telegram to the *True Democrat* of Augusta: "The Cabinet is broken up. Mr. Floyd, Secretary of War, and Mr. Thompson, Secretary of the Interior have resigned. Mr. Holt of Kentucky, our bitter foe, has been made Secretary of War. Fort Pulaski is in danger. The abolitionists are defiant."[50]

In the light of this telegram, on January 2, Governor

---

[47] Speech of Hill, November 15, 1860, *supra*, pp. 43–46.

[48] Samuel Boykin, *A Memorial Volume of Howell Cobb*, p. 31.

[49] *Milledgeville Federal Union*, January 1, 1860.

[50] Phillips, *Life of Toombs*, p. 215.

SECESSION

Brown ordered the seizure of Fort Pulaski, near Savannah, the people of Savannah heartily approving the action.[51]

South Carolina on December 20 had led off in the pathway of secession, followed by Mississippi on January 9, 1861, and Florida and Alabama on January 11. Their ambassadors were seeking Georgia's state capitol.[52]

Close on these events, all highly inflammatory, the Georgia State Constitutional Convention came together on January 16, "without a doubt the most distinguished body of men who had ever assembled in Georgia." Nearly every Georgian of any political importance was a member of the Convention, the exceptions being Governor Brown, Howell Cobb, and Charles J. Jenkins; and these gentlemen were given seats on the floor.[53]

The lines were already drawn in the Convention between immediate secession and "co-operation" with the other southern states in holding a southern convention which should endeavor to secure redress of grievances within the Union.[54] There was no thought of submission to the coming Republican regime without some assurance of redress of past and present grievances.

Hill, representing his own county of Troup, found himself fighting side by side with his old political antagonists,

[51] *Savannah Morning News*, January 3, 1861; also see Avery, pp. 145-46, and Fielder, p. 178.

[52] Rhodes, III, 85, for South Carolina; p. 159 for the others.

[53] Phillips, *Georgia and State Rights*, p. 202; also Avery, p. 150.

[54] *Savannah Morning News*, January 18, 1861, gives the details of organization, the election of ex-Governor George Crawford as chairman, and indicates the prominent rôle played in the organization proceeding by "Hill of Troup."

the two Stephens, Alexander and Linton, and with Hershel V. Johnson in the camp of the "co-operationists."[55] Hill had written a forceful letter against immediate secession, at the time of his acceptance of the position of delegate to the Convention. In this letter he laid bare in unreserved and impassioned terms his love of the Union.[56] He earnestly deprecated passion and petulance in the crisis and pleaded for wisdom and cool firmness. He expressed the opinion that South Carolina had acted hastily and unbecomingly. Let not Georgia be dragooned by friends or foes. Let her rather prefer "discretion to haste" and "wisdom to impetuosity." He further warned the people, pending the assembling of the Convention, to be on their guard against false rumors and the tricks of demagogues. The letter closed with these somber and rather remarkable paragraphs:

> The dissolution of the Union may be a necessity. If so, after being fully satisfied of that necessity, let us decree that dissolution. But I must be allowed to say that I cannot regard such an event as an occasion for rejoicing. . . . .
>
> Unless our grievances are fully redressed and we can have satisfactory guarantees that they will not be repeated, I will aid in the necessity of disunion. But I shall dissolve this Union as I would bury a benefactor—in sorrow of heart. For after all the Union is not the author of our grievances. Bad, extreme men in both sections insult each other, and then both fight the Union which never harmed either. . . . . For myself I shall never ask for more true liberty and real happiness under any government than I have enjoyed as a citizen of this great American Union. May they who would destroy this Union *in a frolic,* have wisdom to furnish our children with a better.[57]

[55] *Columbus Weekly Sun,* January 22, 1861.

[56] Letter, dated La Grange, December 26, 1860, printed in Hill, *Life of Hill,* pp. 38–40.

[57] Letter printed in Hill, *Life of Hill,* pp. 38–40; this extract, p. 40.

SECESSION

In the Convention, on January 18, Judge Eugenius A. Nisbit proposed the critical test resolution, which would reveal the sense of the body on the all important question.

1. *Resolved:* That in the opinion of this Convention it is the right and duty of Georgia to secede from the present Union, and to co-operate with such of the other states as have or shall do the same, for the purpose of forming a Southern Confederacy upon the basis of the Constitution of the United States.

2. *Resolved:* That a Committee of ———— be appointed by the Chair to report an ordinance to assert the right and fullfill the obligation of the State of Georgia to secede from the Union.[58]

On the reading of Nisbit's resolution, Hershel V. Johnson immediately proposed a substitute in the shape of a rather long paper, asserting the favorite "co-operationist" ideas. The paper asserted Georgia's affection for the Union, and called for a convention of all the southern states southward of Pennsylvania, including the seceded states, naming February 16 as the date for the meeting. It further said, that in the event of the failure of such a convention secession would then be resorted to as the very last resort.[59]

The vote was taken on Nisbit's test resolution, and revealed the closeness of the contest; but it was adopted by a vote of 166 to 134, and Johnson's substitute was passed by for the time.[60] In accordance with the resolution passed,

[58] *Journal of the Constitutional Convention of 1861*, p. 15; see also Fielder, p. 177.

[59] *Journal of the Constitutional Convention of 1861*, pp. 16-20; Johnson's resolutions are also found in *Official Records of the War of the Rebellion* (4th Ser., I, 57-60 [referred to hereafter as "O. R."]) with the record of Hill's support of them.

[60] *Journal of the Constitutional Convention of 1861*, pp. 16-20, for the entire fight over the resolutions, test and substitute, with the vote.

on the next day, the nineteenth, Nisbit reported from a special committee, an ordinance "to dissolve the Union between the State of Georgia and other States united with her under a compact of Government, entitled the Constitution of the United States of America."[61]

Hill was not yet through fighting. He instantly moved Johnson's resolutions of the day before as a substitute for the Secession Ordinance, and demanded the vote, but the Convention voted him down by 164 votes to 133.[62] Hill now accepted the inevitable and, believing in truth that the argument was now exhausted, voted yea on the passage of the Ordinance, which was carried 208 to 89; and Georgia was at last out of the Union, so far as the actions of her people could secure.[63]

It remained for Hill to make one more fight in the interest of moderation and continued amity with the states composing the late partnership "under a compact of Government, entitled the Constitution of the United States of America." After secession was an accomplished fact, Hill offered an ordinance, in the Convention, to provide for the continuance of existing postal arrangements and other laws not incompatible with the sovereignty of the state, and for the continued observance of existing treaties and the vested rights of non-residents.[64] Advocacy of these measures, especially of the continuance of commercial relations with

[61] *Ibid.*

[62] *Ibid.* Most of the secondary works carry accounts of this struggle. See Stephens, II, 312–17; Phillips, *Georgia and State Rights*, pp. 202–5.

[63] Phillips, *Georgia and State Rights*, pp. 202–5; also Avery, pp. 150–57.

[64] *Columbus Weekly Sun,* January 29, 1861.

the United States government, brought Hill into a sharp clash with two of the young hotspurs of the Convention, who were both soon to offer up their lives on the battlefield. The men were Francis S. Bartow and Thomas R. R. Cobb.[65]

Bartow replied to Hill's arguments in favor of his resolutions, in rather "spread-eagle fashion." "Let desolation come," he said, "if it must upon Savannah, let every ship lie in her port and rot; let commerce go to ruin for a season; he would never give a vote that compromised the dignity, the fair fame, the honor of Georgia." Whereat the chronicler of the debate writes, "Great applause."[66]

So Hill was again overborne. He had been overborne in 1855 by the Democrats in the Fourth Congressional District, when they elected Hiram Warner; he had been overborne in the presidential canvass of 1856, when Toombs and Stephens won the electoral vote of the state for Buchanan; he had been overborne by Brown and the Democratic onslaught in the gubernatorial contest of 1857; he had been overborne by the Breckenridge party in the presidential campaign of 1860; and now in the Constitutional Convention of 1861 he had been overborne while leading a minority fight. If any public man of note in Georgia was *not* responsible for secession, it was Hill.

Secession had come. The temptation that doubtless comes to any student at this point is to indulge in homily or philosophy after his own kind. Avery, the Georgia his-

---

[65] Avery, p. 254. Bartow was killed at First Manassas, and Cobb at Fredericksburg. Both had been early in the forum as secessionists and in the field as soldiers.

[66] *Savannah Morning News*, January 31, 1861.

torian, in a very few words, covers the subject, perhaps, as well as any other: "Conservative men were powerless, and a moderate party impossible in the heated temper of the era."[67]

Hill acquiesced in the accomplished fact and went with his state, but with sorrow in his heart. In his own phrase, he assisted in the dissolution of the Union as he "would bury a benefactor."[68] Amid the rejoicings and bonfires that illuminated Milledgeville, the state capital, when news of the Secession Ordinance got abroad, he retired into his rooms, and "in darkness grieved for the Union he had loved and labored so earnestly to maintain."[69] So marked was this attitude of aloofness from the general rejoicing that he became very unpopular, and some fiery individuals went so far as to burn him in effigy.[70]

[67] Avery, p. 122.
[68] Hill's letter of December 26, 1860; *supra*, p. 50.
[69] Hill, *Life of Hill*, p. 41.
[70] *Ibid*.

CHAPTER V

CHAMPION OF THE DAVIS ADMINISTRATION

Hill was included in the group of ten strong men who were elected by the state Constitutional Convention to represent Georgia at the Montgomery Congress of the seceded states.[1] This Congress met February 4, 1861, and proceeded at once to the organization of a Southern Confederacy, as had been authorized by the conventions of each of the seceded states.[2]

The Georgia delegation was composed in almost equal part of earnest advocates of secession and of those who had labored equally as earnestly to delay or prevent that consummation. Of the secessionists, Nisbet, Bartow, the two Cobbs, Toombs, and Martin J. Crawford, and of the opponents of secession, Hill, Alexander Stephens, A. R. Wright, and Augustus H. Kenan, were accredited to Montgomery.[3] It is very probable that the Convention took this action in a spirit of conciliation, in an endeavor to forestall any factionalism which might develop around these men

[1] The *Savannah Morning News*, January 26, 1861, gives the vote for the delegate from Hill's district, the Fourth Congressional District. Hill, on the first ballot received 183 votes, scattering 59. On motion, Hill's election was made unanimous. See also, Avery, p. 164, and Stephens, II, 325.

[2] Accounts of the work of the Montgomery Congress, which cannot be covered in this study, are quite numerous. Stephens, who was present, treats it in his *Constitutional View of the War between the States*, II, 325–45. A briefer account is given in Rhodes, III, 178–82, and Dodd, pp. 215–25.

[3] Avery, p. 164; Stephens, II, 325.

within the state.⁴ At first there was slight murmuring at this unexpected action of the Convention, but the course of the erstwhile opponents of secession in the Montgomery Congress soon silenced criticism.⁵

Howell Cobb, elected president of the Congress, records the unaninimity of sentiment actuating the Georgia delegation. On February 6 he wrote from Montgomery:

> I cannot better give you an idea of the sentiment of the Congress than to say that my speech on taking the Chair is approved by everybody. Stephens, Hill, Wright and Kenan are as strong against reconstruction as any of us. The two first made strong speeches yesterday on that line. The delegation from Georgia are acting with perfect unanimity on all questions.⁶

Georgia possessed an embarrassment of riches in the personnel of her delegation. There were not three men in the South better known to the entire section—or to the nation, for that matter—than Toombs, Stephens, and Howell Cobb. Hill, young, and as yet relatively unknown outside of his native state, was quite naturally overshadowed by these more conspicuous figures. And yet the people of Montgomery were not unaware of Hill's presence in their midst, and must have known something of his previous

---

⁴ Phillips, *Life of Toombs*, p. 221.   ⁵ *Ibid.*

⁶ Phillips (ed.), *Toombs, Stephens, Cobb Correspondence*, letter of Cobb to his wife, p. 537. And yet it may be said that the Georgia delegation split, soon after this letter was written, on its choice for president of the Confederacy. Some favored Toombs, and others Howell Cobb, while others wanted Alexander Stephens. Some bitterness resulted. See Phillips, *Life of Toombs*, pp. 223–33, citing T. R. R. Cobb's letters to his wife. Also see Stephens, II, 329–33.

A rather intimate, and undisputed account of the way in which Davis was elected president is given in Stephens, II, 329–33. Also see, Phillips, *Life of Toombs*, pp. 222–26.

THE DAVIS ADMINISTRATION

leadership, for on February 10 a correspondent writes the *Savannah Morning News* of a demonstration that occurred the night before in front of the Exchange Hotel in Montgomery when an insistent call was made for Hill to address the crowd.[7]

Benjamin Harvey Hill, Jr., in his brief sketch of his father, takes the not unnatural position that his father proved a dynamic force at the Montgomery Congress. He says: "It was largely through his influence that the Constitution of the Confederate States was in all essentials like the Constitution of the United States."[8] There seems to be no documentary or contemporary evidence of this influence. Hill was not appointed on the Committee to Draft a Constitution for the Confederate States, Toombs and T. R. R. Cobb being the Georgia representatives on that Committee, which consisted of two from each state.[9] Nor did Hill receive any other major committee assignment, so far as the investigation of this writer has disclosed.[10] He seems only to have served on a committee to adopt a model for a flag for the Confederate States.[11]

Its preliminary work of organization over, the Montgomery Congress, transformed, by its own edict, into a Provisional Congress of the Confederate States, adjourned on March 16 to meet again at the call of President Davis.

[7] *Savannah Morning News*, February 12, 1861. At the time Hill could not be found.

[8] Hill, *Life of Hill*, p. 42.   [9] Stephens, II, 333.

[10] It is not unreasonable, however, to assume that Hill, who was notoriously devoted to the Constitution of the United States, may have exerted some influence in counsels, conversations, and debates, which last, unfortunately, are not preserved.

[11] *Columbus Weekly Sun*, March 5, 1861.

In the various seceded states, adjourned meetings of the state constitutional conventions came back together; and the Confederate Constitution, adopted at Montgomery, was ratified in every state.[12] Hill went to Savannah, where the second session of the Georgia Convention was held, and participated in the concluding deliberations of that body.[13]

The rôle of Hill's future usefulness to the Confederacy was determined by the General Assembly of Georgia on November 19, 1861, when he was elected Confederate States Senator.[14] Hill undoubtedly experienced some surprise at the result of the balloting.[15] Toombs, Iverson, and James Jackson, all ardent secessionists, were known to be candidates, while Hill himself had been one of the last of the prominent Georgians to accept secession.[16] And now in the first year of the new Confederacy, less than ten months after he had stoutly opposed the popular will, that same popular will, as expressed in the General Assembly, swept

[12] For the dates and votes, see Stephens, II, 355–56. The vote of Georgia was unanimous.

[13] Nothing of general import transpired at this session, aside from the ratification of the Confederate Constitution. For Hill's part in a debate over the reduction in the size of the state senate, see the *Savannah Morning News*, March 16, 1861; for a debate in which he urged the district system for congressional representation, see the same newspaper, March 19, 1861. The Convention adjourned on March 23.

[14] Hill's son says his father contemplated entering the military service (Hill, *Life of Hill*, p. 42). But Hill must have known his greatest usefulness would be in a civil capacity, and he had not the vainglory which would seek military fame. In any event he certainly did not rush to arms as did many of his colleagues in the Provisional Congress. From this body Georgia alone had lost Toombs, Howell and T. R. R. Cobb, and Bartow to the military service by the summer of 1861.

[15] Hill, *Life of Hill*, p. 42.

[16] Avery, p. 222.

him into high office.[17] For the first seat in the Confederate Senate, Hill and Toombs were nominated; and Hill was elected on the first ballot, the vote being 127 for Hill to 68 for Toombs.[18] For the other seat, Toombs, Alfred Iverson, James Jackson, and John P. King, the latter a prominent railroad man in the state, were put in nomination. It was not until the sixth ballot that Toombs received a majority of the Assembly and was declared elected to the second seat.[19] This experience was as gall and wormwood to the imperious Toombs, the often acclaimed "Mirabeau of the Revolution." He declined the election in high dudgeon.[20]

The first regular Congress of the Confederate States convened in Richmond on the eighteenth of February, 1862; and on the twenty-second of the same month, amid very depressing circumstances, Jefferson Davis was inaugurated first president of the Confederacy, for a term of six years.[21] Hill was present, representing the state of Georgia in the Confederate Senate;[22] and when the committees were announced, Hill's name headed the Judiciary Committee, which, in view of the fact that the Constitu-

[17] But see Avery's statement that it was charged at the time by opponents of Hill that the Assembly was a Whig body, constrained to vote only for Whigs (Avery, p. 222).

[18] *Milledgeville Federal Union*, November 20, 1861, gives the details of the balloting.

[19] Phillips, *Life of Toombs*, p. 241.   [20] *Ibid.*

[21] The weather was gloomy and news had just arrived of the Confederate reverses at Forts Henry and Donelson (see Rhodes, II, 487).

[22] *O. R.*, 4th Ser., III, 1187; also see *Richmond Daily Dispatch*, February 18, 22, 26, 1862. In the drawing by lot for length of terms for the Senate, Hill drew the six-year term; while Dr. Lewis, who had been appointed by Governor Brown when Toombs refused to serve, drew a two-year term (*ibid.*, February 22, 1862).

tion had left to the Congress the entire task of organizing a Confederate Judiciary, was one of the most important and responsible, as it was one of the most onerous, appointments in the Senate.[23]

And so Hill entered upon a career as Confederate States Senator, in 1862, at the age of thirty-nine years, taking up a fight which he had struggled desperately to avoid. In later years, Jefferson Davis bore witness to the constancy with which Hill served the Confederacy, a government created against his will. "Hill the faithful," he called him, and continued: "If he was the last to engage in the war between the states, he was the last to give it up. If he did not precipitate the controversy, he stood by the wreck of our fortunes." And again: "From the beginning to the end . . . . he was one on whose shoulder I could place my hand and feel that its foundation was as firm as marble."[24]

This steadfast support of a cause, adopted against his judgment and advice, when others who had precipitated, or at least joyously accepted, secession, faltered and carped and sometimes quit, is the outstanding feature of the war period in Hill's life. This is not an essay in moral philosophy, but the student would be less than human who failed to note a fine quality of fidelity in Hill's course as a Senator of the Confederate States. It would have been an easy thing, and a human thing, for him, when Confederate hopes went glimmering, as they were soon to do, to have drawn his mantle about him and, in a superior tone, to have said "I told you so." But on the contrary, in the thick gather-

[23] *Ibid.*, February 26, 1862.

[24] Speech delivered by Jefferson Davis in Atlanta, Georgia, on the occasion of unveiling the Hill statue. See *Atlanta Constitution*, May 2, 1886.

THE DAVIS ADMINISTRATION

ing gloom of the end, he took the stump in Georgia and urged his people to make continued resistance. Lee's surrender found him in Georgia exhorting the suffering people to renewed effort.[25]

In the civil history of the Confederacy nothing was more fateful than the early discord that developed between President Davis' administration and certain popular leaders in the southern states. In its essence, the cause of this friction was the insistence by these anti-administration leaders, oftentimes in a doctrinaire fashion, on extreme and meticulous "state rights." This insistence recognized no expediency and abated no theoretical claim in the interest of a large unity or the successful prosecution of a war for national existence. 'The opinion is growing, and, in the judgment of the writer, will become more and more clearly established, that not the least handicap under which the Southern Confederacy fought was the very political theory upon which it was grounded; that "state rights" and its argumentative advocates did more to defeat the southern cause than did Federal armies.[26] Hill early seemed to ap-

[25] See his speech, delivered in La Grange, Georgia, March 11, 1865, referred to hereafter. This speech is declared to have been "the last one delivered by any southern man in behalf of the Confederacy." The speech is given in Hill, *Life of Hill,* pp. 273–93.

The writer has also talked with Mr. H. H. Cabaniss of Atlanta, who, as a young man, heard Hill several times in his desperate efforts to stir up the Georgia people to resistance in the early spring of 1865.

[26] This view has been recently succinctly stated and carefully documented in the very illuminating study of Professor Owsley—in the opinion of the writer, the most notable monographic contribution to southern history of recent date. See F. L. Owsley, *State Rights in the Confederacy* (Chicago, 1925); also A. B. Moore, *Conscription and Conflict within the Confederacy* (New York, 1924).

preciate this insidious danger, and took the lead in defending the administration and in striving to minimize, in Georgia especially, the grave damage that the enemies of the administration, in that state, were working on the public morale.[27]

By the summer of 1862 Hill was recognized as the outstanding, if not the official, spokesman of the president in the Confederate Senate. The Georgia historian, Avery, writes of Hill and Davis at this period:

> Closely linked to Mr. Davis in sympathy, a constant and devoted personal friend and official adviser, entrusted with frequent and important missions of delicacy, a brilliant and earnest defender and exponent of the Confederate policy, Mr. Hill and Mr. Davis stood in warm cooperation with each other.[28]

The first major resistance to the Confederate government, and particularly the Davis administration, came over the question of conscription.[29] In the spring of 1862, the volunteer system having proved inadequate, in the view of President Davis, and the Confederate Congress, and McClellan's presence on the peninsular of Virginia constituting a serious military menace, the Confederate Congress passed the first of several conscription acts; and the fat was in the fire between the government and the ultra-sensitive advocates of states rights.[30]

---

[27] Avery, p. 255; Dubose, p. 676. Both these writers accord to Hill the leadership in defending the administration.

[28] Avery, p. 255.

[29] The entire controversy over this subject is reviewed in Schwab, *The Confederate States of America*, pp. 193–202, and in Owsley, pp. 203–18. The most exhaustive treatment of the subject, however, is Moore's *Conscription and Conflict in the Confederacy*.

[30] Schwab, p. 193; Moore, pp. 13 ff. For the general military situation, see Rhodes, IV, 2 ff.

THE DAVIS ADMINISTRATION 63

The first act authorized the conscription of able-bodied, male white citizens, with certain exceptions, between the ages of eighteen and thirty-five. On September 27, 1862, a second conscription act raised the age limit to forty-five; but Davis, concerned no doubt about the controversy already raging over the constitutionality and expediency of the whole policy, delayed execution of the second act until July 15, 1863.[31] On February 17, 1864, the age limits were again extended, the act of that date authorizing conscription of male white citizens, not specifically exempted, between the ages of seventeen and fifty. However, those between seventeen and eighteen and between forty-five and fifty were to be required to serve only as a reserve force, not subject to call beyond the borders of their own state.[32] Finally, in a vein of desperation, on March 13, 1865, the Confederate Congress commanded the enrolment of negro slaves, each state being required to provide its quota of the whole, provided this quota did not exceed one-fourth the total of the slave population.[33]

In the meanwhile the Congress had been much occupied all along with the troublesome subject of exemptions under the acts. Legislation on this subject, indeed occasioned almost as much adverse criticism as the conscription policy itself.[34] On April 21, 1862, the first special act re-

[31] Schwab, p. 196. For the act, see Moore, pp. 138 ff.

[32] Schwab, p. 193; Moore, pp. 308 ff. For the act, see *O. R.*, 4th Ser., III, 103.

[33] Schwab, p. 193; Moore, pp. 343 ff. Davis and General Lee both urged this extreme legislation. See J. B. Jones, *Diary of a Rebel War Clerk at the Confederate Capitol*, I, 353 (referred to hereafter as "Jones, *Diary*"). For the act, see *O. R.*, 4th Ser., III, 1161.

[34] See message of Governor Brown to Georgia General Assembly, November 5, 1863, in Fielder, pp. 274–76.

garding exemptions had excepted from the military service those in certain civil occupations and practicing certain professions which were regarded as essential to the body politic.[85] A second exemption act was passed on October 11, 1862, which excused from the military service one white overseer to every twenty slaves within a state, Hill himself proposing the amendment to the original act, incorporating this feature.[86] The act, to remove defects in the first exemption act and satisfy the insistent clamor raised by opponents to the government, also carefully defined the occupations and professions, pursuit of which would secure exemption under the first act, and limited the number eligible to exemption in certain of these categories.[87] Dissatisfaction with the exemption and substitute features of the conscription policy continued, and further amendments were made to the exemption bills from time to time; but this review of the conscription policy must suffice for the purposes of this study.[88]

From the passage of the first conscription act, Brown, Toombs, Alexander and Linton Stephens began a campaign of hostile criticism. Brown, perhaps, was the most vehement and relentless enemy of the policy. He began an acrimonious correspondence with Davis on the subject as early as April 22, 1862, which he continued until Davis

[85] Schwab, p. 196; Moore, pp. 52 ff. For the act, see *O. R.*, 4th Ser., I, 1081.

[86] *Richmond Examiner*, September 24, 1862.

[87] Schwab, p. 197. For the act, see *O. R.*, 4th Ser., II, 160.

[88] Amendments of May 1, 1863, and February 17, 1864. See Schwab, p. 197; also Moore, pp. 73 ff., 83 ff. For the acts, *O. R.*, 4th Ser., II, 553; III, 178.

THE DAVIS ADMINISTRATION

ceased to answer his diatribes. The correspondence, maintained with some reserve and dignity on the part of Davis, became pure defiance on the part of the doughty governor. After arguing through many reams of paper the unconstitutionality and inexpediency of the conscription acts, the governor concludes this correspondence:

> Having entered into the revolution free men, they [the people of Georgia] intend to emerge from it free men. And if I mistake not the character of the sons judged by the actions of the fathers against Federal encroachments under Jackson, Troup and Gilmer, as executive officers, they will refuse to yield their sovereignty to usurpation, and will require the Government, which is the common agent of all the states, to move within the sphere assigned it by the Constitution.[39]

But the combative governor did not rest on epistolary denunciation. Although the Supreme Court of Georgia declared the acts constitutional,[40] Brown in his message of November 6, 1862, to the General Assembly declared the acts unconstitutional and announced they could not be executed in the state, at the same time patiently repeating the arguments which had been addressed to Davis earlier in the year and broadcast in the publication of the Davis correspondence.[41]

---

[39] The entire Davis-Brown correspondence on this subject, embracing five letters from Brown to Davis and three from Davis to Brown, is printed in Fielder, pp. 355–97. To indicate Brown's volubility on this subject, his letter of June 21, 1862, the third of the series, takes up seventeen pages of single-spaced type. The extract quoted above is from the last letter of Brown to Davis, to which no reply was received. It is dated October 18, 1862, and is found in Fielder, pp. 396–97.

[40] Schwab, p. 195, quoting 34 Georgia 139.

[41] For extract of the message concerning this subject, see Fielder, pp. 271–73. Brown's arguments are also repeated in messages and letters con-

Brown's message to the General Assembly created a sensation, resulting in the formation of two factions in that body, the one siding with the governor and the other with the Davis administration. Linton Stephens, a member of the Assembly, addressed the body in a message of "great power," according to Avery, and squarely supported the governor, while condemning the Confederate administration and the Congress. "He showed," says Avery, "that conscription had been put upon the country from no necessity, from no conviction of necessities, but from premeditation and deliberation."[42]

The General Assembly was embarrassed and divided in its allegiance. A joint committee, appointed by the Assembly to consult and report back on the conscription acts, could not agree, and brought in two reports, a majority and minority report, though the division within the committee was almost equal. The majority report indorsed Brown's and Stephens's position, while the minority report "asserted the Conscription Acts constitutional, recommended acquiescence in the decision of the Supreme Court [which Brown had defied], and advised that the Governor counter-

---

tained in the *O.R.*, 4th Ser., I, 1116–20, 1128–29, 1133, 1154–56. Also see Avery, pp. 232–38, for a very sympathetic view of Brown's position. Avery is quite a eulogist of Governor Brown. Brown's entire message of November 6 is found in *House Journal*, 1862, pp. 33–54.

[42] Avery, p. 250. For Linton Stephens's views on the "unconstitutionality" and "impolicy" of the conscription acts, see his letter to J. A. Stewart, dated December 28, 1862, in Waddell, p. 245–48.

There can be no doubt that Brown and Linton Stephens made arguments of great force and cogency. Only the limitations of space and time, imposed by this study, justify the omission of sufficient quotations to demonstrate more fully their positions.

mand all orders suspending the execution of the Conscript Acts."[43]

At this juncture Hill appeared before the Assembly. He had come to Georgia in the autumn, with the approbation of Davis, to endeavor to counteract the disaffection which Brown and other opponents of the administration had aroused in the state.[44] Seeing the critical posture of affairs in the General Assembly, Hill secured an invitation to address that body on the issues of the day and, on December 11, 1862, delivered an impassioned defense of the Davis administration, and particularly of the conscription acts. Inasmuch as this speech, for the time, checked the drift from the administration and rallied support to the government,[45] and reveals Hill, moreover, in his distinctive rôle as the prop of that administration, it seems desirable to analyze this speech of December 11 at some length.[46]

[43] Avery, p. 251; Schwab, p. 200.

[44] See letter from Davis to Hill, written from Richmond to Hill in Georgia, dated October 23, 1862. This letter is largely concerned with conscript problems and concludes "with personal regard for yourself as well as high consideration for your public character." (in Dunbar Rowland [ed.], *Jefferson Davis Constitutionalist, His Letters, Papers and Speeches* [10 vols.], V, 358–59). See Moore, p. 258, for the defeat of Brown's nullification scheme.

[45] Inasmuch as the Assembly adjourned without action, in the face of the governor's message and recommendations and of a report by their own committee favoring the governor's recommendations, after hearing Hill's speech, it seems not unreasonable to ascribe to Hill a victory.

[46] This address is found in Hill, *Life of Hill*, pp. 252–72. The address was not reported at the time delivered, and Hill only wrote it out a few days later, in response to the request of a committee from the Assembly. Hill admits the language is not exactly as used, but says, "the line of argument is precisely the same" (*ibid.*, p. 251).

After a survey of the initial problems of the Confederacy and its early progress in meeting these problems, in which he takes occasion to pay a tribute to the patriotism and constancy of the armies, the civil agencies of the government, and the southern people, Hill approached the subject of the trials incident to all republics.[47]

In republics the disaffected and the dissatisfied generally level their shafts against him who may for the time be Chief Executive. Different conclusions which are always formed when free discussions are universal; personal private griefs which must exist when all cannot be gratified; personal jealousies which will arise when many aspire and few can be chosen must be expected to do their usual share of fault finding in the new Confederacy.[48]

And then he advanced to the mainspring of southern woes:

In addition to these sources of discord inseparable from all free governments, there are others growing out of our anomalous form of double governments. In the nature of things the state governments will be jealous. This jealousy is often legitimate. In the old Union there were many occasions when the southern states were justly resentful and state complaints became popular to the southern mind. It is not strange therefore that the earnest and the ambitious—indeed all the classes first mentioned, should seek to invoke the force of this popular feeling in their own behalf, and in all their clamors against the Confederate Government and the Confederate Executive, in season and out of season, to cry "State Rights."[49]

Hill then took up the delicate subject of Jefferson Davis, against whom Brown and Toombs had directed their

---

[47] *Ibid.*, pp. 252–56.   [48] *Ibid.*, p. 256.

[49] *Ibid.* What an opportunity is afforded to the mind hostile to the South, to exult at this paragraph. It presents a situation little less than ironic; and to the mind hostilely disposed, it must have seemed that "evenhanded justice" was very early compelling the South "to commend the ingredients" of her "poisoned chalice" to her own southern lips.

fiercest onslaughts. Prefacing his remarks with the statement that in earlier years he had differed with Davis, that Davis was not his own choice for president, and that "not one civil commission" had to his knowledge been awarded by Davis "to an old political friend of mine," he pays Davis this tribute:

Thus judging him, I declare to you that if I had now to select a chief magistrate for this trying crisis, I should feel it a duty to select Jefferson Davis. I concede the charge sneeringly made that he is neither a Caesar, nor a Cromwell, nor a Napoleon. He is nobler than either and greater than all, because he has respect unto the laws of the land, and seeks to establish not to destroy constitutional government. In my opinion his great desire, to which all other earthly desires are subordinate, is our final and complete success in this revolution.[50]

Hill then addressed himself to the various "issues" made against the administration, congratulating the country that in a republic of "free opinions," where "minds of men are as variant as the leaves of the trees," these issues had proven so few and had found so few advocates.[51] He represented these issues to be four, each of which he reviewed, attempting to justify the attitude assumed by the Davis administration. The first three he passed over briefly; but the fourth, which had been the source of the liveliest controversy and most bitter animadversions, consumed the remainder of his time, and its discussion constitutes much the larger part of the address.[52]

[50] *Ibid.*, p. 256.   [51] *Ibid.*, p. 257.

[52] The "issues," according to Hill, were: 1st. That the Navy Department has not done its duty. 2nd. That Military appointments have been marked by favoritism, and have proven unsatisfactory. 3rd. That the demands for an invasion of the North have been disregarded. 4th. That the conscription policy is unconstitutional and inexpedient.

This major "issue" was, of course, the conscription policy upon which, at Davis' suggestion, the Confederate Congress had embarked in April, 1862. The vigorous warfare waged on this policy, and on Mr. Davis for sponsoring it, has already been treated.[53] Inasmuch as Hill made a considerable impression on the country in defense of the policy, it remains to analyze his views on the subject.

He repeated the familiar charges made by the opponents of the acts and then proceeded to disprove these charges. The first charge, in substance, was that the previously existing methods of accepting volunteers directly or by requisitioning the states for their quotas of such volunteers "would have secured all the troops needed." Hill exhaustively traced the history of the volunteer system and its workings, from February 28, 1861, when the Provisional Congress at Montgomery made first legislative provision for raising Confederate troops, to January 27, 1862, when the last act concerning enrolments prior to the adoption of a conscription system was adopted. He then announced his conclusions from this review:[54]

> Thus gentlemen and fellow-citizens, you will perceive that Congress adopted every conceivable mode of getting volunteers. Even the humors of states and the caprices of individuals were all consulted. If men wished to come by tender through the States, there was the law. If directly, by offer to the President, there was the law. If as cavalry, artillery, infantry, or mixture of all, or even as independent partisans, there was the law. If they wished to volunteer for three, six, twelve

---

[53] *Supra*, pp. 61–66.

[54] Hill minutely reviewed the passage and workings of no less than eleven acts of the Confederate Congress: the acts of February 28, March 6, May 8, May 11, August 8, August 21, December 11, December 19, all in 1861; and January 22, January 23, and January 27 in 1862.

THE DAVIS ADMINISTRATION 71

months, for three years, for the war, or for any other time, there was the law. If they wished to enter the general service or be enlisted to defend a particular State, or county, or city, or town, or fireside, there was the law. If they wished to come in legions, or regiments, or battalions, or squadrons, or companies, or even singly—all alone and all ablaze with patriotism—there was the law precisely fitting the case, and made to fit the case. Come,—it matters not how, it matters not from where, it matters not with whom, it matters not for how long—come, come, and come quickly, and defend our invaded country—was, and is, and ever has been the earnest appeal of the Government—the President and the Congress—to all our people. Will any complaining, far seeing assailant tell me what other form of tender or acceptance Congress could have adopted to encourage men to volunteer. . . . .[55]

So, we not only provided every mode of volunteering which even caprice could suggest, but also offered every inducement and stimulant that ability would allow, or ingenuity could devise. Men were not only received, and received in their own way but they were sent for and begged to come. Tried veterans filled the country urging those at home to join their glorious ranks. Money was freely offered, and ambition was commissioned to employ all its energies in raising regiments, battalions, squadrons, and companies to secure command. All failed. Our army was still thinning and the enemy still increasing. . . . .[56]

There was no remedy left but to keep all the regiments and organizations we had, and fill them up by a system of compulsory enlistment; and that remedy to be effective, must be speedy and thorough. . . . .[57]

Then Hill advanced to the second major charge directed at the policy, namely, that it was unconstitutional. If the acts are unconstitutional, challenges Hill; if the Confederate government possesses no right, no ability to de-

[55] Hill, *Life of Hill*, p. 260.
[56] *Ibid.*, p. 261.   [57] *Ibid.*, p. 263.

fend itself, then, indeed, it stands a demonstrated failure; and what a sorry spectacle does it present to the world—a nation asking to be admitted into the family of nations and incapable of commanding the obedience of its own citizens or repelling the assaults of foreign foes.[58]

But why are the acts alleged to be unconstitutional, he inquires. First, because "they are said to be contrary to individual liberty and oppressive upon individual rights." But Hill argues that citizens possess obligations as well as rights and that an obligation recognized by all authorities upon government is the obligation resting upon the citizen of rendering military service *according to law*.[59] But in the second place, it is said that "the States alone can exercise this power of compelling military service." Hill answers:

> There is certainly a plain and very easy method of determining this question. Is this power delegated or reserved? If delegated, it belongs to the Confederate Government; if reserved it belongs to the States. The Constitution—the grant—is the only test. That most explicitly declares that Congress shall have power "to declare war" and "to raise and support armies." Here ends the argument but strange to say not the controversy. Men who claim to favor strict construction, to oppose interpolations now begin to construe and interpolate. They say that the Constitution means that Congress shall have power "to raise armies" by voluntary enlistment. By what authority of fact or logic are these words added? Again men who love controversy say the Constitution means that Congress shall have power "to raise armies" by calls on the States. By what authority are these words added? These broad and destructive interpolations upon the Constitution are not only without excuse but in the very teeth of history.[60]

[58] *Ibid.*
[59] *Ibid.*, pp. 263-64.
[60] *Ibid.*, pp. 264-65.

Hill then contends, by a review of the history of the Confederation and the debates in the Constitutional Convention of 1787, that there was no intent so to limit the military power of Congress. But it is said in the third place, he continues, that the power "to raise armies" is limited by the conditions thrown around the power to call on the militia. On this point Brown had made his strongest fight.[61] Hill insists that the militia power is a peace-time power, or, at least, one granted in national emergencies, and cannot be confused with the power "to declare war" or "to raise and support armies," which is a power designed for totally different contingencies.

And so, he says, malcontents, failing in the argument, have attempted "to provoke jealousies and alarm the fears of the people" by a misrepresentation of the motives of those responsible for the conscription legislation. These motives are said to be sinister, to betray a determination "to destroy the people and the States." Hence, for the first time in political logic it is maintained that "to show a power could be abused" is to prove it non-existent. Manifestly by this mode of reasoning, he argues, it could be soon proved that Congress had no power whatever, for what power in the whole enumerated catalog is not subject to abuse.[62]

Hill then launched into a plea for good faith and loyal support of the common government, and a castigation of those malcontents "perpetually snarling, snapping, fault

[61] Correspondence with Davis; see Fielder, pp. 355–97. See especially, Brown's letter of June 21, 1862, pp. 381–84, for an elaboration of the militia argument.

[62] Hill, *Life of Hill*, p. 267.

finding, complaining," at the time when the very national existence was at stake:

> The government is your own. The agents who administer it are of your own choosing from your own citizenship. Choose wise men, good men; then give them your confidence and support. . . . .
>
> Eternal vigilance is the price of liberty. I grant it. But I deny that vigilance means resistance to the government, disaffection to the laws, contumely to authority, or the disorganizing freedom of individual opinion to set itself up against legal enactments and judicial decisions.[63]

In the course of the argument Hill had admitted that he himself had doubted the expediency of the conscription legislation when it had been proposed in Congress, and had expressed himself to that effect. He had preferred "a milder form of conscription."

> But the present proposition became the law of my country, and I shall, as a good citizen, support it, and with equal cheerfulness, whether I voted for it or against it. I will not countenance that sickly patriotism, nor render commendation to that higher law fanaticism, which cannot support as law that which, as a proposition of expediency, did not meet the approval of individual preference.[64]

As has been said, Hill arrested, to a degree, defection from the Confederate administration; but he did not escape virulent personal criticism, as a result of his address before the General Assembly. Old personal and political adversaries were quick to charge him with "inconsistency"

---

[63] *Ibid.*, p. 268.

[64] *Ibid.*, p. 266. Manifestly this last shaft is aimed at Governor Brown, as is a good deal of the address. Brown, it will be remembered, had recommended that the General Assembly disregard the law and the decision of the Georgia Supreme Court (see *supra*, p. 65). Hill's speech drew a public letter from Governor Brown, in which his arguments are combatted. See *infra*, p. 76.

THE DAVIS ADMINISTRATION 75

in his course regarding the conscription acts and to impugn his motives.

An example of this sort of thing is the abuse which appeared over the signature of "Calhoun" in the Georgia press. The anonymous writer points out—as had several, not anonymous—that Hill had voted against the first conscription act and dodged the second by not voting. Then he had had the effrontery to come to Georgia and defend the legislation before the Georgia Assembly.[65] In his speech before the Assembly, sneers this writer, Hill had argued that the acts were constitutional and urgently necessary; but, under oath as a Confederate Senator, the actions of this eloquent apologist had belied his words.[66] "Calhoun" then rather spitefully and weakly disposes of the almost unanimous approval given Hill's address by the Georgia press, and of the manifest effect which the address had exerted over the Assembly, by attributing these results to the fact that it was recognized in Georgia that "Hill will not work in a party unless he works in lead" and that consequently sycophants puff him up, "despite the fact that his leadership usually has ended in a ditch."

Governor Brown also directed his fire against Hill in a public letter which fastened on the alleged inconsistency in Hill's course respecting the conscription acts, and in addition raised the question of motive. The vitriolic governor wrote:

[65] In *Brown Scrap Books*.

[66] Inasmuch as Hill had admitted this so-called "inconsistency" in his address, and explained it satisfactorily to most of his auditors, this criticism seems to have little point. But it was insistently made against him. See also, Avery, p. 255.

Whether the extreme reluctance of the Senator to place himself on record in favor of the Conscription Acts resulted from the over caution of the statesman, or the subtle design of the politician, who was in doubt about political sentiment is a question that the people may be as little embarrassed in deciding as is the Senator in reconciling his record at Richmond with his speech at Milledgeville.[67]

The second major assault on the Davis administration grew out of the legislation authorizing the suspension of the writ of habeas corpus, and the declaration of martial law by the Richmond government. The first act authorizing the suspension of the writ, and the declaration of martial law in exposed or supposedly disaffected areas, came on February 27, 1862, in the period of gloom occasioned by the fall of Forts Henry and Donelson.[68] This act authorized the suspension of the writ during "the present invasion"; but Congress soon amended the law, on April 19, so as to limit the period of suspension to thirty days after the meeting of the next Congress.[69] This law was followed by the suspension of the writ and declaration of martial law in Richmond and in certain coast areas which were regarded as exposed.[70] Little protest attended this legislation at first, though Stephens was soon giving utterance to objections and gloomy prophesies.[71] Nevertheless, on October 13, 1862, the same authorization to suspend the writ

---

[67] See Brown's letter to Alexander Stephens, February 16, 1863, in Phillips (ed.), *Toombs, Stephens, Cobb Correspondence*, pp. 610-11.
The quotation is taken from Dubose, p. 672.

[68] *O. R.*, 4th Ser., I, 954; see also Schwab, p. 186. A comprehensive review of the controversies over the suspension of the writ is given in Owsley, pp. 150-202.

[69] *O. R.*, 4th Ser., I, 1075.

[70] Jones, *Diary*, 1, 113, 115, 116, 120.   [71] *Ibid.*, p. 163.

for a period to include thirty days after the meeting of the next Congress was extended by the Congress.[72]

By the congressional sessions of 1863, however, the opposition to this "despotic" policy had been worked up to a considerable heat. But "by a very urgent message, the President was able to rally the factious congressmen" and secured another law authorizing the suspension of the writ. This act was passed on February 15, 1864, and authorized the suspension during the invasion and until three months after the beginning of the next Congress, that is, until August 1, 1864.[73] "This Act," says Professor Owsley, "precipitated one of the bitterest and in some respects most disastrous conflicts of the whole war between the Confederate and State authorities."[74]

The opposition to this allegedly arbitrary and despotic policy was now so bitter that the Confederate Congress did not dare to renew the authorization to suspend the writ, when this authorization expired by limitation on August 1, 1864. This non-action of the Congress followed the adverse report of the Judiciary Committee of the Senate, which in May, 1864, had reported against the renewal of the authorization to suspend the writ.[75] In the last session of the Confederate Congress, beginning November 7, 1864, the subject of the suspension of the writ again became a bone of contention; but the authorization to suspend was not again granted, and Mr. Davis' sorely pressed administration passed its expiring months without exercising the power which was frequently exercised in the North.[76]

[72] O. R., 4th Ser., II, 121; Jones, Diary, I, 150, 151-58.
[73] O. R., 4th Ser., III, 203-4.
[74] Owsley, p. 177.
[75] Schwab, pp. 187-88.
[76] Ibid., pp. 189-90.

From the first, in Georgia, the states-rights advocates inveighed against the suspension legislation and its execution, although Davis had refrained from suspending the writ anywhere in that state, under the acts of February 27 and April 19, 1862.[77]

Toombs, the two Stephens, Alexander and Linton, and Governor Brown concurred in fulminations against Davis and all his works, and in predicting the direst results, from the direction events were taking at Richmond. Brown wrote Alexander Stephens, at this time: "I fear we have more to apprehend from military despotism than from subjugation by the enemy";[78] and in his message to the General Assembly in this year, he said: "It [the suspension law] places the liberty of every citizen of the Confederacy at the mercy of the President, who may imprison any citizen under this order, without legal warrant or authority, and no court dare interfere to liberate the captive when the imprisonment is illegal."[79]

Judge Linton Stephens, a rather melancholy judge at best, saw nothing for the southern people but subjugation to Davis and his minions at Richmond. He warned that

[77] Owsley, p. 162. However, Bragg, on his own initiative, had declared martial law in Atlanta on August 11, 1862, bringing down on his head the anathemas of the Georgia group of states-rights advocates. See letter of Stephens to James M. Calhoun, Johnson, and Browne, pp. 421-23.

[78] Letter, dated September 1, 1862, in Phillips (ed.), *Toombs, Stephens, Cobb Correspondence*, p. 605.

[79] For Brown's message to the Assembly, dealing with this subject, see *Confederate Records of Georgia*, II, 305-7; for the entire message, see *House Journal*, 1862, pp. 33-54. For the early opposition of Toombs to the suspension legislation, see his letters July 14, 1862, to Alexander Stephens, and August 29, 1863, to W. W. Burwell in Phillips (ed.), *Toombs, Stephens, Cobb Correspondence*, pp. 599-601, 628-29.

THE DAVIS ADMINISTRATION 79

Davis and Lincoln were vying with each other in "usurpations and tyrannies" and were "crushing out constitutional liberties," while their emmissaries and bribed journals were "preparing the sickened and weary hearts of the people for the coup d'etat."[80]

The year 1863 brought to a head another controversy between the advocates of a vigorous central government and the states-rights partisans. This concerned the establishment of a Supreme Court for the Confederacy.[81] Hill had championed the establishment of such a court from the first and, in the course of the long-drawn-out debates on the subject, came into dramatic and finally violent collision with William L. Yancey, the leader of the opposition in the Confederate Senate.[82]

An early act of the Provisional Congress, March 11, 1861, had provided for the establishment of Confederate courts. A Supreme Court whose original and appellate jurisdiction was defined in terms closely resembling those used in the Constitution of 1787, regarding the jurisdiction of the Federal Supreme Court, was, by the terms of the act, to hold annual sessions at the seat of government.[83] In accord with this act, district courts were soon created and began to function.[84]

[80] Linton to Alexander Stephens, April 6, 1863, in Waddell, pp. 257–59.

[81] The controversy over this subject is reviewed by Schwab, pp. 219–20.

[82] Hill and Yancey had long been political adversaries, differing on nearly every political score since as far back as the Buchanan-Fillmore campaign of 1856, in which a personal misunderstanding had arisen to embitter the relation of the two men. See Dubose, pp. 332–33.

[83] Schwab, p. 219.

[84] Acts of May 21, 1861, and January 29, 1862.

But the Congress showed some hesitation in organizing the Confederate Supreme Court. This reluctance to organize was due to the centralizing tendencies ascribed to such a court by doctrinaire adherents of state rights.[85] Consequently on July 23, 1861, the previous act authorizing the Court was amended so as to prevent the meeting of a Supreme Court until authorized to do so by Congress.[86] So matters rested for more than a year, the conscription and suspension of the writ of habeas corpus legislation, together with other pressing measures for the vigorous prosecution of the war, consuming the energies of the Congress.

However, Hill, as chairman of the Judiciary Committee in the Senate, whose prerogative it would be to report a bill organizing the Court, had not given up the project. In March, 1862, a lively debate occurred in the Senate over immediate organization, Hill advocating that action, and being opposed by Semmes of Louisiana. Hill argued, at this time, that the Constitution authorized the Court and that the accumulating cases in the district courts afforded ample evidence of the pressing need of such a Court. Moreover, he stated, the reluctance of the Congress to carry out the plain dictates of the Constitution in this regard was giving aid and encouragement to the enemies of the government.[87] However, the enemies of the Court prevented any affirmative action.

Early in 1863 Hill prevailed on the Judiciary Com-

[85] *Richmond Dispatch*, March 2, 1862, gives account of the opposition of Semmes of Louisiana to the Court; Dubose, pp. 703-4, relates Clay of Alabama's opposition; and the same author, pp. 706-9, recounts the opposition and views of Yancey regarding the Court.

[86] Schwab, p. 219.

[87] See *Richmond Dispatch*, March 27, 1862.

mittee of the Senate to report a formal bill to organize the Court. Unfortunately the report of the Committee to this end was accompanied by two other proposals. It included a measure, popularly known as a "sedition bill," to regulate or suppress the freedom of speech and of the press under certain circumstances, and the nomination to the position of Assistant Secretary of War of former Federal Supreme Court Justice John A. Campbell of Alabama, a former opponent of secession, and peculiarly unacceptable to the Alabama delegation in the Congress. This combination of measures, each one of which was obnoxious to the opposition, produced a fierce resistance from Yancey, Wigfall of Texas, and other anti-administration leaders in the Senate. In the resulting wrangle, Hill's motives and personal integrity were not spared.[88]

The "sedition bill" was soon dropped; the nomination of Campbell was confirmed by the Senate; and the main debate over the triple report of the Judiciary Committee settled down to that part proposing the immediate organization of the Supreme Court. On March 18 the bill, as reported by Hill from the Committee, passed the Senate in modified form. Senator Clay of Alabama, against the combined opposition of Hill and Senator Phelan of Mississippi, had carried through an amendment, striking out the appellate jurisdiction of the Court.[89] The House, however, soon buried the measure; and though another effort was

[88] For the debates mentioned, see Dubose, pp. 689–712; also the following newspapers: *Richmond Examiner*, February 6, 1863, *Charleston Mercury*, March 25, 1863, *Charleston Courier*, February 27, and March 18, 1863. Hill denied authorship or support of the "sedition bill," though accepting its constitutionality (see Dubose, p. 701).

[89] Dubose, p. 700; Schwab, p. 219.

made to organize the Court in the next session of the Congress, it was easily defeated, and the Confederacy went to its death without the services—or, as the advocates of states rights would have said, the disservices—of a Supreme Court.[90]

Hill was far from slavish in supporting the Davis administration. He was ever a close student of constitutional government and, when the practical emergency did not dictate otherwise, seems a bit meticulous in his devotion to and insistence on constitutional forms and principles.[91] Even in the stress of a war for national independence, he insisted that the executive and legislative branches of the government stick to their constitutional functions, where such a course was not clearly incompatible with the vigorous prosecution of the war.[92]

[90] Schwab, p. 220. B. H. Hill, Jr., in his sketch of his father says that he had often heard his father say that had the Confederate government possessed a Supreme Court, President Davis would have appointed Hill's brother, W. P. Hill, an eminent lawyer of Texas, as the first chief justice (see Hill, *Life of Hill,* p. 12). This opens an interesting avenue of speculation for those who are always distrustful of motives.

[91] This is best illustrated in his speeches and writings against reconstruction, notably the Davis-Hall speech of July 16, 1867, the Bush Arbor speech of July 23, 1868, and his "Notes on the Situation" of the summer of 1867, referred to hereafter.

[92] Illustrative of this position, see his action in presenting resolutions designed to prevent the Virginia legislature from appropriating certain property of Georgians engaged in the salt-manufacture in Virginia (*Richmond Examiner,* October 1, 1862); his opposition to certain acts of the War Department in placing conscripts in camps of instruction before their fitness was ascertained ("Let's act according to law," he admonished the executive department at this time) (*ibid.,* September 12, 1862); his sponsoring an exemption bill, against Davis' opposition, on September 21, 1862, in order to obviate what he thought was an unnecessary clash with the state of South Carolina *(ibid.,* September 24, 1862); and his debate

THE DAVIS ADMINISTRATION

It may be further said that the administration and the country at large were not slow to recognize his services. Robert M. Barton, from Tennessee, addressed him on January 23, 1863, as "one of the conservative patriots of the country," and appealed to him for relief in the matter of certain effects of military administration in the state.[93] This letter, forwarded to the president, brought an acknowledgment of Hill's services and a frank expression of the presidential mind on many of the problems of the day.[94] There is good evidence, further, that Hill became very popular with the army, and especially the soldiers of Georgia, for his staunch advocacy of all measures directed to the vigorous prosecution of the war, as opposed to the obstructionist tactics of Brown, Toombs, and the two Stephens.[95]

In 1863 Hill became involved in local political matters in Georgia in at least two cases. Brown's third term as governor expired in 1863, and the local supporters of the Davis administration wished to replace the governor by one sympathetic with that administration. Several likely candidates had been mentioned. Governor Brown's letter to Alexander Stephens explains the relation of Hill to the situation.[96] He writes:

---

with Senator Phelan of Mississippi against the legislative prohibition of cotton planting in 1862 (*Richmond Dispatch,* March 15, 1862). These instances show that Hill is not a slavish supporter of the administration.

[93] Found in *O. R.,* 4th Ser., II, 367-70.

[94] Letter previously cited, *supra,* footnote 44, this chapter.

[95] See Reed, V, 140.

[96] Dated May 29, 1863. Found in Phillips (ed.), *Toombs, Stephens, Cobb Correspondence,* pp. 618-19.

Kenan, I am told, says I shall have opposition, but that it's not worth while to run any of those spoken of against me; that Ben Hill is the man. My own opinion is, while I do not give Ben credit for very superior judgment, that he will not now put himself in the position of a candidate for Governor just simply to gratify Kenan. He would hardly be willing to resign his seat in the Senate for the chance he would have to be elected Governor. If he ran and did not resign he would not be a very formidable candidate.[97]

Brown was right. Hill declined to run. The campaign was a three-cornered one, Brown representing the opposition to Davis, Timothy Furlow being drafted to represent the Davis support, and Joshua Hill running as a Union sympathizer. Brown was easily elected.[98]

The other local political situation into which Hill entered in Georgia in 1863 concerned the election by the General Assembly of a Confederate States Senator to succeed the Brown appointee, Mr. Lewis, who had drawn only a two-year term in 1861.[99] Toombs had gone to Georgia in November with the avowed purpose of securing the election and then using his senatorial position to continue his war on the Davis administration.[100] The situation seemed threatening to supporters of Davis, and Hill hastened to Georgia to exert his influence against Toombs. The election occurred in November, and Toombs was defeated by

[97] Augustus H. Kenan, referred to in Brown's letter, was a former American party associate of Hill. He, too, had opposed secession and had served in the Provisional Congress of the Confederacy. He now represented the Davis administration in the state.

[98] For the election, see Avery, pp. 260–61.

[99] It will be remembered that Toombs had declined the scratch election of 1861 and that Brown had appointed Lewis. See *supra*, footnote 22, this chapter.

[100] Phillips, *Life of Toombs*, p. 250.

Hershel V. Johnson, a man of much less venom and hostility toward the Confederate administration.[101] This was the last great victory of Hill for the administration. Truly, as Professor Owsley says, "Died of State Rights" should be carved above the gravestone of the "lost Cause." Against this ailment, though he was not the logical physician, Hill had labored and prescribed in vain.[102]

[101] *Ibid.*, p. 250. Professor Phillips says: "The determining influence in the contest seems to have been exerted by B. H. Hill who was President Davis's right hand man in Georgia."

[102] Eight major causes of friction between the Confederate government and the states, may be discovered, besides those discussed in the text. They are, briefly stated: (1) the control of the distribution of troops, munitions, supplies, etc., before the conscription acts (see Owsley, p. 4); (2) the control of the appointments of officers among the troops in the Confederate service (*ibid.*); (3) the right of the president to call out the state militia (see Schwab, pp. 214 ff.); (4) appointments to Confederate civil and military service within a particular state (*ibid.*, pp. 216 ff.); (5) the control of interstate commerce (*ibid.*, p. 217); (6) blockade-running and speculations on its profits (*ibid.*, p. 218); (7) the taxation of state bonds (*ibid.*, p. 219); and (8) the impression of property, slaves, and supplies (for extended discussion, see Owsley, pp. 219-71).

CHAPTER VI
RELUCTANT SURRENDER

Hill's most significant contribution to the last year of Confederate history was his opposition to defeatism and his vigorous insistence on the prolongation of resistance to the enemy until the goal of southern independence had been achieved. There still remained during this year abundant necessity to defend the policies of the Davis administration; but at the same time Hill assumed the additional exacting task of frustrating the insidious peace movement which was making a profound appeal to a people wasted by years of war. This peace, urged upon the people and the government, was a peace without victory—in fact, any peace obtainable—and to Hill the idea was intolerable.[1]

The spring of 1864 witnessed the climax of the fight against the policies of the Confederate administration from within the Confederacy. From a military view, the fortunes of the Confederacy were at low ebb. The defeats at Gettysburg, Vicksburg, and Chattanooga, in the summer and autumn of 1863, had shattered the southern morale.[2] Sherman was preparing his thrust into the heart of Georgia, and Grant was projecting the last great offensive against Richmond.[3]

To cope with the increasingly disastrous situation, the

[1] See Hill's speech, delivered at La Grange, Georgia, March 11, 1865; printed in Hill, *Life of Hill*, pp. 273-93, especially pp. 275-81.

[2] For a general account of these southern defeats and their consequences, see Rhodes, IV, 282-98, 300-19, 405-7.

[3] *Ibid.*, p. 448.

Confederate Congress passed two vigorous acts in February, 1864. An act of February 15 authorized renewed suspension of the writ of habeas corpus "during the invasion, and until three months after the meeting of the next Congress."[4] Another, on February 17, extended the ages of those subject to conscription.[5] These acts, especially the first, called forth a veritable torrent of abuse against the Congress and the administration; but more practically effective was a concerted program launched against the policies of the government by the Georgia group, led by Brown and the two Stephens.

While the acts in question were pending in the Congress, Brown and Alexander Stephens were in correspondence, regarding a course of resistance to be inaugurated if they should become law.[6] On February 20 Brown wrote Stephens: "The great wrong which you anticipated has been done by Congress, and I confess I contemplate with horror the suspension of the *habeas corpus*. Every state in the Confederacy should denounce and condemn the wicked act."[7]

The plan of action concerted was that Brown should call the General Assembly in special session and send in a message condemning the act and declaring it a nullity in Georgia. Linton Stephens, a member of the Assembly, then was to introduce resolutions embodying the action proposed in the message. Then Alexander Stephens, whose

[4] *Supra.*, p. 77.   [5] *Supra.*, p. 63.

[6] See letter of Brown to Stephens, dated February 13, 1864, asking that a date be set for a conference between Alexander, Linton, and himself "on the subject of which we have lately corresponded" (Phillips [ed.], *Toombs, Stephens, Cobb Correspondence*, p. 633).

[7] *Ibid.*

influence in the state, as vice-president of the Confederacy, was naturally very great, would appear, by invitation, before the Assembly and argue the adoption of the policy proposed in the message and the resolutions.[8]

This program was carried out exactly as planned. On March 10, Brown sent in his message to the Assembly; on March 14, Linton Stephens proposed his resolutions, concerning which Alexander Stephens wrote Hershel V. Johnson that they had been "prepared by Linton after full consultation with himself";[9] and on March 16, Alexander Stephens addressed the Assembly, urging the adoption of the resolutions. This propaganda was skilfully arranged. The condemnatory and nullifying resolutions were adopted by the General Assembly on March 19; and Georgia, by official action, was arrayed against the Confederate authorities.[10]

Much has been said about Alexander Stephens' opposition to the Davis policies; but until his speech of March

[8] Brown's message to the Assembly is found in part in *Confederate Records of the State of Georgia*, II, 608–18, and is also reproduced by Fielder, pp. 281–306. It is also found in *House Journal*, 1864, pp. 5–51. The resolutions of Linton Stephens are found in *O. R.*, 4th Ser., III, 234–35, and also in Stephens, II, 788–90, and Waddell, pp. 269–71; regarding Stephens's speech, see Owsley, pp. 187–89, and Johnson and Browne, p. 455.

[9] *O. R.*, 4th Ser., III, 279.

[10] Waddell, p. 371; Avery, p. 273. Mr. Avery rather fatuously remarks: "These resolutions have become famous, and stand as a monument of that governing statesmanship that during the Revolution, Georgia so supremely and without rivalry exercised." Avery is a panygyrist of Brown, first, last, and all the time. His book on Georgia history, very excellent in many respects, has been facetiously labeled by some critic, "History of Joe Brown's Georgia."

16 before the General Assembly of Georgia, this opposition had been conducted by means of private correspondence and in personal conferences at Crawfordsville, his Georgia home.[11] He now came out in the open, as Brown, Linton Stephens, and Toombs had been all the while. Stephens from the first saw no virtue in the leaders of the Confederacy and gloomily wrapped himself up in a mantle of self-righteous hauteur.[12]

Governor Brown, whose energy and industry in a political contest is certainly beyond cavil, was determined that the propaganda against the policies of the administration, successful in the Georgia Assembly, should have a wider audience. He sent copies of his message of March 10 and of Linton Stephens' resolutions against the suspension of the writ of habeas corpus to the captain of every company in every Georgia regiment in the Confederate service and to the clerk of every county court within the lines of the Confederacy.[13] But the indomitable governor did not do things half-way. Securing funds from private sources to meet the expense, he sent Stephens' speech of March 16 to the lieutenant of every company, to whose captain he had sent the other documents; and to

---

[11] See Johnson and Browne, pp. 408–54.

[12] Stephens' letters to Linton, his devoted brother, and his conversations with his intimate friend and biographer, Richard Malcolm Johnson, of which copious notes were made by the latter and incorporated in his book on Stephens, afford abundant evidence of the truth of this assertion. As examples, merely see letter to Linton, September 7, 1862, Johnson and Browne, p. 421; and his conversation with Johnson, recorded on p. 414, of the latter's biography. See also Owsley, pp. 184–85.

[13] Brown's statement to Alexander Stephens in letter of April 5, 1864, Phillips (ed.), *Toombs, Stephens, Cobb Correspondence*, pp. 639–40.

the sheriff of every county, to whose clerk the other documents had gone. If one goes awry or meets a rebuff, then it may be that the other will score, is the substance of the explanation which he sent Stephens regarding these actions.[14]

The results of this organized propaganda in Georgia, and to less degree in other states, is seen in the refusal of the Senate Judiciary Committee to recommend renewed suspension of the writ, and in the consequent failure of the Congress to renew the authorization after August, 1864.[15] Davis had been defeated within his own lines.

In the meanwhile Hill had not been inactive while the Georgia opposition was preparing. He was on the ground in Georgia, in March, 1864, endeavoring, as usual, to win support for the Davis administration. Brown and Stephens made overtures to him to join in the fight against the Act of February 15, against which Hill had voted in the Senate.[16] Brown, however, had not put much confidence in getting his support, saying pungently in a letter to Stephens, regarding which due allowance must be made for the governor's own prejudices: "His [Hill's] prejudices are so strong however, against some, who will from their position be obliged to take a prominent part in the matter, that I fear they will control his judgment and his actions."[17]

Hill, as the event proved, did not co-operate with the program of the obstructionists, whether, as the governor

[14] Brown's letter to Stephens, April 12, 1864, *ibid.*, pp. 640–41.

[15] *Supra*, p. 77.

[16] Brown to Stephens, March 14, 1864, Phillips (ed.), *Toombs, Stephens, Cobb Correspondence*, p. 634. For Hill's vote on this measure, see his letter to Stephens, March 14, 1864, *ibid.*, p. 636.

[17] Letter to Stephens, *ibid.*, p. 634.

apprehended, from his "strong prejudices" or not; but he did write a lengthy—and, in the light of his past, rather surprising—letter to Alexander Stephens, which can be viewed as nothing less than the extension of the olive branch to that old antagonist. The letter, indeed, bears a sycophantic note and must have been consciously intended to stir Stephens' vanity.[18]

It opens with a reference to Governor Brown's recent message to the General Assembly, which has just come under Hill's eye. He expresses approval of the latter part of the message, dealing with "the causes of the war, how conducted, and who responsible." Then incense is offered to Stephens in these words:

. . . . I know I must thank *you* for it. The whole country will owe you an everlasting debt for it. Governor Brown can never pay you in kind for the great benefit you have bestowed on him. You have given him a grandeur of conception, an enlargement of views and a perspicuity and power of style which he never could have reached. His only trouble can be that the foot prints are *too plain not* to be recognized.

Regarding that portion of the governor's message dealing with the suspension of the writ of habeas corpus, which Hill says is also Stephens' work, he agrees to the "legal principles" announced. He avers that he will never consent that the "military as such" can take charge of or control the citizen. "The suspension of the writ does not and cannot annul, repeal or modify the citizen's constitutional bill of rights." The Act of Congress of February 15, 1864, Hill admits, "if carried out does infringe in this respect, and therefore I voted against it."

[18] Letter to Stephens, March 14, 1864, *ibid.*, pp. 634-37.

But Hill argues that there are some persons connected with or interfering with the army who "ought to be arrested by order and handled by military authorities." As to "citizens" generally, he agrees with Stephens that the only force of the suspension of the writ "is that they may be held *for trial* after legal arrest and upon proper warrant." This construction, Hill assures Stephens, will be concurred in by President Davis. Then the only difference separating them, Hill suggests, is this matter of confidence in Davis. Hill possesses this confidence, but Stephens does not. But let not Davis be "denounced in advance," pleads Hill. Davis is tenacious of his opinion, Hill is constrained to admit; but his "heart is right," and "nothing could tempt him to be a dictator."

Finally, in the opinion of Hill, admitting the danger of acquiescing in this doubtful law, there is yet a graver danger at this time, and that is to make an issue of the law with the Confederate administration, which can only "weaken us" in the face of the enemy.

Reference has already been made to the peace offensive of 1864. Some disposition toward a peace settlement had cropped out in North Carolina as early as 1862 and never entirely disappeared from that state thereafter. The plan proposed was peace through a separate state convention. Nothing definite had come of it before 1864.[19] However, the peace party in the South received great satisfaction, and the cause a considerable impetus, from peace resolutions introduced in the special session of the Georgia General Assembly by Linton Stephens, at the same time

[19] Schwab, pp. 221-22.

that he introduced his habeas corpus resolutions in March, 1864.

These peace resolutions of Stephens, adopted by the Assembly on the same day that they took favorable action on the habeas corpus resolutions, were captioned: "Resolutions, declaring the ground on which the Confederate States stand in the war and the terms on which peace ought to be offered to the enemy."[20] The resolutions, eight in number, review and reaffirm what are represented as fundamental principles exemplified in the evolution of the American government, and put the Georgia Assembly on record as recommending that the government, after a victory "when none can impute the action to alarm," shall officially propose peace to the enemy on the basis "of the great principles declared by our common fathers in 1776."[21]

The governor in his message of March 10 had also discussed the subject of peace, with especial reference to the essential conditions necessary to safeguard the principles upon which war was waged, and to the methods of procedure in initiating peace proposals.[22]

However, despite fine words and elastic phrases couched in glittering generalities, it is plain enough that

[20] Waddell, p. 271. The resolutions are printed by Waddell, pp. 272-74.

[21] In October, 1864, Linton Stephens reveals the extent to which he would go in proposing separate state action. His letter of October 13 to Alexander Stephens is an argument that Georgia might, in perfectly good faith, secede from secession. He says the contrary idea is a "cant" invented to serve the purposes of usurpation and consolidation. See Waddell, pp. 285-86.

[22] The message is found in *Confederate Records of the State of Georgia*, II, 608-18, and *House Journal*, 1864, pp. 5-51.

the advocates of peace were preparing the southern mind for a peace without victory and for a very probable reunion with the North, with just so much guarantee of state sovereignty and control over "domestic institutions" as could be wrung from the Lincoln government.[23]

Hill, while deprecating the peace propaganda in the form which it assumed—that is, through the individual initiative of the states—was somewhat ambiguous in his utterances on the subject in 1864, while he was trying to effect a conciliation with Stephens.[24] He seemed anxious to assure Stephens that the two of them were in perfect accord on many points and that they had the same conception of the real issues of the war, namely, "state sovereignty and self government." If these principles, which, of course, the student recognizes as so vague and elastic as to preclude their use as a common ground of understanding or settlement between North and South, can be assured, Hill professes to be willing and even anxious to conclude peace.[25]

However, he admits that he differs with Brown and Stephens on the mode of procedure to be followed in initiating peace proposals. They had advocated separate action in the various states, while Hill is very insistent that the states should act jointly in convention, though he is willing that such action shall be subject to "separate ratification"

[23] Schwab says Stephens and Brown were willing to make peace in 1864 "on the basis of States Rights and a guarantee of the right of property in slaves," though I have nowhere found such a specific avowal. See Schwab, p. 221.

[24] See his letter to Stephens, previously cited, *supra*, p. 91.

[25] Letter to Stephens, Phillips (ed.), *Toombs, Stephens, Cobb Correspondence*, p. 635.

by the states. The difference seems more significant and real than Hill affected to believe when he wrote Stephens that "details shall not divide" and that "our paths will meet at the same goal."[26] The impression is unescapable, at this juncture, that Hill is trying to placate the gloomy sage of Crawfordsville and will go very far to do so. But here, as elsewhere, he labored earnestly to maintain the precarious cohesiveness of the Confederacy, without which victory seemed impossible.

For the time, nothing definite came of the peace resolutions and the accompanying propaganda, but there can be little doubt that the agitation of this period left the Confederacy appreciably weaker. Moreover, it is a matter of record that the peace movement of 1864 in Georgia greatly encouraged Sherman in his conduct of the Georgia campaign of that year.[27] The peace movement smouldered in

[26] Letter to Stephens, *ibid.*, p. 636.

[27] The efforts of Sherman, in the fall of 1864, to separate Georgia from the Confederacy by offering a separate peace, make interesting reading and, but for the fact that they seem to bear too slightly on the main subject of this study to justify it, would deserve more than passing mention. Sherman believed that Brown and Stephens would undertake a separate peace. He wired President Lincoln from Atlanta: "I am fully conscious of the delicate nature of such assertions, but it would be a magnificent stroke of policy, if we could, without surrendering principle or a foot of ground, arouse the latent enmity of Georgia against Davis." He sent no less than three messengers to accomplish the business. Mr. William King was sent to both Governor Brown and Alexander Stephens; Judge A. R. Wright was sent to Washington to talk with President Lincoln; and Joshua Hill, a Georgia Unionist throughout the war, was also dispatched to Governor Brown. Stephens and Brown, however, declined to be drawn into the plan, and Sherman's efforts proved abortive. For full discussion of the episode, see Avery, pp. 300–305. For further discussion of Hill's relation to the subject, see *infra*, pp. 97 ff.

Georgia and throughout the South, until it, in conjunction with other developments, virtually drove Davis to sue for the futile Hampton Roads Conference of February, 1865. That episode will be reserved for later discussion in this chapter.[28]

In the meanwhile, events went from bad to worse in Georgia in 1864, and Hill spent most of his time in the summer and autumn of that year in the state, endeavoring to hold up the hands of the disheartened people. On September 2 Sherman entered Atlanta; and Hood, withdrawing toward Alabama, abandoned the state to the mercy of the Federal Army.[29]

Hill's courage and dogged determination seemed to increase with adversity. While Sherman held Atlanta, he made a speech in Macon, remarkable for its stout-heartedness.[30] He cited to the war-weary people the case of the Romans, with Hannibal at the gates of Rome, and enlarged on the ultimate defeat of the Carthaginians. Are Georgians less than Romans, and Sherman more formidable than the Carthaginian? he asked. He insisted that Sherman could and would be destroyed if only the absentees would return to the army, and the malcontents cease whispering peace, when there is, nor can be, no peace, save one of utter submission. He warned the people that he had recently read a letter from Sherman "more intensified with malignity than ever escaped from the lips of man." Sherman, he assured them, meant to exterminate Georgians and re-people

[28] *Infra.*, pp. 102 ff.

[29] Rhodes, IV, 523–24; Avery, p. 285.

[30] *Macon Telegraph and Confederate* (day of month obliterated) in *Brown Scrap Books.*

the state with "Yankees." In Cato-like phrase, he concluded: "We can and will crush the enemy."

About the same time, September 5, 1864, Secretary of War Seddon was writing Hill from Richmond, begging him in view of his "well known influence and high position" to go into southwest Georgia and arouse the people to the "absolute necessity of pressing forward the supplies in their possession," for the use of the army. "You can, I am sure, arouse them to a sense of their danger and their duty," wrote the sorely harassed official.[31]

So Hill labored in a waning cause, but with only indifferent success. The spirit of the people was depressed beyond invigoration. By public addresses and by private and public letters he endeavored to resuscitate the old enthusiasm of the earlier days of the war. Especially did he appeal to men subject to military service, to cease evasion and subterfuge, and return to the armies.[32]

At this time, in early October, the peace overtures extended by Sherman to the Georgia authorities (reference to which has already been made) were the subject of much apprehension on the part of the Confederate administration in Richmond. It is very probable that President Davis was advised, by those sympathetic with the administration, to make a special trip to Georgia, that the inspiration of his presence in the state might serve to counteract

[31] O.R., 4th Ser., III, 621.

[32] See letter October 5, 1864, to James T. McCormick, assistant enroling officer for Troup County, printed in the *Columbus Sun*, October 11, 1864. The letter concludes: "But my only object is to serve the country in this hour of its fate. Neither you nor I can better serve than by getting men in the field."

the influence of the peace party and secure the defeat of Sherman's plan.[33]

At any rate, Davis went to Georgia in early October, and, accompanied by Hill, who also spoke, delivered a speech at Macon, which was the target of much criticism from his opponents.[34] In this speech the president stated that two-thirds of the southern armies were absent from their posts of duty and that the retreat from Dalton to Atlanta had been "a deep disgrace." For such derogatory remarks concerning southern soldiers he was sharply called in question by the critics and accused of encouraging the foe and chilling the southern people. The facts, if true, it was alleged, should not have been stated publicly, as the "revelation was impotent for good."[35]

[33] Avery says: "Lincoln telegraphed to Sherman that the object of Mr. Davis' visit was to see Mr. Stephens and Governor Brown, to stop the peace mischief that General Sherman had inaugurated with those two dangerous gentlemen" (Avery, p. 301).

[34] *Ibid.*, p. 293. As further evidence that Davis had been advised to come to Georgia to offset the peace movement, Hill's letter to Davis of October 11, 1864, may be cited. This letter is found in the Davis MMS Collection in the De Renne Private Library, Wormsloe, Georgia. It is quoted *infra,* p. 99.

[35] In one of his interminable controversies with the Confederate authorities, Governor Brown thus describes the Macon speech of Davis: "Your assertion that my past acts and public expressions have given encouragement to our enemies . . . . may be properly disposed of by the single remark that if we may judge of the encouragement of our enemies by the general expression of their public journals, the President gave them more delight, hope and encouragement, by his single speech at Macon, than all the past acts and public expressions of my life could have done, had I labored constantly to aid and encourage them. He who can satisfy the enemy that two-thirds of our gallant armies are absent from their posts, affords them delight and encouragement indeed, as they will no longer doubt, if this be true, that the spirit of our people is broken, and that our

RELUCTANT SURRENDER 99

Be that as it may, the peace overtures of Sherman were repulsed, and Hill, at least, saw favorable results from the visit of Davis to the state. After the president had returned to Richmond, Hill wrote him on October 14:[36]

> I think your visit here has done us good. The spirit of the people has evidently improved. . . . . I shall do all in my power to arouse the people and hearten the absentees from the army. I suppose you have seen the letter of the Vice President.[37] Under the circumstances it is somewhat better than I expected. He at least talks about *our* cause; says *we* will succeed, and says nothing against the laws and policy of the Government.[38]

Hill certainly lived up to his promise to Davis to do what he could "to arouse the people and hearten the absentees from the army." Even after he had returned to Richmond in November, for the last session of the Confederate Congress, his mind was preoccupied with the situation in Georgia, where Sherman was conducting his famous march to the sea; and on November 14 he telegraphed,

---

brave defenders can no longer be relied on to sustain our cause in the field. All remember the mortification which this speech of the President caused to the patriotic citizens of the Confederacy. If it had been true, surely it should not have been publicly proclaimed" (from letter, dated November 14, 1864, to Secretary of War Seddon, in Fielder, p. 341). See also, attack on the Macon speech of Davis, made in the Senate by Orr of South Carolina and replied to by Hill, reported in *Columbus Sun,* February 18, 1865.

[36] In Davis MMS Collection, in De Renne Private Library, Wormsloe, Georgia.

[37] The reference is to Stephens' public reply to Sherman's peace overtures; see Avery, pp. 302-3.

[38] This private letter, hitherto unpublished, by its emphasis and evident assumptions, reveals that Hill and Davis must have expected that Stephens would co-operate with Sherman's plans.

through military channels, this Spartan message to the people of the state, to be broadcast by the press of the state:

TO THE PEOPLE OF GEORGIA:

You have now the best opportunity ever yet presented to destroy the enemy. Put everything at the disposal of our generals; remove all provisions from the path of the invader and put all obstructions in his path. Every citizen with his gun, and every negro with his spade and axe can do the work of a soldier. You can destroy the enemy by retarding his march. Georgians be firm. Act promptly; fear nothing.

B. H. HILL, *Senator*

On which is the endorsement:

I most cordially approve the above.

JAMES A. SEDDON, *Secretary of War*[39]

In the meanwhile Hill had aroused some feeling of animosity among the classes of citizenry whom he had pressed so hard to undertake military service. Especially had his animadversions on the number of exempted persons employed in the press brought forth some tart replies. In speaking on this subject, he had recommended that the press be operated by old and disabled men not capable of military service.[40]

One cynical editor, in commenting on Hill's Message to the People of Georgia and his animadversions on the press, could not resist a personal fling at the Senator. "Senator Hill himself," says this caustic gentleman, "is young, athletic and able bodied, and will make a good soldier."[41] But the greatest newspaper criticism and backbiting at Hill did not break out until February, 1865, when

---

[39] *O. R.*, 1st Ser., XLIV, 867.   [40] *Columbus Sun*, October 28, 1864.

[41] *Ibid.*, November 20, 1864; also see the same paper, November 24, 1864, for further criticism of Hill along the same line.

he once more came to Georgia, and for the last time, to undertake the work of reviving the dying cause.[42]

In the summer of 1864 Hill became involved in the Davis—Joseph E. Johnston controversy. At the request of Governor Brown he journeyed to Richmond to interview the president regarding the military situation in Georgia. The outcome of the deliberations in Richmond was the well-known order of July 17 relieving General Johnston from his command of the Confederate forces opposing Sherman.[43] A close study of the available material regarding Hill's offices and conduct in this affair has convinced this writer that Hill went to Richmond with an open mind regarding the retention of Johnston; but, learning from the Confederate authorities that reinforcement of Johnston, without which the Confederate general represented successful resistance to Sherman as impossible, was out of the question, he became convinced of the necessity of Johnston's removal. The report current in some quarters that Hill betrayed Johnston seems without foundation.[44]

[42] *Infra.*, p. 108.

[43] *Johnston's Narrative*, p. 349.

[44] Space precludes a detailed substantiation of the conclusions given in the text. A great deal of material has been examined. The following may be cited in the order of importance: *O. R.*, 1st Ser., LII, Pt. II, 693–94, being Secretary Seddon's report; *ibid.*, pp. 704–7, being Hill's report to the Secretary of War; *ibid.*, XXXVIII, Pt. V, 875–76, being President Davis' messages to Johnston; *ibid.*, p. 879, being Hill's message to Johnston. There are several *ex parte* accounts: *Johnston's Narrative*, pp. 78–79, 93–94, 173, 229–52, 262–76, 349–70; Jefferson Davis, *The Rise and Fall of the Confederate Government*, II, 557–61; Edward E. Pollard, *Life of Jefferson Davis*, p. 373 (untrustworthy). In addition I have examined the newspaper controversy of 1874 over this removal, chiefly letters in the Atlanta press reprinted from New York and Philadelphia papers.

BENJAMIN H. HILL

When Davis was in Georgia in October, after Johnston's removal and Hood's evacuation of Atlanta, he continued to advise with Hill regarding the military situation. At Davis' request, Hill was present at an interview between Davis and Hood at Palmetto, Georgia, southwest of Atlanta, as a result of which the disastrous movement of Hood into Tennessee took place. It seems Hill was often consulted regarding military matters, especially as regards the Georgia situation.[45]

The chief interest of the first weeks of 1865 attaches to the famous effort at peace associated with the Hampton Roads Conference, between Lincoln and Seward on the one hand and commissioners appointed by Davis on the other, the chief of whom was the vice-president, Alexander Stephens. The facts connected with the visit of Blair to Davis, of the pressure within the Confederacy on Davis to propose a Conference, and of the complete failure of the negotiations are too well known to require repetition in this place.[46] Of Hill's connection with the episode, less well known, it does seem advisable to speak.

In January, 1865, it was known that Governor Brown

[45] Letter of Hill to Davis, October 11, 1864, Davis MMS Collection in the De Renne Private Library, Wormsloe, Georgia. See also, an interview with Hill published in *Philadelphia Press* and copied in *Atlanta Constitution*, June 26, 1881; also, Avery, p. 293.

[46] This episode is a familiar one to all readers of Civil War history. From a general view it is treated by Rhodes, V, 57–71. All the official documents and reports connected with negotiations leading to the conference, and the reports made by the participants, are found in Stephens, II, Appendix R, 791–803; while Stephens' own narrative of the affair is given in the same work and volume, pp. 576–622.

of Georgia was preparing a message to the General Assembly, recommending a state convention in Georgia to consider a peace settlement.[47] This might precipitate the dreaded "separate-state action," so long feared by the advocates of a continued fight for independence, as the sure harbinger of final disintegration within the Confederacy.[48] To prevent the delivery of this message, Hill and some others of the Georgia delegation in the Confederate Congress repaired to Stephens' room in Richmond, in late January and in effect consummated a bargain with the vice-president whereby, in return for the latter's action in restraining Brown from delivering the message, the Hill group agreed to support resolutions pending in the Confederate Congress to request President Davis to institute proposals for a peace conference.[49] The resolutions were passed in the Congress in the last week in January; and Hill, in person, sought out the president, and in several conferences the commissioners and the instructions to these commissioners were discussed between the two. Hill said later that he knew "why every member of the Commission on our part was selected" and that he "received from Mr. Davis' own lips a full account of the final conversation

[47] Davis MMS Collection, De Renne Private Library, Wormsloe, Georgia, February 17, 1865.

[48] Hill's letter to Alexander Stephens, March 14, 1864, previously cited, *supra*, p. 91.

[49] *Atlanta Herald*, May 3, 1874, "An Unwritten History of the Hampton Roads Peace Conference," written by Ben Hill in 1874. This account is followed where not otherwise indicated.

Also see Hill's letter on the same subject in *Atlanta Constitution*, April 22, 1874.

between himself and the commissioners before their departure from Richmond."[50]

Hill says he had proposed and had insisted on the appointment of Alexander Stephens as one of the commissioners, because, in his opinion, Stephens was more acceptable to the people and government of the North than any other prominent southern man, and moreover, had Stephens not been appointed, and the Conference failed, opponents of the administration would have insisted that its failure was due to Stephens' absence from the commission.[51]

In an historical address in Atlanta in 1874, Hill took occasion to dispute one widely current theory regarding the famous Hampton Roads Conference and its failure. It had long been represented and believed that Mr. Davis had so tied the hands of the commissioners by his instructions as to make failure almost inevitable. It was said that he had made southern independence an ultimatum. Hill maintains that this is not true; that Davis, though expressing his own opinion that independence should not be yielded in advance, gave no written instructions or ultimatum to the commissioners but left much to their own discretion.[52]

[50] Address delivered by Hill before the Southern Historical Society in Atlanta, February 18, 1874, published in the *Atlanta Herald*, March 1, 1874; also in Hill, *Life of Hill*, pp. 399-414. The passage quoted may be found on p. 409, the latter place.

[51] "An Unwritten History of the Hampton Roads Peace Conference," *Atlanta Herald*, May 3, 1874; also letter in *Atlanta Constitution*, April 22, 1874.

[52] "Historical Address," February 18, 1874, *loc. cit*. This address gave rise to a most wordy and acrimonious controversy, conducted in the newspapers, between Hill and Alexander Stephens, who affected to see in it a covert attack on himself.

The "Battle of Intellectual Giants," as the *Augusta Chronicle and*

Hill went to Georgia in his last effort to arouse the people, on February 3, the same date that the Conference took place in Hampton Roads.[53] On February 6, President Davis sent him the following telegram:

HON. B. H. HILL, SENATOR, MACON, GA.

The Commissioners have returned. They met Lincoln and Seward at Fortress Monroe; were informed that neither the Confederate States nor an individual state could be recognized as having power to enter into any agreement prescribing the conditions of peace. Nothing less would be accepted than unconditional submission to the

---

Sentinel called the controversy (April 23, 1874), raged from Stephens' first letter attacking the Address, on April 11, to June 28, 1874. When it was over, Stephens had written six long and bitter letters, and Hill four; but Hill had had the advantage of the Address itself and the "Unwritten History" (see footnote 49, this chapter), which he wrote while the controversy was being aired in the papers. The newspapers used were the *Augusta Constitutionalist* by Stephens, and the *Atlanta Herald* and *Atlanta Constitution* by Hill, though the letters of both were generally copied by the press of the entire state.

The points in the controversy are too numerous and, in many cases, too trivial and personal to discuss here. In general it may be said Stephens resented and denied the vital rôle which Hill had ascribed to himself in the Hampton Roads preliminaries, going so far as categorically to deny that Hill was even present in Richmond while the commission was being chosen and instructed. Hill was able seriously to embarrass Stephens in regard to this point, by securing and publishing affidavits from the other members of the Georgia delegation, proving his presence in Richmond as late as February 3, the day of the Conference itself (see *Atlanta Herald*, May 14, 1874, for the affidavits). Issues of veracity and integrity were often made during the course of the controversy.

The Georgia press divided in its allegiance between the disputants; but the more conservative papers deplored the entire controversy, especially the personal nature of it; and the *Augusta Chronicle and Sentinel*, a neutral, suggested that if it must continue, let it do so in private correspondence, and "thru the medium of the postoffice" (May 9, 1874).

[53] See letter of Hill to Davis, October 12, 1878, Rowland (ed.), *Jefferson Davis, Constitutionalist, etc.*, VIII, 284–85.

Government and laws of the United States and that Congress had adopted a constitutional amendment for the emancipation of all slaves which disposed of that question.

JEFFERSON DAVIS[54]

Whatever the cause of the failure, Hill did not regret it; and it is very probable that Davis was not disappointed at the outcome.[55] For on February 17, 1865, Hill wrote Davis from Macon, rejoicing at the fiasco of the peace commission.[56] It has done "us" splendid service, he informs the president; all talk of a state convention for making peace is now ended, and the war spirit is strong again. He advised Davis, further, that Governor Brown was reported to have changed his message, in process of preparation, and would now say nothing of a state convention. This letter, revealing a cordial intimacy and understanding between the two men, concludes with the expression that it had been a master stroke to put Stephens on the commission.

Hill now began a vigorous speaking tour of the state, attempting to rally the despairing people to a renewed effort, now that it had been demonstrated that peace was an illusory hope.[57]

[54] *O. R.*, 1st Ser., XLVI, Pt. II, 1208.

[55] Hill said: "Mr. Davis had no hope of success or of securing an armistice after he learned that Mr. Seward was to accompany Mr. Lincoln" ("Historical Address, February 18, 1874," in *Atlanta Herald*, March 1, 1874).

[56] Letter in Davis MMS Collection, De Renne Private Library, Wormsloe, Georgia.

[57] See *Columbus Sun*, February 19, 1865, for accounts of speeches made by Hill at Columbus and Macon. I am indebted to Mr. H. H. Cabaniss, of Atlanta, for an account of Hill's speech at Forsyth, Georgia, at this time, when Hill stopped in the home of Mr. Cabaniss.

Governor Brown convened the General Assembly of the state in extra session at Macon on February 15, as the capitol at Milledgeville had been too severely damaged by Sherman to admit of its use.[58] To this Assembly, he delivered his last message as governor of Georgia. He condemned to the last the Confederate administration and all its works, to which he attributed the exising prostrate condition of the state and the Confederacy. He recommended the call of a convention of all the southern states to consider the crisis and provide a remedy.[59]

Hill addressed the Georgia Assembly in an endeavor to provide an antidote to "the poison" of the governor's message.[60] In a letter to a young friend in Mobile at this time he writes of the "upas poison" instilled into the people by certain leaders; and there was very little doubt as to who he meant. He speaks, in this letter, of the necessity of avoiding "conventions as you would reconstruction," and lamented that the "recreants" in the Confederacy are now as "two to the faithful one," while the people can no longer be trusted, so extensive has been the propaganda of the malcontents.[61]

[58] Avery, p. 317; Fielder, p. 308.

[59] Avery, p. 317, gives extracts from the message. Entire message in *House Journal*, 1865, pp. 14–36.

[60] Letter of Hill to a "Young Lady of Mobile" (Miss Augusta Evans, the novelist, who in rather bad faith, or at least carelessly, allowed it to be published), quoted in the *Columbus Sun*, March 26, 1865. Also see Avery, p. 318.

[61] Letter of Hill to a "Young Lady of Mobile," quoted in the *Columbus Sun*, March 26, 1865. Also see Avery, p. 318. The letter is also copied in the *Southern Confederacy* (Atlanta), date undiscernible, in *Brown Scrap Books*.

These views, so disparaging to the people, which Hill had not meant for publication, in connection with his address before the General Assembly in March, when he had paid his respects to original secessionists, now turned peace advocates, brought down on their author vindictive sarcasm and abuse. He was satirized as merely a "talking Senator"; and some editors asserted that instead of representing Georgia in the Confederate Senate as he had been commissioned to do, he preferred to dodge that responsibility and make stump speeches in Georgia villifying his personal opponents.[62]

But despite the irresistibly mounting tide of defeatism and the personal abuse which his dogged course was bringing on himself, the Confederate Senator, "last in secession," proved himself to be the last to give up the hope of establishing that secession. On March 11, 1865, he delivered what has been designated "the last speech made by any southern man in behalf of the Confederacy."[63] This speech has been preserved; and since it may be taken as revealing the arguments used to inspire continued resistance, by Hill, in these last days of the Confederacy, it seems worth while briefly to analyze it.[64]

Hill first considered the terms of peace proposed by

---

[62] *Columbus Sun*, April 1, 1865, quoting the *Milledgeville Federal Union*, a Brown paper. For disparagement of Hill at this period also see, *Columbus Sun*, February 24, and March 26, 1865; and letter from Milledgeville, dated April 8, 1865, in *Southern Confederacy*, date undiscernible, in *Brown Scrap Books*.

[63] Hill, *Life of Hill*, p. 273.

[64] This speech was delivered in Sterling Hall, La Grange, Georgia, Hill's own home. It was published in 1874 by Hill and is found in Hill, *Life of Hill*, pp. 373–93.

Lincoln at the Hampton Roads Conference in the previous February.[65] He summarizes his conclusions on this score:

I have shown you that he requires us:

1. To accept a new Constitution and new laws made by our enemies.

2. To accept this new Constitution and these new laws without reservation or qualification as to the consequences that may follow.

3. That we must agree in advance that our slaves are emancipated; and that the Federal Congress shall in future exercise the power to enforce that emancipation by such laws as they may deem appropriate.

4. I have shown you that to enforce this emancipation it must necessarily be deemed appropriate: 1. That the freed negro must have this country to inhabit. 2. That he must be furnished with lands to cultivate, and with means to cultivate them. 3. That he must have civil rights, civil and political power and social equality with us. 4. That he must have power to protect himself in all these rights . . . . and that too, to this end: the negro will be armed, and the former master, the white race, will be disarmed.

I need scarcely add that in order to carry out this policy it will become necessary to obliterate all state lines, and have all the states of the Confederacy reduced to one vast territory. For this territory there will be but one law-making power, the Federal Congress; and from this territory in that Congress the negro, or the white man willing to be his equal, will be the only fit and accepted representative.

As an inducement and the only inducement offered, to accept these terms, Mr. Lincoln promises us a liberal exercise of the pardoning power. And doubtless those at the north who support him, will consider this indeed a liberal offer, since they claim the right to exterminate us for the sins already committed.[66]

[65] The papers and reports respecting this conference, and including Lincoln's terms, may be found in Stephens, II, Appendix R, 791–803.

[66] Hill, *Life of Hill*, p. 279. The prescience shown by Hill in forecasting the "consequences" of surrender on these terms, or no-terms, is little less than remarkable. So exact is his prediction of what reconstruction

Such terms, Hill declares, are manifestly impossible. Defiance to such an insolent enemy is the only answer that a proud people can make.

> Oh dastardly is the cowardice of that trooper who lingers from the battle now; hopelessly suicidal is that avarice which can withhold its offering now; and hateful, hateful far beyond the darkest thought of the traitor's mind is that ambition which cannot forget its personal griefs and personal schemings and cease to divide our people now.[67]

Moreover, Hill maintains, a peace on such a basis as Lincoln offers, would avail the southern people nothing. The old Constitution, which many of them loved and would gladly embrace again, is gone beyond recovery; and by the very terms proposed, southern property is confiscate. Why accept such a peace while hope or resistance remains? But "darkest thought of all," in such a peace, that blackest of all libels must be written over the graves of dead comrades: "Traitors lie here. Whose hand shall write it and not grow paralyzed? Whose tongue shall utter it and not grow speechless? .... Enough, enough!" cries Hill. "Away with the thought of peace on such terms. 'Tis the wildest dream that restless ambition, or selfish avarice or slinking cowardice could conjure. . . . ."[68]

What then are southern resources for prosecuting the war? First, Hill enumerates physical resources. He reveals that he has just served on a joint committee of the Congress to inquire into this very subject, and he divulges

---

brought to the South, that one wishes one might have seen the manuscript of the address as it was delivered in 1865 and before it was published by Hill after the event in 1874.

[67] *Ibid.*, pp. 279–80.   [68] *Ibid.*, p. 281.

some startling and little-known facts which indicate that the Confederacy is not nearly so poverty stricken and resourceless as is popularly supposed.[69] But moral resources are the real reliance of a people, he says; and here Hill warms to his theme, his favorite theme—loyalty to the government. Lincoln, says Hill, had recognized the critical southern weakness, and in his last message to Congress had pithily expressed it. "If the southern people fail him, he is beaten," he had said. Fail whom?—the president. Here, the issue is narrowed to its true, its focal point.[70] Hill then chastises in burning words those who early in the field for secession had, by every word and deed, promoted the work of disaffection to the government. And yet, he insists, even now, such allusions are "not so much to chastise as to cure, and to make friendly to the republic."

He then reviews caustically, and yet with a certain wistful note, as though of sorrow more than anger, the various classes of "fair-weather" secessionists and Confederates who are now failing the cause. Among these are those who had gone into the war to make money, to reap honors "in liberty's new struggle," "the croaker, the critic, and the traitor, the triune curse of all revolutions," the avaricious, the ambitious, the office-holding speculator: these, he affirms, are the present enemies of the country; these are breaking down the morale of a brave people. He declaims:

There is but one way to fight these enemies among us. The people must support the government, which Mr. Lincoln, and these, his co-workers, fight. It is your government, my countrymen. . . . . Support the President; support the generals; supply the army; drive off the traitors; confound the critics; and then you will be able to

[69] *Ibid.*, pp. 281–82. [70] *Ibid.*, p. 283.

defy the enemy, arrest disasters, and win independence. There are many roads to failure and bondage. You may drift there by lethargy; you may wind there by treason; you may rush there by faction. There is but one road to success and freedom. It may be narrow, and require toil and patience and sacrifice, but you are certainly travelling that road when you support your own regular Confederate Government. Every man who teaches you otherwise is your enemy.[71]

This is followed by passages of glowing tribute to Davis as president, to the armies for their valor, and the Confederate government officials for their fidelity. These, all these, are worthy of the patriot's full measure of devotion. Hill concludes with this entreaty:

Let us dedicate all that we are, and have, anew to the contest. Let us from this day think no thought, speak no word, do no deed, but for our country, until that country shall be free. Let us have no friends but the friends of our country, let us have no enemies but the enemies of our country.[72]

It was too late. Less than a month after Hill had finished delivering this speech, Lee had surrendered at Appomattox. Hill had led another minority fight in vain.

In May after the surrender, while Hill was quietly living at home in La Grange, he and former Secretary of the Navy Stephen D. Mallory, who was in Hill's home with him, were arrested and transported to Fort La Fayette in New York Bay, where Hill was detained until paroled by President Johnson in July and allowed to return to his Georgia home.[73]

[71] *Ibid.*, p. 290. [72] *Ibid.*, p. 293.

[73] The orders relating to Hill's arrest and imprisonment are found in *O. R.*, 1st Ser., XLIX, Pt. I, 369, 379; *ibid.*, Pt. II, pp. 883-84, 901-2, 923, 927; *ibid.*, 2d Ser., VIII, 577, 640, 652.

CHAPTER VII.
COMING OF CONGRESSIONAL RECONSTRUCTION

Hill had freely predicted the direst evils as certain to follow in the train of southern surrender on the terms remaining to the South after the failure of the effort at negotiations at Hampton Roads in February, 1865.[1] It is very probable that his arrest and detention in a northern prison, together with the publicity given at the same time to President Johnson's threats against southern leaders, contributed nothing to a relief of his gloomy apprehensions. It will be remembered that Johnson in April and May of 1865 was breathing "fire and hemp" and voicing such utterances as, "Treason is a crime and must be made odious" and "Traitors must be punished."[2] Even conservative opinion at the North was beginning to fear that the new president was about to precipitate wholesale executions and political proscription.[3]

Hill was released in July and, as any prudent man in like circumstances, went home and kept quiet. A diligent search of the press for the period fails to disclose any pub-

---

[1] Speech at La Grange, Georgia, March 11, 1865. Found in Hill, *Life of Hill*, pp. 273-93. See especially, pp. 275-81. See also Hill's warning to the people at Macon that Sherman intended to exterminate Georgians and repeople the state with "Yankees" (*supra*, p. 96).

[2] Ellis P. Oberholtzer, *History of the United States since the Civil War*, I, 8-12; William A. Dunning, *Reconstruction, Political and Economic*, p. 20.

[3] *Ibid.*, p. 21.

lic letters from him, or any reference to public activity on his part, for the remainder of the year. This somewhat unwonted silence and inactivity, however, was not solely due to that discretion indicated in the circumstances, but, no doubt, in part to the necessity pressing on nearly every southern man who had whole heartedly and with full purse supported the war, to provide a livelihood for himself and family during the first trying years of transition from war to peace and from a slave-labor to a free-labor economy.[4]

Moreover, Hill approved Johnson's plan for Reconstruction, which, announced for North Carolina on May 29, came to relieve the southern leaders of their worst fears.[5] In his letter to the president, written July 4, 1865, from Fort La Fayette, New York harbor, in which he requested a parole, he disavowed any desire for public position but stated that as a private citizen he would "aid in restoring harmony and prosperity on the new basis of labor." At the same time he characterized the president's plan of Reconstruction as "a great benefaction to the southern people when compared to other plans proposed."[6]

Therefore, it seems reasonable to conclude that the silence and inactivity imposed on himself from 1865 to 1867 was due in equal parts to discretion, to necessity, and to an

---

[4] Hill, *Life of Hill*, p. 48.

[5] The Johnson plan for North Carolina, substantially followed in proclamations soon issued for the other southern states, is found in Walter L. Fleming, *Documentary History of Reconstruction*, I, 68 (hereafter referred to as "Fleming").

[6] Letter in Hill, *Life of Hill*, p. 47. See also Hill's testimony before the so-called "Ku Klux Committee of Congress in 1871," found in *Reports of Committees*, 42 C., 2 S., No. 22, Pt. VII, p. 753 (hereafter referred to as "*Ku Klux Report*").

acceptance of the president's plan, which seemed to call for no interference from himself. Since his championship of Fillmore in 1856, he had remained out of public life no such length of time and was never to do so again, when once his silence was broken by the Congressional Reconstruction Acts of 1867.

In the meanwhile the work of reconstructing Georgia under the Johnson plan was going forward.[7] Military rule had been gradually extended over the state in April, May, and June, following the cessation of armed resistance.[8] Governor Brown on May 3 had summoned the General Assembly to meet in extraordinary session on May 22.[9] However, the military authorities by special order prohibited the meeting of the Assembly; and on May 11, despite the parole issued by General Wilson, Brown was arrested and sent under custody to Washington.[10] He was allowed to return to Georgia, however, after a week, and then issued a

[7] There are two excellent monographs treating the reconstruction of Georgia. The more exhaustive is that of Miss Mildred Thompson, *Reconstruction in Georgia, Economic, Social, Political*, in the "Columbia University Studies in History, Economics, and Public Law," Vol. LXIV, No. 1, and a shorter one by Edwin C. Wooley, in the same series, Vol. XIII, No. 3 (these are referred to hereafter as "Thompson" and "Wooley").

Avery and Fielder, previously used for the war period, continue to be of service for the period of Reconstruction, although Avery writes in a partisan spirit and Fielder continues to write primarily as the apologist and panygyrist of Brown.

[8] Thompson, pp. 136-44, gives the details and incidents of the extension. There seems to have been little hardship attendant on the process. But see Hull, *Annals of Athens* (Georgia), pp. 302-27, for some contrary evidence.

[9] *Milledgeville Federal Union*, May 9, 1865.

[10] *O. R.*, XLVII, Pt. III, 505; XLIX, Pt. II, 630.

formal resignation of the governorship, thereby leaving to the military authorities the undisputed control of the state.[11]

It is very probable that Brown, while in Washington, reached an understanding with President Johnson that he would actively promote the work of Reconstruction. There was in Brown's character and record somewhat of the representative of the plain people, rather than of the slavocracy, that commended itself to Johnson. It is suggested that Brown may have been "one of the influences that changed Johnson from severe to moderate measures."[12] Certain it is that Brown and Johnson were in frequent communication regarding governmental affairs after the governor's return to Georgia.[13]

The proclamation providing for Georgia's Reconstruction was issued on June 17; and on the same day the president appointed James Johnson, a Georgia citizen who had opposed secession and had taken no part in the war, as provisional governor.[14]

Pursuant to the plan set forth in the president's proclamation, Governor Johnson on July 13 announced a date for the election of delegates to a Constitutional Convention whose work it would be to remodel the state constitution conformably to the new order. Only citizens who had taken the amnesty oath, and this excluded certain influential

---

[11] *Ibid.*, XLIX, Pt. II, 1064.   [12] Thompson, p. 145 n.

[13] *Ibid.*, citing some of the correspondence. Also see Wooley, pp. 13-14.

[14] Thompson, pp. 145-46; Wooley, p. 13; Avery, p. 341. The appointment of Johnson was not unpopular when made, but by a speech at Macon, July 15, Johnson alienated the conservative sentiment of the state. See Avery, p. 341.

classes, were eligible to vote for, or be members of, this Convention.[15] The elections were duly held, and on October 25 the Convention came together to carry out its deputed task.[16]

The personnel of this Convention of 1865 to restore Georgia to the Union was far less brilliant than that which took Georgia out of the Union in 1861; but it was a reputable body, composed largely of moderate and patriotic individuals, who were disposed to accept the new dispensation in good faith.[17] Of the brilliant galaxy of Georgians who had played such a conspicuous part in Georgia history for the past decade, only Hershel V. Johnson and Charles J. Jenkins were included in the Convention of 1865. Johnson was elected president, but the leader of the deliberations of the Convention seems to have been Judge Jenkins, who was the chairman of the Committee on Business.[18]

The Convention speedily went to work, and after a session of thirteen days had revised the constitution of the state in a manner acceptable to the president.[19] The most significant measures of the Convention were the repeal of

[15] *Milledgeville Federal Union,* July 13, 1865.

[16] The entire proceedings of this Convention, including the Constitution adopted, may be found in *Sen. Ex. Doc.*, 39 C., 1 S., No. 26. The Constitution is given on pp. 82–89.

[17] Thompson, p. 149; Wooley, p. 14; Avery, pp. 347–48. Thompson describes the body as "unprogressive; mostly old men, with a conspicuous lack of prominent men and rising politicians." Wooley calls it, "a body distinguished for the reputation and ability of its members." Avery says, "The body was an able one, and patriotic and conservative."

[18] Thompson, p. 50; Avery, p. 348.

[19] The Convention, assembling on October 25, adjourned on November 8, subject to the call of its president. See *Journal of the Constitutional Convention of 1865,* p. 194.

the secession ordinance, the abolition of slavery, and the repudiation of the state's war debt.

There was no opposition to the repeal of the ordinance of secession; but it is not without significance that the Convention elected to "repeal" this ordinance rather than to declare it null and void, as had conventions in several other states.[20] This action indicated that the Georgia Convention accepted the original legality and validity of the secession ordinance.[21]

The abolition of slavery was also accomplished without opposition, although a provision was incorporated in the measure relating to it, which expressly stipulated that the abolition "is not intended to operate as a relinquishment, waiver, or estoppel," of any future claim for compensation which any Georgian "may hereafter make upon the justice and magnanimity of the government."[22]

The repudiation of the war debt was only accomplished with considerable difficulty and after an appeal had been made to President Johnson for assistance. The president telegraphed that repudiation was essential to the restoration of the state to the Union; and with this fortification, the advocates of repudiation carried the measure by a narrow margin.[23]

Elections for state officers and Congressmen, under the

[20] *Ibid.*, pp. 17–18.

[21] Mississippi, Alabama, Florida, and North Carolina nullified the ordinance, the North Carolina Convention saying: "The said supposed ordinance is now and at all times hath been null and void" (see Rhodes, VI, 20–21).

[22] *Journal of the Constitutional Convention of 1865*, p. 38.

[23] *Ibid.*, pp. 135–36, 185–234. Governor Johnson wired President Johnson: "We need some aid to repeal the war debt . . . . what shall the

revised constitution, took place on November 15; and Charles J. Jenkins was elected to the governorship without opposition. Jenkins had been an old-line Whig and an opponent of secession. His election at this time constituted a conservative expression of the popular mind.[24]

Of the seven Congressmen elected at this time, none were able to take the test oath, but neither had any of them been prominently identified with secession or the prosecution of the war.[25] In these state elections no persons were disfranchised, as certain classes had been, in the election for the Constitutional Convention; and it was perhaps natural that the resulting General Assembly should be less controlled by the Unionist and anti-secession element than had been the Convention.[26]

Before the state could be turned over to its own elected officers, under the Johnson plan, one further thing was necessary. The Assembly, elected November 15, must ratify the Thirteenth Amendment to the Federal Constitution, abolishing slavery. The Assembly, therefore, came together on December 4, and promptly took this action.[27] Howell Cobb, in retirement on his plantations, could not refrain from this gibe when informed of the Assembly's action: "I think they will get the 'peculiar institution' disposed of

---

Convention do?" The president responded: "The people of Georgia should not hesitate one single moment in repudiating every single dollar of debt created for the purpose of aiding the rebellion against the government of the United States" (see *Sen. Ex. Doc.*, 34 C., 1 S., No. 26, p. 81. For the final vote on repudiation, see *ibid.*, p. 93.

[24] Thompson, p. 153; Avery, p. 351.

[25] Thompson, pp. 155–56; Avery, p. 351.   [26] Thompson, p. 153.

[27] *House Journal*, 1865–66, pp. 16–17; *Senate Journal*, 1865–66, pp. 9, 16–18.

after awhile. It has now been abolished by Congress, the President, war, state conventions, legislatures, etc. If all that don't kill it, I would like to know what will."[28]

On December 14, Jenkins was inaugurated as governor of Georgia, in accordance with instructions from President Johnson; and five days later, when the provisional governor was removed, it was presumed that the work of Reconstruction in Georgia was over.[29]

Only one untoward event in this progress toward normalcy in Georgia had occurred to disturb President Johnson's peace of mind. For the most part, he felt, with reason, that he had cause for gratification at the readiness with which his suggestions had been adopted. But the increasing likelihood that the Assembly, on convening in December, would elect Alexander Stephens to represent the state in the United States Senate had gravely disturbed him. On November 24 he sent the following telegram: "I am free to say it would be exceedingly impolitic for Mr. A. H. Stephens' name to be used in connection with the senatorial election. . . . . If elected, he would not be permitted to take his seat . . . . he could not take the oath required.[30] He stands charged with treason."[31]

[28] Letter to his wife, December 7, 1865, Phillips (ed.), *Toombs, Stephens, Cobb Correspondence*, p. 673.

[29] *Sen. Ex. Doc.*, 39 C., 1 S., No. 26; *Milledgeville Federal Union*, December 19, 1865.

[30] The reference is to the "iron-clad" or test oath, exacted by an act of July 2, 1862, of all persons taking federal or state office, that they had never voluntarily participated in rebellion or given aid and comfort to the enemies of the United States (see Rhodes, VI, 26 n.). Of course this oath excluded the majority of southern leaders from office-holding so long as it should be exacted.

[31] *O. R.*, 2d Ser., VIII, 818.

CONGRESSIONAL RECONSTRUCTION 121

Again, on December 11, the president, by telegram, had urged the election to the Senate of Provisional-Governor Johnson;[32] but to no avail. The Assembly insisted upon its freedom of choice and, after a stiff fight, named Alexander Stephens and Hershel V. Johnson.[33] The reception of this action in the North, when it was known, abundantly proved that the president had at least used a mild word when he referred to the election of Stephens as being "impolitic."[34]

Despite the fact that Hill had been in retirement since the surrender and had not participated in the work of Reconstruction, there were some who urged him to stand for election to the United States Senate before the Assembly in December. His reply to these gentlemen constitutes his only utterance of this year on public affairs, and it was not intended for publication. He disavowed any concern about candidacy for public office, affirming his distaste for office-seeking at any time, and especially at so critical a period in the people's fortunes, when the office should seek the man. But he leaves the matter open by concluding in these words: "I leave the whole matter where the Constitution and people have placed it, in the hands of an unsolicited

[32] Thompson, p. 154; Avery, p. 352.

[33] *House Journal*, 1865-66, pp. 44-45, 120-201.

[34] See Thompson, pp. 154-55, for the various interpretations put upon the action of the Assembly in naming Stephens. It may be remarked that Stephens and Johnson had always been moderate men where sectional questions were concerned. Indeed, Hill cited the election of Jenkins as governor, and Stephens and Johnson as Senators, as evidence of the Union and conservative sentiment in the South after the war. See *Ku Klux Report*, pp. 763-64.

and freely acting Legislature."[35] But Hill's name was not presented to the Assembly, as indeed it would have been folly to send to the United States Senate at this time a man who, notoriously, had counseled resistance to the United States government up to the very last of the war.

In the same letter regarding candidacy for the Senate, Hill evidenced some understanding and anticipation of the course soon to be followed by the northern Radicals, who were, at the time (January 12, 1866), on the point of the violent warfare they were soon to launch on President Johnson and his entire Reconstruction program. The Republican House, under the driving spur of Thaddeus Stevens, it may be remembered, had in December refused admission to the representatives from the southern states reconstructed under the presidential plan. A Joint Committee on Reconstruction had then been created whose purpose should be to inquire into the conditions of the former Confederate States "and report whether they, or any of them are entitled to be represented in either House of Congress."[36]

Hill, on January 12, in the light of the developments foreshadowed by the early days of the Thirty-ninth Congress, maintained that these Radicals had always been the bitterest enemies of the Union, and that they had forced the South into an "unwise secession," which was utilized as an "excuse" for war. And now that the South had surrendered, abandoning the war issues in good faith, the Radi-

[35] Letter, January 12, 1866, to Messrs. Ridley and Frost, representatives in the General Assembly from Troup County, in Hill, *Life of Hill*, pp. 48-49.

[36] Rhodes, VI, 29-30.

cals reject the offer to restore the Union, for partisan purposes, seeking to control the government until they shall have fastened on the country a "new Constitution, suited to their fanatical purposes." "The great original error of the South," says Hill, repeating his favorite thesis, "was in mistaking her enemy and making war upon the Union instead of upon these common enemies of the South and the Union."[37]

The Georgia General Assembly, in the meanwhile, passed to a consideration of the legal status of the negro freedmen—probably the most difficult problem facing the newly constructed states. Its legislation on this subject constitutes the most significant accomplishment of the session.[38]

Moderate and constructive counsel on this subject had already been advanced by several leading statesmen. Hershel V. Johnson in closing the state Constitutional Convention on November 8, 1865, had made a plea for full civil justice to the negro, which should be rendered by "ourselves" and not by others.[39]

Governor Jenkins, in his inaugural address, had won the approval of the North by his kindly and progressive views respecting the new freedman.[40] After paying tribute

[37] Letter to Messrs. Ridley and Frost, cited in footnote 35, this chapter.
Compare these views with Hill's statements in his speech against secession, December 15, 1860. He shows restraint in not emphasizing that he had expressed the same sentiments in almost identical words in 1860. See above, pp. 43 ff.

[38] *Acts of the General Assembly*, 1865-66, pp. 234-35, 239-40.

[39] Sidney Andrews, *The South since the Civil War*, p. 336.

[40] Thompson, p. 160, quoting editorial in *New York Times*, December 18, 1865.

to the loyalty of the slave to his master during the war, the governor said: "As the governing class, individually and collectively we owe them unbounded kindness, thorough protection. . . . . Their rights of person and property should be made perfectly secure. . . . . The Courts must be open to them."[41]

Alexander Stephens had expressed similar views in an address before the General Assembly on February 22, 1866. "Ample and full protection," he advised, "should be secured to the negroes, so that they may stand equal before the law in the possession and enjoyment of all rights of person, liberty and property."[42]

Ex-Governor Brown, in a long letter, written in response to a request for his views, had advised that the negro be awarded complete civil equality. A wise man, cautioned the astute governor, is always governed, in part, by existing circumstances. Times have changed since slavery days. There should now be no separate "black code" enacted by the Assembly. The black man, moreover, must have the right to sue, and be sued, to be accepted as a witness in court, his credibility only subject to the determination of the jury, and there must be the same laws respecting his rights of inheritance, guardianship, etc., as govern the rights of the white man in these particulars. Only by fol-

[41] In *Appleton's Annual Cyclopedia*, 1865, p. 399; also see Avery, p. 353.

[42] Johnson and Browne, p. 605. Stephens' entire speech on this occasion is printed as Appendix C, pp. 597–609, in this book. For the same views entertained by Hill respecting the freedman, see the *Ku Klux Report*, Pt. VII, p. 763. Hill's views, however, were not published at the time.

CONGRESSIONAL RECONSTRUCTION 125

lowing such a course, warns the canny governor, will the southern states escape the obnoxious interference of the Freedmen's Bureau.[43]

The Assembly was not, it then appears, without the benefit of wise counsel; and moreover, the hostile criticism already seething in the northern press against other southern states who had enacted separate "black codes" of no such enlightened character, could not have been without effect. The consequence was that the Georgia Assembly enacted very liberal legislation respecting the freedman.[44] The most important statute on the subject reads:

> Persons of color shall have the right to make and enforce contracts, to sue and be sued, to be parties, and give evidence; to inherit, to purchase, lease, hold and convey real and personal property, and to have full and equal benefit of all laws and proceedings for the security of person and estate; and shall not be subject to any other or different punishment, pain or penalty, for the commission of any act or offense than such as are prescribed for white persons committing like acts or offenses.[45]

So far as Georgia is concerned, then, it seems indisputable that one year after the surrender, the state was accepting the results of the war in good faith. Secession, slavery, and the war debts were abandoned without resistance; the amnesty oath was being freely subscribed to; and, the rights of the freedman were adequately safeguard-

[43] Letter, dated February 18, 1866, in *Atlanta Intelligencer*, in *Brown Scrap Books*.

[44] Other states, notably Mississippi, had assigned the negro a distinctly inferior civil status. For the discriminating "black codes," and resultant northern criticism, see Dunning, pp. 54–60; Rhodes, VI, 40–44; Oberholtzer, I, 125–30.

[45] *Acts of the General Assembly*, 1865–66, pp. 234–35.

ed by appropriate legislation.[46] It is true that the negro was not extended political privileges or granted social equality, but most northern states had not gone this far.[47] It is equally true that here and there in Georgia occurred outrages against the freedman and the northern immigrant, even as similar outrages might and did occur in Ohio or New York.[48] And, finally, it is true that this profound revolution in the structure of Georgia society had occurred "without enthusiasm," a deficiency in the view of Carl Schurz, a German idealist with less than twenty years of American background, which could not be understood or condoned.[49]

While Georgia had been working out its salvation as best it could, a conflict, ominous for the peace of the country, and especially the stricken South, was developing between the executive and legislative departments of the national government. It will be impossible within the limits

---

[46] Thompson, pp. 160–65, gives a mass of documentary evidence to show that Georgia was accepting the situation in good faith.

[47] Mr. J. G. de R. Hamilton has made a comprehensive survey of the legislation of the Southern legislatures respecting the status of the freedman. His conclusions are that the southern states acted moderately and in good faith, and in no spirit of defiance; and that the Mississippi code, the severest, was not representative, though it was falsely or ignorantly portrayed as such by the Radicals who wanted arguments and pretexts, not facts. See *Studies in Southern History and Politics*, pp. 139–58.

[48] General Steedman to President Johnson, August 15, 1865, in the Johnson MSS, quoted by Miss Thompson, p. 163.

[49] Schurz's unfavorable report on conditions in the South, which was so potent in strengthening the case of the Radicals against the Johnson plan is found in *Sen. Ex. Doc.*, 39 C., 1 S., No. 2. The report of Schurz was deprived of some of its sting by reports of General Grant, Henry Watterson, and Truman submitted at about the same time.

of this study to do more than indicate the most general causes and significant incidents of this conflict; but it does seem necessary to do this much in order to make intelligible the transition from presidential to Congressional Reconstruction, which transition called Hill back into public life and into the most dynamic and spectacular fight of his entire career.

Andrew Johnson was personally unacceptable to the Radical Republicans in the Congress. A southern man and old-line Democrat, with well-known states-rights proclivities, he was viewed as an accidental president and had only received a momentary allegiance from the Radicals when it had seemed likely that he would be an executioner of southern rebels. Since the announcement of his liberal reconstruction policy, in the proclamation of May 29, 1865, he had been steadily losing favor with the Radicals.[50]

When the first session of the Thirty-ninth Congress convened in December, 1865, the Radicals, led by Stevens in the House and by Wade and Sumner in the Senate, openly declared war on the president by refusing to admit representatives who presented themselves from the states reconstructed according to the Johnson plan. Congress then began the work of legislation, on its own account, which ended in a complete rupture between the executive and legislative departments of the general government, and later to the enactment of Congressional Reconstruction.

On January 11 Lyman Trumbull reported from the Judiciary Committee of the Senate a bill to extend the time and enlarge the functions of the Freedmen's Bureau, which

[50] See Oberholtzer, I, 41–44; Rhodes, VI, 16–19.

had been established by act of March 3, 1865, for only one year. The bill passed the House and Senate in due time and was vetoed by the president on February 19 in a message attacking its constitutionality and declaring, among other objections, that it was designed for a state of war which no longer existed, created a dangerous and expensive bureaucracy, and would coddle the negro to his own detriment. Another grave objection, said the president, lay in the fact that "the bill was passed by a Congress from which eleven states were excluded."[51]

On the same day, January 11, Trumbull reported a Civil Rights bill, which, when passed by both houses of Congress, also received the executive veto on March 27, in a message which reiterated much the same objections on the ground of constitutionality that had been advanced regarding the Freedmen's Bureau bill.[52]

The president's veto had been sustained on the first bill, but the Civil Rights bill was passed over the veto on April 9, and from that moment it is very probable that Johnson and his Reconstruction policies were doomed.[53]

In the meanwhile the Congress was endeavoring to agree on an amendment to the Constitution, which, in their view, seemed necessary to safeguard the legitimate fruits of the war. The Joint Committee on Reconstruction had reported an amendment on January 31 which was defeated, more because it was considered inadequate than for any

[51] See *Congressional Globe*, 39 C., 1 S., p. 915, for the veto message.
[52] *Ibid.*, p. 1679.
[53] *Ibid.*, p. 1861. The Civil Rights Act is found in Walter L. Fleming, *Documentary History of Reconstruction*, I, 197–201 (hereafter referred to as "Fleming").

other reason. It was not until May 10 that the recognizable germ of the Fourteenth Amendment appeared in the form of a joint resolution proposed by the House. Subsequently modified and supplemented, this House resolution came forth as the Fourteenth Amendment to the Constitution on June 13.[54] Consisting of four distinct sections, no one of which sustained any necessary relation to the other, "but united by the bond of a relation to the issues of the war, and sustained by the pressure of partisan political necessity, they served to support one another and to consolidate the requisite majority."[55]

On July 16 Congress adopted a new Freedmen's Bureau bill, overriding the president's veto to do so.[56] Its own counter plan to the president's now being complete, Congress adjourned on July 28; and the relative merits of the policies of Congress and president became a matter for the people's decision in the Congressional elections of 1866.[57]

In summarizing the conflict thus far, it may be observed that the Congress had asserted its determination to share in the process of Reconstruction. It had refused to admit southern Congressmen and Senators, taking refuge

[54] Rhodes, VI, 79-81, traces the legislation of the Fourteenth Amendment through its various stages.

[55] Dunning, p. 68. Professor Dunning, in the same passage, says no one of the sections of the amendment would have passed on its own merit.

[56] Fleming, I, 321-26, gives the act.

[57] For a comprehensive review of the work of the Thirty-ninth Congress in its first session, and the presidential opposition thereto, see the following secondary accounts: Rhodes, VI, 50-96; Oberholtzer, I, 150-88; Dunning, pp. 51-70. The account in the text above is confessedly inadequate, but the limitations of space hardly seem to justify a more extended treatment.

in its Constitutional privilege of passing on the qualifications of its own members.[58] It had then demonstrated its sense of the inadequacy of the presidential plan by enacting a Civil Rights bill, designed to counteract the allegedly discriminating "black codes" of the southern states, and a Freedmen's Bureau bill, said to be necessary to protect and uplift the negro, who otherwise, it was professed, would be at the mercy of the cruelty of the southern whites. And finally it had proposed a Fourteenth Amendment to the organic law, defining citizenship and imposing certain disabilities and obligations on the southern people, which disabilities and obligations were represented as essential in order to preserve the legitimate fruits of the war.

While the Congress did not explicitly promise admission to the southern states on the basis of the acceptance on their part, of these terms, it was tacitly understood that such admission would be granted if the states ratified the Fourteenth Amendment and were otherwise good until Congress came together again.[59]

While the Congressional elections of 1866 were pending, both sides to the controversy made energetic efforts to organize and direct public opinion, as it was recognized that the elections were tantamount to a popular referendum on the events of the dispute between the executive and legislative departments. It was naturally to be expected

[58] Constitution of the United States, Art. 1, Sec. 5.

[59] The action of Congress in admitting Tennessee, July 28, indicates its temper on this point, were there not abundant other evidence in the Congressional debates. See Rhodes, VI, 82–83. It may be noted that the extreme Radicals are not yet in control at the conclusion of the first session of the Thirty-ninth Congress.

that the sympathies of the South would be with the president, who now seemed the only bulwark between the southern states and an irate Congress.[60]

The chief interest in the political maneuvering of the campaign, from the viewpoint of this study, attaches to the National Union Convention, assembled in Philadelphia on August 14 in response to a call from the supporters of the president. The Convention was planned as a great national demonstration which, by assembling delegates from all sections and moderate men from all parties, should prove that Johnson and the administration presented a true rallying-point for all lovers of the Constitution and the Union, as against the dangerous and subversive Republican Congress.[61] The plan was part of a shrewd move to create a new Constitutional Union party and, conducted in behalf of any other leader than Johnson, might have been dangerous to Republican ascendancy. It was proposed to include the old Democrats, North and South, former Whigs, and any moderate Republicans who might be willing to rest content with the accomplishments of the national government to date in preserving the integrity of the Union and abolishing slavery. It would make its appeal to all who feared centralization of power in the national government at the expense of the states, or who viewed with apprehension the encroachment of the legislative department of the national government upon the executive. Favoring a lenient course

[60] For a review of these efforts, see Oberholtzer, I, 384-418; Rhodes, VI, 99-111; Dunning, pp. 71-82.

[61] For the Philadelphia Convention, see Oberholtzer, I, 384-91; Rhodes, VI, 99-102; Dunning, pp. 73-76.

toward the South, it might be expected to secure solid southern adherence.

Hill favored the participation of the southern states in this Convention and, in response to a request from the editor of the *Augusta Constitutionalist and Sentinel,* broke his self-imposed silence to the extent of a letter setting forth his views on this subject.[62] "I think that every southern state should take immediate steps to be represented in that Convention," he wrote. And then at some length he explains his reasons for this opinion.

The Radical Republican party, he thinks, has demonstrated in the legislation of the session of Congress just closing, that it is unwilling to save the country or to respect the Constitution. Hill then reiterates his familiar view that the unconciliating, uncompromising extremists of both sections were always the natural enemies of a constitution founded in concert and administered in concert. "This theory has ever been the corner-stone of my policies."

It will be easier, he says, to reconcile the South to the Union than to reconcile the North to the Constitution. The movement at Philadelphia, he understands, is designed to save the Constitution; and in attaining such an end, he thinks that every other issue should stand adjourned. By a combination of all conservative men, Constitutional government may yet be saved. The South, he thinks, sought to save the Constitution out of the Union, and failed. "Let her now bring her diminished and shattered strength, but united and earnest counsels and energies to save the Con-

[62] Letter dated July 4, 1866, reprinted in *Savannah Daily News and Herald,* July 9, 1866, from which the analysis in the text is taken.

stitution and the Union." Such had always been his desire and advice.

He continues: "The Union must remain. So it is settled. Shall the Union be without the Constitution? Shall it be with a new Constitution formed by a section, and formed in farce? Shall it be bread to one section and stone to another section of a common whole?"

The Philadelphia movement is represented as standing for a "Union of equals, according to a Constitution made by all, and administered by all and for all"; and therefore he approves it.

In this letter Hill indicates that he considers his public life is concluded. The letter ends: "These are my views; and though I consider that my days as a public man have been counted, you may lock them in your drawer, or throw them in the fire, or give them to the public as you please."

It would not be fair to dismiss these views respecting Constitutional government as the disgruntled or jaundiced expression of a disappointed politician, or even as a mere defense armament put on in the exigency of defeat and danger. Hill's public utterances before secession abound in similar sentiment.[63] He had almost made a fetish of the Constitution, and the flippancy with which that revered document was treated by the Radicals in Congress had gravely alarmed and outraged him.[64]

[63] See speech delivered at Macon, Georgia, June 30, 1860; speech delivered before the Georgia General Assembly, November 15, 1860; letter of acceptance as delegate to the Georgia Constitutional Convention, December 26, 1860—all found in Hill, *Life of Hill*. Particular references are to pp. 236, 246–48.

[64] See Stevens speeches in Congress, December 18 and 20, in *Congressional Globe*, 30 C., 1 S., pp. 72, 92.

In appearing before the committee of Congress investigating the Ku Klux Klan operations in 1871, Hill enlarged on his political views and expectations of 1866. He said: "I advised our people to go into a new party arrangement." Then referring to the letter he had written in 1866, he continued: "In this letter I used this expression: We will not go into the Democracy, because if secession was wrong, the Democrats instigated it, and if secession was right, the Democratic party of the North joined in the war to put it down. In no event, therefore, should we of the South trust the Democratic party."[65]

Hill, before the committee, then explained the hopes and anticipations of the old Whigs in the two years immediately following the war, which hopes and anticipations were destroyed by the failure of the Johnson plan and the enactment of Congressional Reconstruction.[66] He reminded the committee that the old Whigs had never favored secession as a Constitutional remedy, though they had acquiesced in it rather than oppose their native state. But Congress made the supreme mistake, says Hill, when it

lumped the Old Union Democrats and Whigs together with the secessionists and said they would punish all alike, would put us all under the negro. That naturally created a sympathy between us and the secession Democrats. Congress by that act prevented us from saying to the secession Democrats that all they had said was untrue; that the northern people had no desire to oppress them, because the Acts of Congress proved that they were right. I wish to state once more as an evidence that the old Union Democrats and Whigs might have come to the surface and controlled the country, we elected an

[65] *Ku Klux Report*, Pt. VII, p. 762.
[66] *Ibid.*, p. 763.

old Union Whig as the first Governor in 1865, whom the Democrats had repeatedly rejected before the war, whom we never could elect before the war.[67]

The Philadelphia Convention was held in due season, but whether it accomplished anything of value is a matter of conjecture.[68] The campaign waxed warm over the country; and when the elections for members of the Fortieth Congress were over, it was found that the country had overwhelmingly sustained the Congress, giving the Radicals a working majority of considerably more than two-thirds for the next Congress.[69]

The President had gained nothing by his appeal to the country. He had asked the Republicans to follow him; only Democrats did so. He had read himself out of his party . . . . and encouraged by the popular endorsement the leaders prepared to conduct the nation's affairs with a high hand.[70]

When the second session of the Thirty-ninth Congress came together in December, 1866, it did so with a feeling that it possessed a mandate from the people to take Reconstruction out of the hands of the executive. Its determination to do so was but increased by the fact that southern state after state was refusing to ratify the Fourteenth Amendment. James A. Garfield, heretofore a moderate, expressed the common opinion when he said on February 8, 1867, when news came that the last southern state to act

[67] The reference is to Charles J. Jenkins, for whose antebellum career see Phillips, *Georgia and State Rights*, pp. 146, 167, 168, 179, 202, 208.

[68] Rhodes thinks "it bade fair to influence public sentiment" favorably, (VI, 101); Oberholtzer is non-committal but says the leaders at the close were "overflowing with their success" (I, 390).

[69] Rhodes, VI, 110.

[70] The quotation is Oberholtzer's (I, 419).

had turned down the Amendment: "The last one of the sinful ten has at last with contempt and scorn flung back into our teeth the magnanimous offer of a generous nation. It is now our turn to act."[71]

It would be almost an endless task to prosecute the query as to whether the southern states were justified in repudiating the Fourteenth Amendment at this time, and in the end this will remain a matter of individual opinion. It is, however, easy enough to ascertain the reasons which were advanced in the southern legislatures for their action in defeating ratification of the amendment. The main reasons were two, the one constitutional and the other sentimental.

From the constitutional view, it was alleged that if the southern communities were indeed states, as was implied in the request that they ratify the amendment, then the amendment had been proposed in an unconstitutional manner, since ten states were unrepresented; but that if the southern communities were not states, as sometimes appeared from the course of the argument, then it was utterly superfluous to require them to ratify the amendment, and their act in so doing would have no binding force.

The sentimental reason for repudiating the amendment related primarily to that section which placed former Confederate leaders under political disabilities. The state legislature took the position that whatever guilt attached to these leaders was shared by the southern people, for whom they had merely exercised a mandate; and it little became

[71] *Congressional Globe*, 39 C., 2 S., p. 1104.

the southern people now to acquiesce in penalizing men who had merely carried out the popular will.[72]

The second session of the Thirty-ninth Congress, assuming the approbation of the electorate because of the overwhelming victory scored by the Radicals in the elections of 1866, came together in December, 1866, and set to work on the deliberation which resulted in the passage over the president's veto of the fateful First Reconstruction Act, of March 2, 1867.[73] This act declared that "whereas no legal state governments or adequate protection of life or property" now exists in the rebel states, it remanded them to military rule. After stipulating the divisions and manner of this rule, the fifth section of the act provided a plan by which escape from military rule and a reconstruction of the state government might be accomplished.

This act proved to be the first of three enactments, which collectively are designated the "Reconstruction

[72] These reasons will be recognized by the student of the period, as being commonplace. The literature regarding the subject is pervaded by them.

However, it may be said, in particular, that they represent a consensus of opinion expressed by Joe Brown, General John B. Gordon, Augustus R. Wright, Ambrose Wright, and Alexander Stephens. The testimony of the first four named is found in the *Ku Klux Report* as follows: Brown's testimony, Pt. VII, pp. 810–27, especially, p. 821; Gordon's testimony, Pt. VII, p. 304–34, especially, pp. 316–18; Ambrose Wright's testimony, Pt. VII, pp. 264–304, especially, pp. 278–79; Augustus R. Wright's testimony, Pt. VII, pp. 88–149, especially, pp. 110–111. Stephens' views are given in numerous places. See Fleming, I, 234–48, for his views before the Joint Committee on Reconstruction, and for other documents explaining the defeat of the amendment.

[73] The act is found in Fleming, I, 401–3. Its passage had been the result of much labor, conference, and amendment, of which a good account is given in Rhodes, VI, 124–34.

Acts," but in the southern literature of the period, quite frequently are called the "military bills." When the Fortieth Congress assembled in special session on the same day on which the preceding Congress expired, that is, March 4, 1867, it applied itself to the work of filling out the details and providing the machinery, for the process of Reconstruction outlined in the Act of March 2, 1867. This Second, or Supplementary, Reconstruction Act became law over the president's veto on March 23.[74]

Yet a third act was necessary to the completion of the Congressional plan. The former acts had possessed certain ambiguities and had been subjected to unacceptable constructions at the hands of executive officers; so to clear up these ambiguities and nullify the injurious interpretations the Act of July 19 passed the Congress again over the president's veto.[75]

The Congressional plan, as developed in the three Reconstruction Acts as a whole, may be briefly summarized. The former state governments, set up by Lincoln and Johnson, were scrapped, except where military commanders might see fit to utilize them in part. Military rule became paramount.

A plan of reorganization or reconstruction of state government was then prescribed. The first step in the plan concerned the registration of voters and the qualifications for the suffrage. There should be a registration of all voters, qualified to exercise the suffrage, for the purpose of having an election on the question of assembling a state

---

[74] The act is found in Fleming, I, 407–11.

[75] *Ibid.*, pp. 415–18. For the occasion of its passage, see *ibid.*, pp. 411–15; also, Rhodes, VI, 171–75.

CONGRESSIONAL RECONSTRUCTION 139

constitutional convention whose work should be a revision of the state constitution: All adult males, including the negro, could exercise the suffrage except those under the disabilities of the Fourteenth Amendment or who were disfranchised for participation in rebellion or for felony.[76] The Third Reconstruction Act had given the boards of registrars wide and inquisitorial powers in the supervision of the registry lists, that none ineligible under the Acts might be registered.

After such a registration the commanding general was to set an election date at which time the registered voters should express an opinion of the advisability of having a constitutional convention. If the majority of the registered voters desired a convention, the convention should be called, but none are eligible to seats in the convention who could not, under the Acts, exercise the suffrage for the election on the convention.

This convention must then adopt a constitution prescribing the same suffrage for state elections as was imposed in the Reconstruction Acts; and the constitution must otherwise be acceptable to Congress.

The constitution, as adopted, must then go before the people of the state for ratification. If a majority of the reg-

[76] This clause barring those disfranchised "for participation in rebellion" seems to have had little practical effect, judged by the interpretation of the attorney-general, Stanberry: "The actual participation in a rebellion does not amount to a disfranchisement. . . . . No law of the United States has declared the penalty of disfranchisement for "participation in rebellion" alone. Nor is it known that any such law exists in either of these ten states, except perhaps, Virginia, to which special instructions will be sent" (memorandum to the president from Stanberry, Fleming, I, 413).

istered voters approved the constitution, it should be declared in effect; but not otherwise.

And finally, when the state legislature elected under this new constitution should have ratified the Fourteenth Amendment to the Federal Constitution, and Congress shall have approved the state constitution, then, and not until then, "said state shall be declared entitled to representation in Congress" and may resume its own local self-government.

It seems impossible to escape the query as to the necessity, the expediency, and the justice of these Acts; and it is equally impossible to arrive at any final or incontrovertible conclusion on the score of any one of these points. Reputable, and in some cases learned authority, might be quoted almost without end, on either side of any one of the three questions.

It would seem that a very good case can be made for either side of the question as to the necessity of the legislation. Miss Thompson, however, who has made the closest and most exhaustive study of the conditions in Georgia, is very positive that so far as Georgia is concerned, at least, the Acts were unnecessary.[77] The preponderance of evidence tends to support this view.

The question of expediency is the easiest to answer. There can be little doubt that the Acts were most inexpedient and ill-adapted to the situation. The entire subsequent

[77] Thompson, p. 165. Rhodes, after reviewing southern conditions in 1865, says: "It may be affirmed with confidence that there was nothing in the condition of the South which required the stringent military rule provided for in the Reconstruction Acts" (Rhodes, VI, 139).

CONGRESSIONAL RECONSTRUCTION

history of Reconstruction might be supposed to demonstrate the egregious inexpediency of the Acts.

The justice of the Acts presents a question which is not admissible of a satisfactory answer because any answer must be made in the light of an interpretation of the whole war period. And the words in that period had come to possess different meanings to the participants and are only slowly being reduced to uniformity by latter-day students. When the words "treason" and "loyalty" had come to be applied to one and the same act, the parties to the different usage could hardly be expected to agree on the content of the word "justice."

Mr. Rhodes, among the professedly dispassionate and non-sectional historians, has delivered the severest judgment on the Reconstruction Acts. "No law," he says, speaking of the Acts of March 2 and 23, "so unjust in its policy, so direful in its results had passed the American Congress since the Kansas-Nebraska Act of 1854."[78] And again: "Steven's Reconstruction Acts, ostensibly in the interest of freedom, were an attack on civilization."[79]

---

[78] Rhodes, VI, 134.

[79] *Ibid.*, p. 146. The scope of the foregoing study and the necessity to get on with the work of Hill has precluded the use of a mass of documentary material that has been examined, regarding the transition from presidential to congressional reconstruction. The most important documents which have been examined, bearing on this subject, are the reports of Carl Schurz and Ulysses Grant on conditions in the South, found in *Sen. Ex. Doc.*, 39 C., 1 S., No. 2; and the majority and minority reports of the Joint Committee on Reconstruction of the Thirty-ninth Congress, with the accompanying mass of testimony taken by the Committee (found in *Reports of Committees*, 39 C., 1 S., No. 30). The majority report disapproved the presidential plan and recommended additional legislation, which eventually took shape in the Reconstruction acts.

CHAPTER VIII

THE FIGHT AGAINST THE RECONSTRUCTION ACTS

In the fight against the acceptance of the Reconstruction Acts, or the "military bills" as they were designated in the South, Hill became the most outstanding figure in Georgia and attracted the attention of the entire nation. Before this period he had usually shared the limelight with other leaders, in some cases leaders of equal or superior distinction to himself. In the lurid struggle of 1867, Hill stood forth in a unique rôle as the unchallenged leader of an embattled cause.[1]

The South was somewhat stunned and leaderless as the full force of the Reconstruction policies of Congress began to be revealed in the early months of 1867.[2] Georgia leaders were either counseling submission, as in the case of Brown; were in exile, as in the case of Toombs; or were in gloomy retirement, as in the case of Stephens.[3] Under these circumstances, a small group of Atlanta citizens summoned Hill to Atlanta for a conference on the course to be

[1] One contemporary writer called Hill "the Moses of the entire South" (see Reed, p. 141). Other such views will appear in the sequel.

[2] Joel Chandler Harris in the *Atlanta Constitution*, quoted in Hill, *Life of Hill*, p. 51; also see Fielder, pp. 435-36.

[3] For Brown's counsel see especially his letter of February 23, 1867, in *Atlanta Daily New Era* for February 26 (*infra*, p. 151); for Toombs's exile, see Phillips, *Life of Toombs*, p. 256; for Stephens' course, see Johnston and Brown, pp. 492 ff.

FIGHT AGAINST RECONSTRUCTION ACTS

pursued. He secured a copy of the Reconstruction Acts and promised within a few days to return and make known his advice.[4]

The result of this conference and Hill's study of the Acts was his speech of July 16, 1867, which came to be known as the Davis Hall speech from the hall in Atlanta in which the speech was delivered. This proved to be the initial gun in a struggle of great intensity to be waged in the state. In this speech Hill took advanced position against southern voluntary participation in the Congressional plan of Reconstruction and became at once the acknowledged leader of the movement in opposition to the Acts.[5] The praise that was showered on him for his Davis Hall effort seems fulsome to the dispassionate student; but if there be any virtue of truth in contemporary evidence, where passions are rife and prejudices strong, the speech must have been a very powerful one and must have exerted a prodigious effect. The following editorial comment is no more superlative than the average:

> This speech is alive with the characteristics of Mr. Hill's mind when aroused to the noblest action. Here is displayed in thoughts that breath and words that burn, his deep insight into the philosophy of history and government—his logical dissection and apt ideas and words—his sublime moral courage not to be moved by the frowns of the tyrant, nor the wicked passions of the multitude—his withering invective that blisters as it falls on his victim, and the religious trust

[4] Hill, *Life of Hill*, p. 51.

[5] *Columbus Sun*, July 20, 1867; *Savannah News and Herald*, July 26, 1867; *Atlanta Daily Intelligencer*, July 18, 1867, in *Brown Scrap Books;* Reed, p. 150. These are but a few of the acknowledgments of Hill's leadership.

of a patriot who thinks only of his country. . . . . If our country is not doomed to destruction, surely his eloquent voice will not fall on closed ears, and his right arm be not bared in vain.[6]

The speech was delivered under singular, and, what must have been for the speaker, forbidding circumstances. In a dimly lighted hall, the military staff of General Pope were seated in full regalia on the front seats, facing the speaker. The audience expected the momentary arrest of Hill as the speech progressed. Indeed, just before he arose to speak, Hill had been presented with a slip of paper which proved to be an order from General Pope forbidding the delivery of a controversial or incendiary speech.[7]

In the speech Hill's main argument against the Acts is that they are unconstitutional, and he passionately urged that the southern people will have nothing to do with the "nefarious" plan proposed. By refraining from voting for a convention, and, if the convention is held anyway, by voting against the ratification of the constitution adopted by the "illegal" body, the "infamous" scheme may be defeated. There is no occasion for violence or force, even were force possible.[8]

[6] *Columbus Sun*, July 20, 1867. See also Reed, p. 140. Mr. Reed says of Hill's speech: "A bright light shot up which seemed to illuminate all the helpless South." Such characterizations might be multiplied almost endlessly.

[7] Mr. H. H. Cabaniss, of Atlanta, who was present, in a conversation with the writer related the circumstances of the Davis Hall speech. Mr. Cabaniss says that he himself read the order of General Pope immediately after the speech. Mr. D. M. Bain, of Atlanta, also present at the speech, has confirmed the narrative. Mr. Bain says that nearly every person present possessed a "six-shooter." (Conversations of July 8, 1926.)

[8] The speech is reported by J. Henley Smith in the *Atlanta Daily Intelligencer*, July 18, 1867, and widely copied in the state press. The most accessible copy is in Hill, *Life of Hill*, pp. 294-307.

FIGHT AGAINST RECONSTRUCTION ACTS

He approached the subject with his usual praise of Constitutional government:

> .... The great symptom of the decay and death of government is the disregard of the fundamental law of that government. Whenever a people come to treat lightly the fundamental law, they have arrived at the most dangerous point short of entire destruction. Republics above all other kinds of governments are maintained by respect for law. If the people of the United States fail to have a sacred regard for their own law . . . . they will deserve that awful fate which awaits them. . . . . I charge before Heaven and the American people this day, that every evil by which we have been afflicted is attributable directly to the violation of the Constitution. Tinkers may work, quacks may prescribe, demagogues may deceive, but there is no remedy for us, and no hope to escape the threatened evils, but in adhering to the Constitution.[9]

But if it be admitted, as Stevens was reported to have done, that the Acts were outside the Constitution, or that the Constitution was dead, as was alleged by some southerners who advocated acceptance, why, asked Hill, must southerners be forced to take oath to support the Constitution on every occasion? To take such an oath, and then acquiesce in this violation of the Constitution in almost the same breath, is to commit perjury; and Hill avows that he will never so perjure himself.

But again, if it be argued that the end justifies the means, and that the end, in this case restoration to the Union, is such a supreme good that it outweighs the evil of the means employed, Hill replies that restoration to such a Union as will result from this legislation will avail the South nothing. It is not even sure that representation in Congress will follow; and if it does, it will be conditioned

[9] Hill, *Life of Hill*, p. 295.

upon an abject submission to Radical rule.[10] The whole purpose of the nefarious business is to perpetuate Radical control, and by accepting the proposed measures, Hill says the South will abandon her only protection against that rule, namely the Constitution.

Again, if it be argued that refusal to accept the proposed restoration will be followed by confiscation and other severer terms, he replies, citing authority, that confiscation is a war measure and will not be dared even by the Radicals; and, as for worse possibilities, there are none. The continuation of military rule is far preferable to rule by the negro, the scalawag, and the carpetbagger, which will be the inevitable sequel of the success of the Congressional scheme.

Hill quotes Roman and English history to show that Roman decline began through such demagoguery as he attributes to the Radicals in Congress, and that in England resistance to unconstitutional measures of the Stuarts preserved the English Constitution and English liberties. Some had counseled "necessity" then; but Hampden and others defeated usurpation.

The Radical program is destined to sure failure, continues Hill in more optimistic vein. It will fail "because it is not possible to perpetuate a government of force under the forms of democracy" and "because it is sought to be accomplished by deceit and fraud which cannot long escape detection."

But how may the measures be resisted? it is asked.

[10] He cites the case of Kentucky, in the Union, but recently deprived of its representation because it is alleged her representatives were voted for by "disloyal" persons.

FIGHT AGAINST RECONSTRUCTION ACTS 147

First, by not approving them; and second, by peacefully refraining from having anything to do with their execution. He advises the whites to register, but thereafter to refuse to vote for a convention, and if a convention is held, to vote against ratification of the resultant constitution. Thus will the Radical design of making the southern whites the instruments of their own infamy fail.

Throughout the entire speech runs a bitter note of condemnation and scorn of southern men who either from weakness, cowardice, or selfish calculation counsel the acceptance of the Reconstruction Acts. Regarding such men, he declares:

> Some of you who favor the acceptance of the military bills take an oath to support the Constitution and still intend to vote for a Convention which you admit to be contrary to the Constitution. . . . . If you vote for the Convention you are perjured. . . . . You prate about your loyalty. I look you in the face and denounce you. You are morally and legally perjured traitors. You perjure yourselves and perjure the poor negro to help your treason. You may boast of it now while passion is rife, but the time will come when the very thought will wither your soul and make you hide from the face of mankind.[11]

It is impossible to convey by means of extracts or a condensed version the sustained invective and close constitutional reasoning contained in this fierce philippic of Hill's. The *New Orleans Crescent* compared it with the best of Demosthenes's philippics.[12] George Prentice, of the *Louisville Courier Journal*, declared: "It is a remarkable speech. It is stirring, splendid and scathing. And withal

---
[11] Hill, *Life of Hill*, p. 297.
[12] Quoted in the *Savannah News and Herald*, August 2, 1867.

it is as sound as the Constitution and as loyal as the Union."[13]

Hill's entire heart and brain were enlisted in the fight against what he considered the iniquitous policy of the Radical Congress; and, abandoning that silence which he had imposed upon himself in 1865, he indited a series of letters to the *Augusta Chronicle and Sentinel* which he called "Notes on the Situation" and which created a profound impression in the state and aroused echoes throughout the nation. Henry W. Grady, in writing of these "Notes" in the *Atlanta Constitution*, said:

> In my opinion they stand alone as the profoundest and most eloquent political essays ever penned by an American. They were accepted as the voice of the South, uttering her protest and her plea, and as such were discussed on the streets of London and the Boulevards of Paris, no less than in the cities of the North. Even now they stir the blood and kindle the pulses of the most phlegmatic reader, but this is but a hint of the sensation they produced when they were printed. Had Mr. Hill never spoken one speech his "Notes on the Situation" would have stamped him as one of the greatest men Georgia ever produced.[14]

The "Notes on the Situation" are twenty-two essays or letters attacking the Reconstruction policies of Congress on the ground of constitutionality, expediency, and justice.[15] In the "Notes" Hill analyzes minutely the Reconstruction

---

[13] Quoted in the same paper, July 26, 1867.

[14] August 17, 1882. Discounting some hyperbole, there is much truth in this assertion.

[15] Beginning June 19, 1867, and extending through August 1 of the same year, these "Notes on the Situation" were published at frequent intervals in the columns of the *Augusta Chronicle and Sentinel*. They were widely copied in the press of the state, and the entire country. They are found most conveniently in Hill, *Life of Hill*, pp. 730-911.

Acts, the motives behind the Acts, the issues of the war, the terms of the surrender, and the consequences which in his opinion will follow the execution of the plan proposed by the Reconstruction Acts. The "Notes" embrace eighty-one closely printed pages, and an extended analysis of them is impossible within the limits of this study. However, Hill himself has provided a summary of the points he "sought to establish." They are:

1. That the Military Bills were contrary to the Constitution, and destructive of all the principles and guarantees of free government in America.

2. That they were contrary to every code of civilized nations, and in infamous bad faith to the terms of the fight and the conditions of the surrender.

3. That the reasons urged to justify these measures—such as a desire to restore the Union, elevate the black race, secure guarantees of future peace, etc., etc., were utterly untrue, inconsistent and insidious—were pretexts to cover the *only real* purpose which was to perpetuate the power of the Radical party.

4. That the acceptance of the plan proposed by these bills could only result in a permanent subversion of the Government, in the degradation of the people, in a long and bloody reign of anarchy, with social, civil and agrarian wars, resulting after unparalleled horrors, in despotism for the whites in the whole United States, and in the extermination, exclusion or political re-enslavement of the African race.

5. That the only remedy for these evils both threatened and existing was a speedy return, by the people of all sections to the Constitution, and a vigorous enforcement of its remedies against all violators.[16]

It seems to have been the universal opinion that the chief service Hill rendered in these "Notes" was the en-

[16] Note No. 15. The summary is found in Hill, *Life of Hill*, p. 778.

couragement, the stiffening of morale, they gave to a crushed people. "Far and wide they went," says one writer, "among a downtrodden people and whoever read any one of the numbers recovered strong hope."[17] Another writes: "He could not go into every hamlet, but his influence went. He was a Greatheart to whom the new Pilgrim turned."[18]

From far outside the state came echoes of approval, awakened by the "Notes." A Kentucky judge who described himself as abhorring secession wrote:

> My opinion is that they contain the most thorough, all sufficing exposure, yet made of the tyrannical usurpation attempted in the territorializing acts for non-reconstruction. . . . . A reprint of them by the ten thousand, and sent broad cast throughout the North would reach and arouse the northern conscience.[19]

Even Alexander Stephens expressed approbation, saying that the "Notes" were destined to create a powerful impression wherever read, North or South.[20] This, coming from Stephens, who had never seen any good in Hill, was high praise.

But there were some few in Georgia and the South who demurred sharply to the paean of praise which went up from the South to Hill. And most notable and industrious

---

[17] Reed, p. 141.

[18] Joel Chandler Harris in the *Atlanta Constitution*, quoted in Hill, *Life of Hill*, p. 51.

[19] Judge Nicholas in a letter to the *Louisville Courier Journal*, reprinted in the *Columbus Sun*, July 25, 1867.

[20] *Savannah News and Herald*, September 26, 1867. See also *Columbus Sun*, July 9, 1867, and Fielder, pp. 437–48, for similar views.

FIGHT AGAINST RECONSTRUCTION ACTS

of his critics at this period was his old political antagonist, Brown. Brown had counseled acceptance of the Acts in a letter addressed to some gentlemen who had requested his advice when it was deemed that the passage of the Acts was certain.[21] This was in February, 1867. Brown had just returned from Washington, where he had reached the conviction that the terms proposed in the Reconstruction Acts was the minimum that Congress would offer. His advice, therefore, to the South was to "agree with thine adversary quickly," lest worse conditions be attached as a penalty for non-acceptance. Let a convention be called and let it take the required steps, counseled the prudent ex-governor. "Because we have lost much," he asked, "must we sacrifice the little we have?" He admitted that the terms proposed were hard, even humiliating, but he suggested that such was the fate of the conquered. And, moreover, he pointed out, the conditions now exacted were really no more humiliating than other conditions which had already been accepted by the South without such a grimace.[22] Let not sympathy for southern leaders, disfranchised under the Congressional acts, although quite natural, cause the people to continue their wives and children in beggary.

Moreover, what the South needs, he suggested, is the northern immigrant and capitalist, so much potential wealth; and these cannot be secured until Reconstruction is accomplished. As for negro enfranchisement, the south-

[21] In *Atlanta Daily New Era*, February 26, 1867, in the *Brown Scrap Books*. The letter is dated February 23.

[22] He refers, no doubt, to the exactions made by Johnson as to abolition of slavery, repudiation of war debts, etc.

ern whites, in due time, would be able to control the negro's political views.[23]

It is easy to recognize much of practical wisdom in these views of Brown. He had convinced himself that the South could get peace on no better terms, and he saw that peace was essential to the rehabilitation of the shattered fortunes of the section. He was willing to waive points of constitutionality and consistency and accept what could not be bettered. And it is a very strong argument in his favor that eventually, and at no remote date, the Democratic party of the South and of the entire nation came over to his position. The Democratic platform of 1872 took virtually the identical position on Reconstruction assumed by Brown in 1867.[24] But in the meanwhile the Democratic party was to wage desperate war against the Reconstruction policies of the Republican Congress.[25]

Whatever the calculating wisdom and subsequent vindication of Brown's advice, his course recommending acquiescence in the Reconstruction Acts brought down on him unparalleled obloquy. His name became a byword and a cause for hissing among all Georgians of Confederate or Democratic affiliations, and this embraced nearly all the better classes. He was the "unmentionable," and endured

---

[23] Brown's views were pressed in a vigorous campaign. Besides the letter of February 23, 1867, previously cited, and Brown's "Review of Hill's Notes," to be discussed later, his views were expressed in the following: speech in Savannah, April 18, 1867, reported in the *Atlanta New Era*, April 24, 1867; speech in Augusta, April 27, 1867, reported in *Augusta Daily Press*, April 28, 1867; speech in Milledgeville, June 6, 1867, reported in *Milledgeville Federal Union*, June 11, 1867; interview in *Cincinnati Commercial*, May 7, 1867. All the foregoing in *Brown Scrap Books*.

[24] Rhodes, VII, pp. 43, 53.   [25] *Infra.*, pp. 161–200.

FIGHT AGAINST RECONSTRUCTION ACTS

a degree of political reviling and personal ostracism rarely equaled in the annals of the state.[26]

It was represented that Brown, in order to save his own neck from the hangman's halter for his alleged treason in resisting federal authority, and for seizing the Augusta arsenal and Fort Pulaski[27] prior to secession and while Georgia acknowledged allegiance to the Union, and to save his own property from confiscation, had turned his back upon his country, and betrayed the people who had honored and raised him to official power, and whom he had led into secession and its disastrous consequences. And now in order to save himself and his ill-gotten gains, it was charged, he had joined the Republican Radicals, the enemies of his people, and was aiding them in completing the humiliation and dishonor of his deserted compatriots.[28]

The doughty ex-governor was a hard fighter and, not

[26] The press of the state teemed with bitter invectives against Brown from 1867 well into the 1870's. The following is a typical example: "Brown, portentuous name! Brown, synonym of Georgia's disgrace and humiliation! Brown, indicative of treason and knavery! . . . . Judas Iscariot, and Benedict Arnold. What a fall is there my countrymen . . . ." etc., for several columns (from the leading editorial in the *Augusta Chronicle and Sentinel*, August 14, 1868).

Miss Sally Brown, the daughter of the war governor, has related to the writer many incidents in the social ostracism of her family in the Reconstruction period.

[27] *Supra,* p. 49.

[28] Fielder, pp. 425–26. Brown was a good business man, and his accumulation of wealth was always regarded with suspicion by the less fortunate or successful. The most complete defense of Brown's course during the reconstruction period is given in his speech before the Georgia General Assembly in October, 1879, copious extracts of which are given by Fielder, pp. 428–31. Judging by the results, this proved a complete vindication of the much traduced ex-governor, as he was shortly thereafter elected to the United States Senate (see Avery, p. 602).

daunted by the avalanche of vituperation, began a vigorous campaign in behalf of the Reconstruction Acts. He issued a series of letters which he called a "Review of Notes on the Situation," and which were given publication in the same Augusta journal publishing Ben Hill's "Notes."[29] Hill and his partisans charged that the "Review", was merely a scurrilous attack on his political record and that it studiously begged all the real points raised in the original "Notes." In a letter to the *Augusta Chronicle and Sentinel,* Hill offered to aid Brown in getting down to the real issues, by proposing ten questions, which should engage the governor's attention rather than the immaterial task of writing his (Hill's) biography. He asks a reply on these questions:

1. Are the military bills constitutional?
2. Are they in accord with the laws of nations?
3. Has Congress any existence outside the Constitution?
4. Can the conqueror add to the terms of surrender *after* the surrender?
5. Is there not a difference in executing a law possibly unconstitutional (before the Court rules) and executing one palpably and avowedly unconstitutional?
6. Would not the execution of a citizen without trial under military law in Georgia be *murder?*
7. Is Georgia not a state in the Union?
8. Can the white race be forced under the black race without violence and race war?
9. Can the Union be restored and peace secured by violating the Constitution?
10. Are the reconstruction enormities more tolerable because perpetrated merely to continue Republican Power?[30]

[29] Consisting of seven numbers, running from August 1, 1867, to August 9, in the *Augusta Chronicle and Sentinel.*

[30] Letter dated August 2, 1867, and published August 4.

FIGHT AGAINST RECONSTRUCTION ACTS 155

Brown does not seem to have replied categorically to these questions, as indeed they permitted of no categorical answer, as Hill was shrewd enough to know. Definitions and premises had first to be established, and a generation succeeding these antagonists has hardly reached an agreement on the underlying definitions and premises involved in the dispute.

But there was one other man in Georgia who addressed himself to some of Hill's questions. Hill had made much of the contention that the Reconstruction Acts were "outside of the law of the peace," that they were conditions exacted after the terms of surrender, and therefore in bad faith and contrary to the law of nations.[31] Benjamin F. Yancey argued, in a letter published in the *Atlanta Daily Intelligencer*, that there had been no "law of the peace" but merely an unconditional surrender. There had been no one authorized to make a "law of the peace" at the time of the surrender, said Mr. Yancey. Sherman had proposed such a law in his first agreement with Joseph E. Johnston in North Carolina but had been overruled by the government.[32] But if it be contended that Georgia's acceptance of Johnson's terms in 1865 constituted a "law of the peace," which could not be changed thereafter, Yancey replied, first, that Johnson had no more constitutional right than had Sherman to determine a "law of the peace"; and second, that Johnson's terms were just as *outside* and beyond what Hill represented as the "law of the peace" as were the hated terms of Congress, against which Hill in-

---

[31] "Notes" Nos. 6 and 7, Hill, *Life of Hill*, pp. 743-51. See Hill's fourth question addressed to Brown.

[32] See Rhodes, V, 166-68.

veighed so bitterly. For had not Johnson required humiliating action at the hands of the "sovereign states," such as the repudiation of war debts. Yancey then turned on Hill: "Were you Mr. Hill so perjured, so traitorous, having vowed to support the Constitution, as to engage immediately in its violation by consenting to terms—to action *outside* that very document." In conclusion, Yancey counseled immediate acceptance of Congressional terms, lest worse conditions be imposed.[33]

General James B. Longstreet also wrote a letter advocating prompt acceptance of the Reconstruction Acts.[34] The military bills and amendments are "peace offerings," he said. The highest of human laws is the law that is established by an appeal to arms. Southern principles have ceased to exist and northern principles are now "laws," advised this self-confessed authority on military strategy who was soon to hold the position of surveyor of the Port of New Orleans.[35]

It is not likely that a conclusion satisfactory to all parties can be reached on the question of the constitutionality or unconstitutionality of the Reconstruction Acts, which engaged so much of the argument of Hill in 1867. Mr. Rhodes has given the following opinion, and his opinions regarding Reconstruction problems certainly merit serious consideration:

[33] Yancey's letter was a reply to certain gentlemen who had requested his views. It was published October 6, 1867. Clipping in *Brown Scrap Books*. Mr. Yancey was a resident of Athens, Georgia.

[34] *Savannah Daily Republican*, June 10, 1867, in *Brown Scrap Books*. Letter also in Longstreet's book, *From Manassas to Appomattox*, pp. 636–37.

[35] Mrs. Helen D. Longstreet, *Lee and Longstreet at High Tide*, p. 105.

FIGHT AGAINST RECONSTRUCTION ACTS

Had the cases of Mississippi and Georgia[36] been considered on their merits little doubt can exist, to argue from the decision in the Milligan case[37] the preceding December, that a majority of the Judges would have pronounced the Acts unconstitutional. . . . . One thing is sure; the Republican majority in Congress and among the Northern people was determined to have its way, and would no more be stopped by legal principles and technicalities than it had been by the President's vetoes.[38]

This seems a frank avowal, and is substantiated by the tone of the press and the debates in Congress. Indeed, some of Hill's friends had phlegmatically wanted to know why he expended so much argument on a self-evident proposition. The student of the period can hardly reach any conclusion but that the second session of the Thirty-ninth Congress and the Fortieth Congress were revolutionary bodies; and then if some extenuation or explanation is desired, it may be provided by the statement that the American constitutional system had contemplated no such contingency as faced the men of this period, and that they had to work out their own salvation without chart or compass. No doubt there were reckless and unprincipled Radicals, and Conservatives too, in these Congresses, but it is

---

[36] Rhodes refers to the injunction proceedings instituted by officials of Mississippi and Georgia to prevent the execution of the Acts, which action was denied in each case by the Supreme Court, for want of jurisdiction. See Rhodes, VI, 184–85. For Governor Jenkins' action as respects Georgia, see Avery, pp. 366–67.

[37] The decision in the case *ex parte* Milligan (4 Wallace 2) declared that military commissions and the other incidents of martial law were unconstitutional save where flagrant war made the actions of the ordinary courts impossible (See Dunning, p. 89).

[38] Rhodes, VI, 185.

a doubtful procedure to indict a whole Congress, as it is to indict a whole people.

While Hill escaped arrest as a result of his alleged "incendiary" utterances in the Davis Hall speech, he became the subject of epistolary discussion between General Pope and the General of the Armies, Grant, in Washington.[39] In the *Augusta Chronicle and Sentinel* for August 21, 1867, appears the following communication from General John Pope:

Hq. 3d Mil. Dist.
  Atlanta, Ga., July 24, 1867.
    To General Grant

GENERAL: I have the honor to send enclosed a newspaper containing a speech made in this city by B. H. Hill of this state, late a Senator in the Rebel Congress. This person only a few weeks since was pardoned by the President, and in common with almost every pardoned rebel, this is the use of the clemency of the Government. You can readily see from the speech the character of the man, who is representative of a large class, and the hopelessness of any satisfactory reconstruction of the Southern States while such men retain influence. . . . .

The letter continued at considerable length to expound the vices of Hill and the men of his class and to advance views of the writer's own concerning reconstruction.[40]

In August of the same year General Pope closed the State University at Athens and withheld the funds due to the University from the State Treasury in Milledgeville.[41]

---

[39] The Washington correspondent of the *New York Times* is quoted in the *Savannah News and Herald*, August 27, 1867, as saying: "It is generally believed here, Grant will order the arrest of B. H. Hill."

[40] Letter widely copied in state press. See *Columbus Sun*, August 23, 1867, and *Savannah News and Herald*, August 23, 1867.

[41] Hull, *Annals of Athens*, p. 327.

FIGHT AGAINST RECONSTRUCTION ACTS

The order affecting the University is alleged to have been due to certain occurrences at the annual University commencement in August. A young student, Cox by name, made a speech objectionable to the general. At its conclusion, Hill, who was present and on the platform as a trustee of the institution, arose and grasped the young student warmly by the hand. General Pope is said to have become incensed, and issued two military orders, one closing the State University instanter and the other withholding the state funds. On the same day Chancellor Lipscomb of the University visited Pope, who was in Athens, and secured the withdrawal of the first order. The general at the same time intimated to the chancellor that if Hill were forced to resign his trusteeship and the professorship of law to which he had recently been elected,[42] the whole matter would end.[43]

Hill soon went to Washington, following Pope's visitation of his wrath on the State University, and interceded with President Johnson and General Grant, the latter of whom wrote Pope in a mild vein of displeasure, to which Pope replied in an argumentive manner.[44] He declared that Hill and the young student, A. H. Cox, were "unrepentant rebels" and "incendiaries," and that in closing the Univer-

---

[42] To succeed Judge Wilson Lumpkin, deceased. Hill did not accept the office. See *Savannah News and Herald,* August 15, 1867.

[43] Hull, p. 327; *Columbus Sun,* August 24, 1867. Amusing scenes occurred at this commencement when Hill and Brown, as trustees of the University, were thrown together in public; and the audience enjoyed their efforts "to edge away from each other." See *Savannah News and Herald,* August 15, 1867.

[44] Letter dated October 22, 1867, printed in *Atlanta Constitution,* November 8, 1867.

sity he had but followed the precedent set by Georgia authorities who on a former occasion had closed the University on account of a political demonstration.[45] He said he would rescind his order "very reluctantly." It was with considerable difficulty, and only after a special meeting of the University trustees had addressed an appeal to Johnson and Grant, that an order was secured setting aside Pope's action.[46] Early in January, 1868, the removal of General Pope from his position in Georgia occasioned much rejoicing in the state.[47]

While in the North on this trip connected with the State University, Hill thought that he observed signs of a reaction from the policies of the Radical party among the rank and file of the northern people, and wrote a very optimistic letter back to Georgia. He advised that if the people would but defeat the Reconstruction Acts by keeping hands off, and at the same time be kind to the negro and disprove the campaign lies circulated about southern outrages, that escape from the black pall is imminent, because the North is coming to recognize the purpose of the Radicals and to resent the heavy taxation required to support the military and civil bureaucracy maintained in the South.[48]

[45] Referring to a demonstration made in favor of Troup for governor over his rival Clarke.

[46] Hull, p. 327. An account of this episode is also found in Avery, p. 372.

[47] For reasons for the removal and circumstances connected with it, see Thompson, pp. 177–79. Pope was freely referred to as a "military satrap."

[48] Dated October 14, 1867, published in *Augusta Chronicle and Sentinel.*

FIGHT AGAINST RECONSTRUCTION ACTS 161

There had been no political party organization in Georgia since the war.[49] From the announcement of the Congressional policies, however, Georgia, as did most southern states, began to divide between those advocating acceptance, who were called Radicals and were more or less affiliated with the Republican party, and the party of opposition to the Acts, usually designated the Conservative party. From the attitude assumed by the national parties, it was inevitable that this latter group in Georgia, and elsewhere, should become affiliated with, and indeed identified with, the Democratic party, although many of its members had always heretofore opposed the Democratic party. It was thus, as Hill explained at great length before a Congressional committee in 1871, that he and many other old Whigs were forced into the Democratic party.[50]

Hill now, in the autumn and winter of 1867, assumed the leadership of this party and went about the work of perfecting an organization which might combat the execution of the Acts. A convention was held at Macon, on December 5, 1867, which named Hill as its president.[51] Speeches were made "of an exciting character," among the chief of which was one made by the president in which he summed up his message: "Hold on, hold on, hold on at all hazards and through all sacrifices to the Constitution of your Fathers."[52] Details of organization were arranged,

[49] Avery, p. 373.

[50] Hill's testimony before the Ku Klux Committee, *Ku Klux Report*, Pt. VII, pp. 760-68.

[51] *Atlanta Daily Intelligencer*, December 8, 1867, in *Brown Scrap Books*.

[52] *Ibid.*

and a committee named to issue an address to the people of the state, condemning Radical Reconstruction.[53] The convention called itself a "Conservative Convention," and the absence of the former Georgia dictators, Stephens, Toombs, Cobb, and Brown is notable. Hill had now become the uncontested leader of the former following of these gentlemen.

In the meanwhile the first steps in the execution of the Congressional plan for restoration of state government had gone forward. Registration under the Acts being completed in September,[54] General Pope ordered an election to take place on October 29, 30, and 31, on the question of holding a convention, and at the same time directed that delegates to the convention be named in the same election.[55] Despite the efforts of the Conservatives, the convention carried by a large vote. The customary charges of fraud were made against the successful party.[56]

When the Reconstruction convention assembled in Atlanta on December 5, 1867, it was found to consist of

---

[53] Besides account cited, see Avery, pp. 373–75, and Fielder, pp. 438–41. Hershel V. Johnson, Absolom H. Chappell, B. H. Hill, Warren Aiken, and Theodore Guerry were named as the committee to draft an address, for text of which see Fielder, pp. 440–41.

[54] The Georgia registration figures were: whites, 96,333, colored, 95,168, according to table in Rhodes, VI, 194. Thompson, p. 186, gives only slightly different figures.

[55] Avery, p. 373.

[56] *Ibid.* Rhodes gives the figures: for a convention: whites, 32,000; colored, 70,283; total, 102,283 (table, VI, 196). Avery (p. 373) agrees with these figures. There was little vote against the convention. Hill and the Conservatives had hoped to defeat it by what Avery calls "the suicidal non-action policy," that is, by staying away from the polls entirely. This course was followed by 60,333 whites, according to Rhodes's figures.

about 170 members, the large majority being what were known as "scalawags" or native whites who had gone over to the Republican party. There were about 35 negroes, 9 "carpetbaggers," and about 12 "good and true Democrats," who no doubt had a hard task to leaven the whole.[57] The great majority of the membership was without political experience, and of mediocre or inferior abilities of any kind.[58]

The guiding spirit of the convention seems to have been Brown, and he succeeded in moderating its tone and preventing such harsh and discriminatory measures as were adopted by convention in other southern states.[59] Brown was not a member of the convention, but he occupied a unique rôle in that he was universally looked to as a sort of high priest of the Republican party in Georgia. Negroes, "scalawags," and "carpetbaggers" accepted, almost without challenge, any dictum coming from him.[60]

Brown addressed a very constructive letter to the con-

[57] The figures respecting the personnel of the convention vary slightly. Thompson (p. 189) gives the total as 169, with 39 negroes, 9 carpetbaggers and 12 "conservative whites" (Democrats); Rhodes (VI, 190) gives the total as 166, with 33 negroes; Avery (p. 375) merely gives the total as 170 and says there was a "sprinking of good and true Democrats." Statistics as to color are difficult throughout the Reconstruction period, as the color line was so thin at times as to be almost indistinguishable.

[58] See review of the work of the convention, Thompson, pp. 189-98.

[59] As Mississippi and Alabama, whose constitutions went beyond the requirements of Congress. See Rhodes, VI, 201-6.

[60] Thompson, pp. 193, 198, attributes the moderation of the convention to Brown's influence. The press of the state uniformly, and as a matter of common knowledge, recognized him as the head of the party—"the chief Beelzebub," as they expressed it (see *Augusta Chronicle and Sentinel*, August 14, 1868).

stitutional convention, counseling it to go no farther than the Congressional acts required in its discriminatory enactments. He especially urged that the convention avoid political proscription, such as was incorporated in the constitution of other states, disfranchising large numbers of so-called "disloyal" whites and imposing exacting test oaths for office-holding designed to exclude former Confederates. He also cautioned against bestowing political and social rights or privileges upon the unprepared negro, beyond the stipulated right of suffrage contained in the Reconstruction Acts. He advocated the enactment of some "relief" measures for the sorely burdened debtor class. The letter of Brown, extremely moderate, failed to reveal the cloven hoof which Conservatives had taught the people to expect in anything connected with the reviled ex-governor.[61]

The chief subjects engaging the convention proved to be the determination of the suffrage, qualifications for office-holding, and the relief question. Due, in large measure to Brown's influence, as aforesaid, the convention adopted a very moderate policy on the suffrage and qualifications for office. Although the attempt was made to disfranchise a large proportion of the "disloyal" whites and to enact a rigid office-holding qualification which would have excluded ex-Confederates, the convention in the end defeated those efforts;[62] and the constitution as adopted

[61] Letter dated January 11, 1868, in the *Atlanta Daily New Era,* January 11, 1868, *Brown Scrap Books.*

[62] *Journal of the Convention of 1867–68,* pp. 148–50, 299–30, 311–12, give the efforts and the failure.

went no farther in these particulars than the Congressional acts had gone.[63]

The convention, however, adopted liberal measures of "relief," virtually canceling all debts incurred prior to June 1, 1865, and enacting a liberal homestead law. These features were incorporated in the constitution, but the greater part of the relief clause was stricken out in 1868 by order of Congress.[64]

The convention adjourned on March 11, 1868, after having appointed April 20 as a date for the vote on ratification.[65] There followed a month of bitter political campaigning between the Conservative party led by Hill, opposing ratification, and the Republican, or, as it was popularly known, the Radical, party, led by Brown and advocating ratification. When reading, a half-century later, the opprobrious epithets and deep venom with which these bitter days were filled, it is hard to see how the antagonists spared each others' lives.[66]

Hill had opened up the attack on the "corrupt instrument called a Constitution" turned out by the "negro-radical, so-called State Convention"[67] in a rousing speech before the Young Men's Democratic Club of Atlanta on the night of March 10, the report of which in an Atlanta

[63] Constitution of 1868, Art. 2.

[64] Thompson, p. 194 n. Miss Thompson gives an excellent review of the work of the convention, pp. 192–98.

[65] Avery, p. 383.

[66] There was at least one duel fought during the political contest. See Avery, p. 383.

[67] *Atlanta Intelligencer*, March 13, 1868. The quotations are the editor's not Hill's. See, also, John C. Reed, *History of Atlanta*, p. 238.

paper necessitated the printing of an extra edition in order to supply the demand.[68] In this speech and in subsequent utterances and letters, Hill centered his fire on three particular features of the proposed constitution. These were: (1) that the constitution bestowed the right to hold office on negroes; (2) that it provided for social equality of whites and negroes; (3) that the relief clause was unconstitutional and a "cheat," designed merely to ensnare votes.[69]

Of course, before attacking these specific intolerable features of the "corrupt instrument," Hill and the Conservatives generally, expressed their nausea at the whole proceedings of the "so called State Constitutional Convention." The "mongrel character of its authors" was always good for a cheer or a column; it was a "nigger-New England" conclave, etc., dominated by the "Beelzebub of the fallen" (Brown).[70]

Hill charged that the constitution underwrote negro office-holding in the state. Brown, in a speech in Marietta,

[68] *Atlanta Intelligencer*, March 13, 1868. The speech is reported entire by Eugene Davis, "especially for the Intelligencer." See also *Columbus Sun*, March 15, for editorial comment, lauding the speech, and an entire page given over to its publication.

[69] *Ibid*.

[70] The following are some sources for Hill's utterances in the campaign, besides the speech of March 10 in Atlanta, previously cited: letter to editor of the *Macon Telegraph*, March 24, 1868, taken from reprint in *Augusta Chronicle and Sentinel*, March 29, 1868; address to people of Georgia, April 8, 1868, originally appearing in *Macon Telegraph*, taken from *Savannah Daily News and Herald*, April 14, 1868; letter to editor, *Atlanta Intelligencer*, dated April 11 in edition of April 14, 1868, *Brown Scrap Books*.

Georgia, March 19, vigorously denied this statement.[71] The question was an ambiguous one under the constitution, and its explanation was somewhat complicated. It came about in this way: A section to the constitution had been proposed providing that all qualified electors for the convention, and none others, should be eligible to hold office. This would have qualified all negroes and disqualified a large class of whites.[72] It was represented to the negroes that they were eligible to office anyway, without this distinct clause; and by a vote of 126 to 12, the negroes voting affirmatively, the section was stricken out.[73] It now appeared that the omission of the section was giving the Radicals a two-edged sword; in negro circles and constituencies the Radical leaders represented that negroes were eligible to office, while in areas where prejudice against the negro was strong, as in the Cherokee country of Georgia, Brown was representing that they were not eligible. There is some ground for suspicion of this action, and Hill freely charged Brown with duplicity.[74]

Hill further charged that the constitution made social equality of the whites and negroes inevitable, and depicted a forbidding array of horrors such as miscegenation, intermarriage, and the like. He based his view on a clause in the constitution that read: "The social status of the citi-

[71] Speech in *Atlanta Daily New Era*, March 20, 1868, *Brown Scrap Books*.

[72] *Journal of the Constitutional Convention of 1867–68*, pp. 148–50.

[73] *Ibid.*, pp. 311–12.

[74] *Atlanta Intelligencer*, April 14, 1868. It may be observed, at this time, though it will be discussed later, that Brown, when chief justice of Georgia, ruled that negroes *were* eligible to hold office under the constitution of 1868 (see Thompson, p. 215).

zen shall never be the subject of legislation," and construed this to mean that no social discrimination against the negro might be made.[75] Brown denied any such construction, saying that Hill had either willfully or ignorantly confused his definitions and terms and that the clause in question would not have such effect as alleged.[76]

But it was the "relief" features of the proposed constitution that called forth the most concentrated invective of the Conservatives. It was designated a "fraud and a cheat," intended from the first merely as a bid for votes. Hill devoted almost three printed columns in a published letter to expounding the evils and the falsity of the relief laws.[77]

The laws he declared unconstitutional because they impair the obligations of contract. Moreover, the scheme is a mere device to get votes and will be repudiated once the election is over, leaving many evils in its train. It is a "dirty bribe," and its authors know it for such.[78]

Brown struck back right lustily at Hill and the Conservatives. Especially did he take great delight in exposing Hill's alleged political inconsistencies. He charged that the leaders of the Conservative, or Democratic, party, Hill, Ranse Wright, E. G. Cabaniss, and Nisbet, were really hereditary enemies of the Democratic party—old Whigs

[75] Speech at Atlanta, March 10, 1868.

[76] Speech at Marietta, March 18, 1868.

[77] To editor, *Macon Telegraph*, March 24, 1868.

[78] Hill's position on "relief," which has not been developed in the text, would appear to have been vindicated by the Radical Congress in demanding the elimination of the feature from the constitution. See Thompson, p. 194.

and Know-Nothings. The real leaders of the Democracy, Cobb and Hershel V. Johnson, said Brown, were relegated to a back seat, while these new and self-assumed leaders were trying to appeal to the prejudices of the people and arrogating to themselves spokesmanship for the party. Let not the Georgia Democracy follow blindly such false prophets, warned the former Democrat and present high priest of the Republican party in the state.[79]

Each side resorted to the use of flaming handbills and every device known to the political agitator. One such handbill emanating from the Conservative camp read:

> White men of Georgia! Read and Reflect! Rescue Georgia.
> The issue involved in the election on the 20th of April is Whether or not Georgia shall pass into the hands of negroes and Yankee political adventurers! Can Georgians rule Georgia? They can! Then go to the polls and vote the Democratic-Conservative ticket.[80]

The Republican job printers were not without business. A flaming handbill coming from the *New Era* job office and signed "Dougherty" was headed: "Hon. B. H. Hill," and was addressed to the "Poor White Men of Georgia." After scoring the efforts of the "Hon. B. H. Hill" who "figures so conspicuously as the mouth piece of the tail end of the National Democratic Party (so called)," to appeal to the poor white men of the state against the "relief" laws, the manifesto concludes:

> Be a man! Let the slave holding aristocracy no longer rule you. Vote for a constitution which educates your children free of charge; relieves the poor debtor from his rich creditor; allows a liberal home-

[79] Speeches at Marietta, March 18, and Rome, March 20, in the *Atlanta Daily New Era*.

[80] Quoted by Miss Thompson, p. 204.

stead for your families; and more than all, places you on a level with those who used to boast that for every slave they were entitled to three-fifths of a vote in congressional representation. Ponder this well before you vote.[81]

At the same time that the people voted on the constitution, April 20, they were to elect a governor and other state officers. The Republicans, not without some internal friction, had put in nomination Rufus B. Bullock for governor.[82] The Conservative-Democratic organization had also experienced difficulty, for other reasons, in arriving at a candidate; but finally General John B. Gordon, a soldier with a brilliant war record, had been put forward as their candidate for governor.[83] Hill, in addressing a special appeal to the citizens of the Cherokee section of Georgia, urged Gordon's election in the following language: "Even if you do ratify the hated Constitution, influenced by fraud and force, at least give us the noble Gordon, native to your hills, to administer it."[84]

When the votes were counted after April 20, it was found that the "hated Constitution" was indeed ratified by a majority of about 17,972, but that the "noble Gordon" was outdistanced by the "New England express-man" by

[81] This handbill is found in the *Brown Scrap Books.*

[82] Thompson, pp. 201–2; Avery, p. 383.

[83] Judge Reese and David Irwin, named in this order, had been nominated; and on investigation both were found to be under the disabilities of the Fourteenth Amendment and therefore ineligible. General Gordon had held no political office before the war and was not otherwise debarred by the disability clause of the amendment. See Thompson, p. 201, and Avery, p. 383.

[84] Address of April 8 in *Macon Telegraph.*

FIGHT AGAINST RECONSTRUCTION ACTS

some 7,171 votes.[85] Charges and counter charges of fraud in the election were made by both sides.[86] Reconstruction had carried in Georgia despite the labors of Hill and the Conservative-Democratic party. A moderate constitution, "mulatto-tinkered" according to the Conservatives, went into operation; a Republican governor was to take office; and a legislature whose exact political complexion could not be foretold would soon convene.[87]

[85] Thompson, p. 204; Avery's figures on p. 384 are approximately the same.

[86] Thompson, p. 206; Avery, pp. 384–85.

[87] Thompson, p. 207.

CHAPTER IX

CONTINUED RESISTANCE—
THE GREELEY CAMPAIGN

Although defeated at every step so far in their resistance to the execution of the Reconstruction Acts, the Georgia Conservatives, or Democratic party, were not yet ready to abandon the fight. The continuation of the agitation against so-called "Radicalism" in Georgia became a part of the larger national campaign of 1868 when the National Democracy, and with it the Georgia Conservatives, pinned their hopes upon Horatio Seymour and Frank P. Blair.[1]

Before the campaign got under way, however, Congress, by the so-called "Omnibus bill" of June 25, 1868, had declared that Georgia, along with certain other southern states, was entitled to admission to the Union and to representation in Congress when its legislature should have ratified the Fourteenth Amendment.[2] However, there were certain "fundamental conditions" attached, to wit: "That the constitutions of neither of said states shall ever be so amended or changed as to deprive any citizen or class of citizens of the United States of the right to vote in said state who are entitled to vote by the Constitution thereof, herein recognized."[3] This, of course, was a discrimination

---

[1] For the national campaign, see Rhodes, VI, 269–79, 303–11; Oberholtzer, II, 151–204.

[2] Rhodes, VI, 287–88; Oberholtzer, II, 59–61.

[3] Rhodes, VI, 288; the act also required that Georgia repeal the relief provisions in her recently adopted constitution (Oberholtzer, II, 61). See above, p. 168.

against the states to which it applied, circumscribing their future action in a way which did not obtain in the case of other states; and it provided Hill with much political thunder against Radicalism.

The Georgia General Assembly elected under the "mulatto-tinkered" constitution of 1868, as it was characterized by the Conservatives,[4] convened on July 4, 1868; and its session proved to be a "strange blending of farce and melodrama."[5] The Assembly on July 21 ratified the Fourteenth Amendment to the Federal Constitution, and thereby entitled the state to admission to the Union and representation in Congress.[6] On the next day the Republican governor, Bullock, was inaugurated.[7]

On the following day, the twenty-third of July, a monster political demonstration was staged in the city of Atlanta to inaugurate the campaign in the state for the election of Seymour and Blair on the National Democratic ticket. This occasion, known as the "Bush Arbor meeting," has become famous in Georgia tradition. The demonstration was staged in the middle of the city, near the present Union depot, and received its popular designation from the fact that the speakers' platform was shaded, because of the heat, by an immense bush arbor constructed

[4] *Columbus Sun*, March 15, 1868.

[5] Avery, p. 394; Miss Thompson gives an excellent review of the work of the Georgia Assembly of 1868, pp. 207-25.

[6] *Senate Journal*, 1868, pp. 44-46; *House Journal*, 1868, pp. 49-51.

[7] Avery, p. 397; see also Reed, *History of Atlanta*, pp. 240-41, for a graphic description of the inaugural ceremonies. At the climax of the ceremony a voice from the gallery created quite a commotion by yelling, "Go to it niggers!"

for the purpose. It was estimated that twenty thousand people, from all parts of the state, flocked to this political rally, making it "the largest political mass meeting ever held in Georgia" up to that time.[8]

The National Republican Convention which met in Chicago in May, 1868, had adopted a platform which approved the entire Reconstruction program, as worked out by the Radical Congress. The Convention nominated Grant and Colfax, and clearly expected to base its campaign on the war popularity of Grant and the imperative necessity of carrying out Radical Reconstruction in the South.[9] Brown had represented Georgia in the Chicago Republican Convention, thereby capping his infamy in the view of Georgia Conservatives.[10]

The National Democratic Convention in New York in early July nominated, after considerable difficulty, Horatio Seymour and Frank P. Blair. But the most important action of the Convention, as regards Georgia and the South, was the adoption of a plank in the platform, which declared: "We regard the Reconstruction Acts of Congress as usurpations and unconstitutional, revolutionary and void."[11] Here indeed was an omen of good cheer to the southern Conservatives, and their enthusiasm for the new

[8] Avery, pp. 391-92; Reed, "Reminiscences of Ben Hill," *South Atlantic Quarterly*, V (April, 1906), 141-42.

[9] For the Chicago Convention, see Oberholtzer, II, 154-59; Rhodes, VI, 269-70.

[10] Avery, p. 385. The press of the state exhausted its vocabulary in damning Brown. So numerous were the castigations, and so commonplace the sentiment, that I have failed to make specific citation.

[11] Rhodes, VI, 276. For the Convention, see *ibid.*, pp. 270-78; and Oberholtzer, II, 171-80.

Daniel come to judgment was increased when the famous Brodhead letter of the vice-presidential nominee, Frank Blair, was published. General Blair, it may be remembered, had written to Colonel James A. Brodhead on June 30:

> There is but one way to restore the government and Constitution, and that is for the President-elect to declare these acts null and void, compel the army to undo its usurpations at the South, disperse the carpet-bag state Governments, allow the white people to organize their own governments and elect senators and representatives.[12]

This Democratic platform and vice-presidential candidate, then, were considered worthy of all the support that an embattled Georgia Conservative party could render it, and the Bush Arbor meeting was the inauguration of the hectic campaign. Blair's position had been the exact position assumed by Hill and the Conservatives all along; and, leaving out of account its expediency or judiciousness as a basis for a national campaign, it could certainly be expected to rally the masses of the southern whites, and seemed to open up a way of escape from the black Republican rule that was fast closing in around them. Hill had gone to the New York Convention as a member of the Georgia delegation, and returned to Georgia full of enthusiasm and optimism regarding the platform and the candidates.[13]

[12] Quoted in Fielder, p. 447; also, Rhodes, VI, 303.

[13] James G. Blaine, *Twenty Years in Congress*, II, 397; *Columbus Sun*, March 15, 1867; Oberholtzer, II, 171. Further, see Hill's speech in Atlanta, July 23, 1868, cited hereafter. For Hill's advice to the Georgia delegation, see *Savannah Daily News and Herald*, June 10, 1868. Hill had advised that the southern delegates should say little in the convention either as regards the platform or nominee of the party; that the platform should

At the monster rally of July 23 in Atlanta, Toombs and Cobb made the first speeches; but the evidence is conclusive that Hill was the favorite of the crowd and that his appearance was the most eagerly awaited. When he arose to speak, following the somewhat disappointing efforts of Toombs and Cobb, the demonstration is described by one present, as having exceeded anything of the kind he had ever witnessed.[14] Hill acknowledged the ovation, which was really an indorsement of the previous "Davis Hall speech" and the "Notes on the Situation," as the "reward of fidelity to one's people."[15]

The Bush Arbor speech of Hill's is a companion piece to the Davis Hall utterance. In sustained invective and fierce philippic tone, it is the equal, if not the superior, of the former, though perhaps it lacks something of the former's close constitutional argumentation, as Hill may have deemed that the argument had been sufficiently set forth and that what was now needed was to arouse the people to action.[16]

---

be brief, merely stipulating as regards suffrage that the subject appertained solely to the states, and that in the interest of harmony the South should accept whomsoever the North desired to defeat Radicalism.

[14] Reed, "Reminiscences of Ben Hill," *South Atlantic Quarterly*, V (April, 1906), p. 141; Hill, *Life of Hill*, pp. 52–53. See also in substantiation the *Augusta Chronicle and Sentinel,* August 6, 1868.

[15] Reed, "Reminiscences of Ben Hill," *South Atlantic Quarterly*, V (April, 1906), 141.

[16] The speech was printed in pamphlet form, of which I have examined a copy, by the *Augusta Chronicle and Sentinel,* and offered for sale at five cents the copy, or in orders of fifty or more at two and one-half cer the copy. An effort was made to put it in the hands of every Democr? club in Georgia. See the *Chronicle and Sentinel* for August 6, 1868.

THE GREELEY CAMPAIGN

Hill first expressed a note of optimism. One year before, he had come to Atlanta and met only a handful of faithful citizens determined to resist the infamous designs of the Radical Congress, and now he witnesses a host of twenty thousand enlisted in the righteous cause.[17] And he states further that he is proud of Georgia, whose white people have refused to be "bought" and who, by large majorities, have opposed Radicalism at every step. The Georgia whites have at least saved their "honor as a people" from the wreck of their fortunes, since they have not cravenly consented to their own "infamy."[18]

But the issue has somewhat changed in the last twelve months. By fraud and violence the Congressional scheme has been put in operation. The question now becomes whether the Congressional program shall continue or whether the "glorious tramp of the Democracy" shall not tread it out and bury it in the infamy and oblivion it so richly deserves. At this point Hill descants at some length upon the Omnibus bill by which Congress had recently declared Georgia entitled to admission to the Union, and upon the "shame" of the Assembly which, pursuant to the bill, had, two days before, ratified the Fourteenth Amendment. By the Omnibus bill, Hill declares, the Congress has enacted a revolutionary principle, namely, that the American Union is a Union of *unequal* states. For, according to the

---

speech is more easily found in Hill, *Life of Hill*, pp. 308-19, to which, for convenience' sake, as in the case of many of Hill's speeches, citations are made.

[17] This is a reference to his conference of July, 1867, preceding the Davis Hall speech (*supra.*, p. 142).

[18] Hill, *Life of Hill*, pp. 308-12.

express terms of this bill, the southern people could not "change their Constitutions at will." This legislation put the southern states on a different basis from the other states. In effect, this legislation declared that Georgia was not equal to Rhode Island, and that Virginia, "proud old Virginia . . . . shall not be the equal of Kansas," than which, it may be inferred, there could be no worse degradation.[19]

Hill's indignation at this shameful and unconstitutional legislation to which the Georgia Assembly has basely subscribed, seems to find one, and only one, relief. It is tempered somewhat by a disappointment which he attributes to many of the Georgia Radicals, because of the terms of the Omnibus bill. He alleges that some "whites" who had supported the Reconstruction Acts had done so, saying that after they had gotten Georgia into the Union they could do as they wished. On these, Hill turns, not without a note of triumph:

Ah you renegades, ye men, that adopted the Reconstruction measures for the purpose of getting back in the Union, and then catching the Radicals by changing the Constitution afterwards. Are you not caught—caught by Thad. Stevens—caught by Charles Sumner? I don't know but one thing that is worse, and that is agreeing to be a negro, to get rid of your debts and then, after becoming a negro, having your debts to pay.[20]

[19] *Ibid.*, p. 315. Hill might have discovered that the act in question did not relate to Virginia.

[20] Hill here refers to the clause in the bill admitting Georgia which stipulated that the "relief" feature, cancellation of debts accruing before 1865, contained in the Georgia constitution, as the Conservatives alleged, for political purposes, should be striken out as a condition precedent to admission.

A good deal of the speech is mere ringing denunciation, especially of the Georgia Reconstruction convention and the General Assembly convoked under the constitution of 1868. As, for example:

> Ye vile miscreants of the Convention, who stole the money of the state to pay your *per diem*, I give you notice that you shall pay it back.[21] . . . . Ye constitution makers that sprung [*sic*] at one bound from the penitentiaries of the country, to frame constitutions for honest people;[22] ye men who oscillate from grand jury rooms with charges of perjury upon you, up to legislative halls and other high places in the land. . . . . And you, members of the Legislature, I will talk to you kindly—you who voted for this infamy, the other day, the Fourteenth Amendment. . . . . At the peril of your respectability, go and take it back. It is a record whose stain will reach your children.[23]

But Hill would receive back into the ranks of decency even these southern whites whose "infamy no epithet can describe, and no precedent parallel." He invites them to return, for the "day of grace is almost passed. Reform now and we will forgive you." But if not, if they will persist in their infamy, what measure shall be meted out when the day of victory, augered by the "glorious tramp of the Democracy, growing more and more distinct," shall have

[21] Governor Jenkins had been removed from office by General Meade, who succeeded Pope, because he would not sign a warrant on the Treasury for $40,000 for the expenses of the convention. The money was then secured through General Ruger appointed as governor by Meade. See Thompson, pp. 179-80.

[22] A. A. Bradley, a notorious negro member of the convention, and later the Assembly, was expelled from the Assembly on evidence that he had served a term in a New York state prison, convicted of the felony of seduction. See *Senate Journal*, 1868, pp. 13, 121-27, 129, 134-35, 137.

[23] Hill, *Life of Hill*, pp. 317-18.

arrived. For Hill is sure that November will bring a "verdict" that shall gladden the hearts of patriots now and forever. When this victory shall come, what shall be done with the "criminals"? He answers:

> I would not hurt a hair of their heads, do them no personal harm, and deprive them of no right. Give them over—oh, give over the miscreants to the inextinguishable hell of their consciousness of infamy. But some things you must do for the protection of your children and of yourselves, and for the vindication of your honor. . . . . Not one man that dares record his vote for the inequality and vassalage of the southern states and the degradation of his own race, ought ever to be received into a decent family in Georgia; or in the South, now or hereafter.[24]

But, says Hill, the return of liberty, the redemption of the southern states at the November election, must be followed by one more thing, "necessary to a proper expression of the abhorence of our people for the infamous attempt to destroy the Union by destroying the equality of the states, and for the measures, authors and advocates of the whole scheme to degrade the states and people of the South":

> . . . . We must gather all the journals, and constitutions and enactments, and records of every character of the conventions and assemblies, thus forced upon us by force, and fraud, and usurpation, and catching fire from heaven, burn them up forever.
>
> And right here my countrymen, I want you to understand that I am a candidate but for one office on earth. When the glorious day shall come . . . . let the office be mine to kindle the flames.[25]

At the conclusion of this impassioned oration with its fiery peroration, a contemporary who was present relates that

[24] *Ibid.*
[25] *Ibid.*

THE GREELEY CAMPAIGN

Hill was embraced by Bob Toombs, amid the indescribable uproar of the crowd.[26]

The comment in the state and in the nation on the Bush Arbor assemblage, and especially on the speech of Hill's, depended, of course, on the political affiliations of the commentator. The Conservative press of the state, for the most part, praised the speech highly; but there was a note of doubt voiced by some cautious Conservatives, who alleged that Hill was proving a "trouble maker" and an "obstacle to peace." This was vehemently denied by other Conservatives.[27]

The *Augusta National Republican* voiced the reaction of the Radical party in Georgia and elsewhere when it called the Bush Arbor meeting "the grand pow-wow of the Ku Klux Klan." As for the fervid oratory of the day, this journal professed to believe that "no better campaign documents for Grant and Colfax can be disseminated throughout the country than the speeches of Toombs, Cobb and Hill," which are described as abounding in abuse of "better men than they" and as an "incitement to revolution on the Blair ticket."[28]

Hill seems to have given over the month of August to a stump tour of the state in the interest of the Seymour and Blair ticket. His familiar views on the danger to constitu-

[26] Reed, "Reminiscences of Ben Hill," *South Atlantic Quarterly*, V (April, 1906), 142; see also Hill, *Life of Hill*, p. 53.

[27] See the controversy on this score between two correspondents, "Confederate" and "Russell," rehearsing the respective views in the *Columbus Enquirer* under date July 28, 1868, in *Brown Scrap Books*.

[28] July 25, 1868. Blaine in his book, as might be expected, characterizes Hill's speech of July 23 as "incendiary" (*Twenty Years of Congress*, II, 404).

tional government presented by the continuance of the Republican party in power, and on the iniquitous features of the Congressional Reconstruction, were broadcast throughout the central and eastern part of the state.[29] But the demands on his time were so great, and the invitations to speak so numerous, that on August 24 he adopted the expedient of writing a public letter which he hoped would be accepted as reply to such letters as he could not answer personally, and would be used in localities where he could not possibly speak. He says he could not "possibly attend one-tenth of the meetings" to which he is urged to come.[30]

Hill's speech in Augusta, the center of a powerful Radical clique, attracted most attention at the time, next to the Bush Arbor effort. Augusta was an interesting and strategic point in Georgia for this period. Bullock, the governor, and a group of his most intimate advisers counted Augusta as their legal residence.[31] The Republicans there were strong and controlled the municipal government, and yet two of the most powerful Conservative journals in the state were published there, the *Chronicle and Sentinel* and the *Constitutionalist*.[32] The situation, then, challenged

[29] I have discovered newspaper reports of meetings addressed by Hill in this campaign, at Harlem on August 8, Lexington on August 11, Augusta on August 21, Abilene church (near Augusta) on August 22, Waynesboro on September 3. These reports are all in the *Augusta Constitutionalist* and the *Augusta Chronicle and Sentinel* of approximately the dates concerned. They represent, however, only a few of the meetings which he addressed at this period.

[30] Letter, dated August 24, 1868, and addressed to the editors of the *Augusta Chronicle and Sentinel*, published August 25.

[31] See Thompson, pp. 221–22, for the so-called "Augusta ring."

[32] For brief review of these papers, see Avery, pp. 610–11.

Hill's best efforts. On his arrival in the city, he was received like a conqueror by the Conservatives; and extensive preparations were made for a huge rally on the occasion of his speech, August 21.[33]

Hill began his Augusta speech with a plea for forbearance and a new view, adapted to the new situation.[34] He seemed to sense that his past vehemence had created enemies, some of whom were in his audience; and he would disarm them with moderation. He praised the terms of surrender granted by Grant and Sherman, and sketched the new terms exacted by President Johnson and the additional ones added by the Radical Congress in 1867. He argued that the South had accepted all, all, until the humiliating Fourteenth Amendment, which it could not, in honor to its living heroes and its dead, accept. He then reviewed the prosperity which had set in from 1865 to 1867, and which was swiftly brought to an end by the acts of 1867 with the evils which came in their wake—low wages, low land values, carpet-baggers, and corrupt Radical state governments.

He then launched into a plea to the negroes, arguing that their real friends were the Democratic whites; that the Radicals but meant to exploit and, if desirable, desert them. He labors the argument somewhat that the southern whites really emancipated the negro, out of gratitude and a new view of economy; and that the southern whites will allow, indeed have already allowed, the negro full civil rights. This appeal to the negroes elicited sarcasm from the Re-

[33] *Augusta Chronicle and Sentinel* and *Augusta Constitutionalist* for August 21, 1868.

[34] The entire speech, six and one-half newspaper columns, is printed in the *Augusta Chronicle and Sentinel*, August 23, 1868.

publican press of Augusta. The *Augusta National Republican* commented after the speech:

> Ben Hill in his speech at the Court House on Friday evening last almost ignored the whites. The white people were disgusted at the manner in which the great apostle of the white man's party got down on his marrow bones to the colored men. The colored men on their part said they had heard of the invitation of the spider before and would not walk in, knowing the fate of the poor fly.[35]

Hill, in the Augusta speech, repeated his attacks on the constitutionality of the Reconstruction Acts, saying they were acknowledged to be unconstitutional by Radicals, North and South. He represented the Radicals as growing desperate, and the election of Seymour and Blair as certain.[36] Finally, he was at some pains to disprove the charges of Radicals and Loyal Leaguers that the southern Democrats desired a new war, renewed secession, and the re-enslavement of the negro. His chief argument in rebuttal of these charges was that the southern Democrats own the land in the South and have, indeed, what little property is left in the section; and that they would not be so foolish as to desire another war in which this would be lost too. Rather do they, above all others, fervently desire and pray for a real and lasting peace.

It was three days after the Augusta speech that Hill wrote the public letter on the political situation previously referred to. He repeated much of his arguments and de-

---

[35] August 23, 1868, under caption "Ignoring the Whites."

[36] It was commonly said that the rather hurried Omnibus bill of June 25 admitting southern states had been passed in order to secure the electoral votes of states supposedly now "safe" for the Republican ticket. Rhodes ascribes "eagerness" to the Republicans to secure the southern electoral votes (Rhodes, VI, 285).

nunciation already familiar, but he struck out on a new vein in predicting the business and agricultural revival that must surely follow for the southern states in the train of Democratic victory. "If the Democratic party shall be successful," he writes, "confidence will return, harmony between the races will be restored, war and strife and discord will then certainly be avoided; capital and a better class of immigrants will then come among us from the North; business will revive, the price of our property will enhance, and we can afford to increase *the wages* of labor." If, on the other hand, the Radicals shall again succeed, "much of the capital now here will be carried away, the price of property will still further decline, the products of industry will be lessened, and labor must still more decline in price."[37]

In another connection Hill, in urging the negroes to support Seymour and Blair, had said:

If you do this, colored people, I will guarantee to you that your wages will be increased fifty per cent by Christmas. I am a farmer and I am willing to enter into a bargain with you if, whether with or without your help, the Democratic candidates are elected, to give you the next year, fifty per cent more than I am giving you in 1868.[38]

The Radical and Conservative press seemed to vie with each other in the use of billingsgate and opprobious epithets. Toombs and Cobb often spoke on the same platform with Hill in this canvass.[39] Toombs was characterized by the Radicals as "blustering Bob, always drunk and ob-

[37] Letter in *Augusta Chronicle and Sentinel,* August 25, 1868.

[38] In Augusta speech, August 21, 1868; previously cited.

[39] As at Harlem and Lexington, see *Augusta Constitutionalist,* August 6 and 12, 1868.

scene"; Cobb and Hill are "secessionists who save their own carcasses when in danger."[40] And both Toombs and Hill were lumped together in the jibe of the Radical editor who said: "Ben Hill and Bob Toombs are good for two things. They are excellent hands to get up a fight and remarkably successful in keeping out of it."[41]

But it is Hill who is the target for the severest Radical strictures. The Radical journals, such as the *Augusta National Republican* and the *Atlanta Daily New Era,* the latter credited with being Brown's organ, rarely printed an issue in the summer and early autumn of 1868 without a long diatribe against Hill, or, at the very least, some slur on his activity or his record. The following from the *New Era* is typical:

> Ben Hill . . . . that poor political maniac who is the scourge of every political party with which he acts, and whose popular advocacy of a cause never yet in a single instance failed to produce its defeat. It is simply the misfortune of the so called Democratic leaders that Ben Hill has attained fellowship among them, and knows their secrets, and has no better sense than to disclose them. If they could control his judgment, they might turn his diarrhea of words to account in exciting the populace. . . . . If they will only let Ben canvass the state thoroughly, he will unfold their secrets so fully, that Grant's election can, I suppose, be questioned by no one, as all will have discovered the revolutionary purposes that lie at the bottom of their movement.[42]

The very vehemence of the Radical press, and its oft reiterated assertion that Hill was really serving the course

[40] *Augusta National Republican,* September 6, 1868.

[41] *Ibid.,* August 22, 1868.

[42] *Weekly New Era,* August 27, 1868, in *Brown Scrap Books;* see also *Augusta National Republican,* August 22, September 6, 18, 20, 22, 23, 27, 1868.

of the Republican party, seems strong evidence that the Radicals feared him; and the fact that Georgia finally went for Seymour, the only southern state to do so except Louisiana, tends to show that Hill's campaigning was far more successful than the Radicals were willing to admit.[43] The Conservative press, on the other hand, acclaimed his leadership throughout the campaign, and almost unanimously praised his speeches. The following editorial comment on one of Hill's speeches gives the characteristic contemporary Conservative opinion:

Hon. B. H. Hill made one of those earnest eloquent and telling speeches for which he is so distinguished. For more than an hour he held his audience enraptured and spellbound by his earnest and burning eloquence. No report of this gentleman's speeches can do him justice. There is something in his eye, in the tone of his voice—in his manner—a certain electrical influence which he possesses which enables him to claim the attention, and sway the feelings of the multitude in a manner which we have rarely seen equalled and never excelled. To get the full value of his speeches you must hear him deliver them as only he can do. His speech here will do good—particularly that portion in which he advised the people as to their duties toward the black man.[44]

In the meanwhile, since the campaign had started in Atlanta on the Bush Arbor occasion, July 23, significant events, pregnant for the future, had transpired in the state. Two events in particular need to be examined briefly, because of the effect they exerted on the course of Reconstruction in Georgia and the very probable effect they exercised on the national political campaign. The reference is

[43] Rhodes, VI, 306.

[44] *Augusta Chronicle and Sentinel*, August 23, 1868. The editor is reporting a speech at Abilene church, August 22, near Augusta.

to the expulsion of the negro members from the General Assembly and to the so-called "Camilla riot" that occurred in September. Hill had nothing to do with either of these affairs; but he was charged with responsibility, especially for the latter, by the Radicals, who said his revolutionary and incendiary utterances had produced the riot.[45]

Some reference has been made to the disputed subject of negro eligibility to office.[46] It will be remembered that the Constitution was ambiguous on this point and that conflicting interpretations were advanced during the campaign for ratification. Especially interesting and significant had been Brown's opinion, advanced to the citizens of the Cherokee section, that negroes were not eligible to office under the Constitution.[47]

Thirty-two negroes had been returned to the Assembly which met on July 4. On July 25 Milton A. Candler, the Conservative leader, made the following motion in the Senate:

WHEREAS, Ex-Governor Joseph E. Brown, one of the ablest lawyers of the Republican party of Georgia, as well as persons distinguished for their knowledge of constitutional law, held during the late election canvass that persons of color were not entitled to hold office under the existing Constitution. . . . .

Resolved, That the Committee on Privileges and Elections be directed to inquire into the eligibility of the several persons of color holding seats as Senators, and report at the earliest day practicable.[48]

[45] *Augusta National Republican,* September 23, 1868.

[46] *Supra,* pp. 166–67.

[47] Speech of Brown in Marietta, March 19, in *Atlanta Daily New Era,* March 20, 1868.

[48] *Senate Journal,* 1868, p. 84.

THE GREELEY CAMPAIGN

It was a neat turn that the Conservatives gave in thus prominently playing up Brown's recorded opinions. Although no immediate action followed Candler's resolution, early in September the House and Senate by resolution expelled the "persons of color" and seated those white men who had possessed the next highest number of votes in the districts affected.[49]

Whatever the proper legal aspect of the negro eligibility case, the game was not worth the candle from the Conservative viewpoint; and Mr. Rhodes is probably within reason when he says: "Georgia compared with other southern states was doing so well that it was a pity she furnished campaign ammunition for the Northern Republicans."[50] For this was the immediate result of the negro expulsion; the "high handed injustice" of the Georgia legislature was blazoned across the land; and Governor Bullock, in protesting against the expulsion, took occasion to say that in Georgia a "reign of terror exists."[51] Eventually, the negro expulsion would be the cause of the refusal to admit Georgia representation to Congress and of another Congressional reorganization of the state.[52]

[49] Miss Thompson, pp. 211-16, gives a full treatment, and in her usual clear and thorough manner, of the whole process of the expulsion of the negro members; Avery, pp. 401-2, gives it a briefer treatment. Mr. Avery quotes one colored member, G. H. Clower, as saying on this occasion: "Whenever you cast your votes against us, dis nigger will take his hat and walk right out; but like Christ I shall come again. I go to prepare a place for them. Stop, Democrats! stop, white folks. Draw de resolution off the table and let's go to work."

[50] Rhodes, VI, 301.

[51] *Ibid.*, p. 295; Avery, p. 404.

[52] *Infra.*, pp. 201 ff.

Unfortunately, in the same month of September (always a critical month in a national election) occurred a bloody mêlée at Camilla, Georgia, between a body of negroes, led by two carpetbag Radicals, and the greater part of the citizenry of the town. The responsibility for this affair and the merits of the dispute are too involved for a discussion here; but the broad fact was evident that several negroes were killed and many wounded, while practically none of the whites were hurt.[53] Governor Bullock, in his official proclamations and utterances, fastened the blame on white Conservatives and printed conditions in the worst possible light, giving rise to the accusation that he was conducting a "slander mill" against the white population of his adopted state, for partisan political purposes.[54]

These occurrences, and others similar, made the southern question the most important issue in the presidential campaign. The *Augusta National Republican* said: "Christianity shudders at the outlawry of the Democratic party of Georgia, lashed as it has been into blind fury by the diabolical utterances of Cobb, Hill, Toombs, and other mutinous and unprincipled ingrates."[55]

In the *Columbus Sun* for September 5, 1868, among the "Personals" occurs the following: "Ben Hill is going on a stumping tour in the north western states at his own expense." This is the first public word that seems to have

---

[53] Avery, p. 404, says: "7 persons were killed and 40 wounded"; Rhodes, VI, 302, says: "8 or 9 negroes were killed but no white men; 20 or 30 blacks were wounded, and but few of the Camilla inhabitants were even slightly hurt." For discussion, see Avery, pp. 404–5; Rhodes, VI, 301–3.

[54] Avery, p. 404.   [55] September 23, 1868.

come to light regarding a plan that Hill had matured in his own mind, to spend part of September and October in the North and there render any service to the South or the Democracy which the circumstances might indicate. The Georgia press was soon more or less agog over Hill's proposed trip, and, for the most part, expressed itself favorably.[56]

Hill went North, to New York in the middle of September, where were also Howell Cobb, General Gordon, and ex-Governor Vance of North Carolina.[57] But no speeches, or rather, only one speech, delivered before the Young Men's Democratic Union in New York City on October 6, 1868, materialized. Hill did not speak over the country or before a mixed electorate. The evidence as to the real reason for this failure is very scanty. The *Columbus Sun* says that "at the advice of friends" Hill has "foregone his stumping tour" in the North but in his interviews and letters to the *New York Tribune* "is doing yeomanlike service."[58] Hill himself asserted that he had not come North to make political speeches but only to ascertain true northern sentiment.[59] The Georgia Republican press was jubilant that Hill and Toombs, who have "been felicitating themselves with the idea of swinging around the circle at

[56] *Savannah Daily News and Herald*, September 8, 1868. Editorial in *New York Times*, reproduced in *Augusta National Republican*, October 15, 1868, says the entire Georgia press friendly to Seymour had predicted good results from Hill's tour in the North and West.

[57] *Augusta Constitutionalist*, October 8, 1868.

[58] October 9, 1868.

[59] Letter to *New York Tribune*, October 9, 1868, reprinted in *Columbus Sun*, October 17, 1868; speech before Young Men's Democratic Union in New York City, October 6, referred to hereafter.

the north" have received an "unexpected rebuff" and have been informed by northern Democrats that their services are not wanted.[60] From a review of the various explanations and interpretations put upon Hill's trip and his several weeks sojourn at the North with only one political speech, and that before a *Democratic* club, there cannot be much doubt that it was concluded, either with or without Hill's assent, that his appearance on the stump in the North would not aid the Democratic cause.

But Hill was not silent during his three weeks' sojourn in New York City. On September 10 he wrote a letter, two columns in length, to Horace Greeley's paper, the *New York Tribune,* undertaking to present the southern white side of the Camilla riot (about which the *Tribune's* columns had been full of distorted accounts), in Hill's view. This first letter was followed by three others which the *Tribune* printed, before it finally closed its columns to the southern champion.[61]

Hill's second letter regarding the Camilla riot had been printed in parallel columns along with the account of the riot written by a Georgia negro, one Turner. In a third letter, of September 29, Hill thanked the *Tribune* for according him an equality in this respect with the negro Turner, which the Reconstruction Acts denied him; and after a further review of the Georgia disturbance, went on to de-

[60] *Augusta National Republican,* September 18, 1868.

[61] Hill's letters to the *Tribune* are dated New York, September 20, 24, 29, October 9, 1868. I have used reproductions of these letters as follows: letters of October 20 and 24 in *Augusta Chronicle and Sentinel* for September 30 and October 6; letters of September 29 and October 9 in *Columbus Sun* for October 9 and 17.

THE GREELEY CAMPAIGN 193

fend himself against personal abuse and misrepresentation, of which he accused the *Tribune* and the northern press of being guilty. He says his southern speeches had been distorted and mutilated and made to stand for things which he had never advocated. He denies that he is an extremist or has ever counseled violence, but admits that he had advised and will practice social ostracism of the southern Radicals pandering to negro prejudice.[62]

In a letter to the *New York Times,* he says:

You speak of me as a wild southern extremist. A political extremist! My whole life is directly the contrary. I defy you to find in all my utterances against the reconstruction measures a single sentiment of hostility to the Union, or to the Constitution, or of unkindness to the negro. Directly the reverse pervades everything I ever wrote, spoke or felt and any report to the contrary is false.[63]

Passing from defense of himself, in the letters of September 29 and October 9 to the *Tribune,* which are in the same key, Hill presents very much the same arguments against the Radical program, which are reviewed in his speech of October 6 before the Young Men's Democratic Union in New York City and which are set forth later in this study[64]

In his letter of September 29, he concludes a flaming appeal against the Reconstruction policies:

But I warn you, the same Government cannot administer force at the south and freedom at the north. The time has come when emphatically the country must be all free, or all slave.

[62] The letter of September 29 is followed up by another of October 9, pursuing the same argument. They are treated together in the text.

[63] Also dated October 9, 1868; in *Augusta Chronicle and Sentinel*, October 14, 1868.

[64] *Infra.*, pp. 195–98.

And the same note is struck in a passage of his last letter to the *Tribune,* October 9, after which Greeley closed his paper to Hill:[65]

But the whites of the south never have and never will, because they never can consent to the reconstruction measures, nor to the Governments formed by them. To consent to these is to consent to her own immolation and ruin. Others far away, may not so believe, but we so know.[66]

But Hill wrote other letters than those to the *Tribune.* In fact he must have spent most of his sojourn in New York City laboring at this pursuit. He wrote three letters, all long ones, to the *New York Times;* and two to the Democratic paper, the *New York Herald.* The arguments employed are familiar to readers of Hill's speeches; but there can be no doubt that in thus spreading these arguments on the pages of journals of such wide circulation as the *Tribune,* the *Times,* and the *Herald,* he reached a very large audience which otherwise would never have heard the southern side of the question.[67] Besides the nine letters to the three New York papers, he gave one interview to a *Trib-*

---

[65] *Augusta Constitutionalist,* October 22, 1868. *Columbus Sun,* October 9, 1868, says Hill is "making Horace squirm"; that Greeley has met an adversary "outside of editorial ranks of more force and skill than himself."

[66] It may not be amiss to remark that these prophesies have, in the large, proven true, though Hill gave up hope himself in 1870. No one pretends that the Fourteenth and Fifteenth amendments are effective in the South; and in 1877 the last Reconstruction governments broke down.

[67] The letters to the *Times* are dated October 9, 11, and 12 and are found as follows: letter of October 9 in *Augusta Chronicle and Sentinel,* October 14; and letters of October 11 and 12 cut from the columns of the *Times* in the *Brown Scrap Books.* The two letters to the *Herald,* dated October 3 and 8 are also found clipped from that paper in the *Brown Scrap Books.*

une reporter, which was printed in the New York paper and widely copied throughout the country.[68] The interview but expressed the sentiments contained in the speech some days later before the Young Men's Democratic Union of New York City.[69]

In many respects, this speech of Hill before the Democratic Club in New York on October 6, 1868, is the best utterance of his entire career on the issues involved in Reconstruction. Speaking before a northern audience, with the consciousness that invective and denunciation are not the proper modes, he voices a plea for justice and fair play toward the South which probably had not been equaled; and gives an exposition of the southern viewpoint in the whole post-war imbroglio, which for charity, for fervor, and for convincing argument is not equaled elsewhere in his speeches or writings.

He began his speech in New York with the statement that he departed from his "original intention not to make a speech in New York" only at the insistent request of friends and a committee from the Young Men's Democratic Union. In the first place, he affirmed, it is absolutely necessary that the North realize that southern men are not criminals, but in the matter of secession had acted honestly and in good faith. This idea of the criminality of the South, he asserts, is the "sum of all your politics and statesmanship." It must be abandoned, or else "peaceful reunion under free institutions" is impossible. For, "you must hold them as friends, or let them go as foreigners, or govern

[68] Found, among other places, in the *Columbus Sun*, October 3, 1868, and *Augusta Chronicle and Sentinel* of same date.

[69] The speech is found in Hill, *Life of Hill*, pp. 320–31.

them as subjects. If you govern them as subjects, you must share the penalty, for the same government can never administer freedom to one half and despotism to the other half of the same nation."

The South, he continued, has accepted every legitimate result of the war which "could have benefited you, or strengthened the Union, or not dishonored themselves." In an incisive review he attempted to prove this: From Grant, the southern armies, and the people after them, had accepted an end of secession and yielded obedience to the laws of the Union in force at the surrender. From Johnson, when this proved inadequate, the South accepted conditions imposed on their new state governments, the repeal of secession ordinances, the abolition of slavery by state action, and the repudiation of war debts. From Congress, when these concessions to the executive were declared inadequate, the South had peacefully accepted taxation without representation, the Freedmen's Bureau, and a Civil Rights bill which, moreover, merely re-enacted what Georgia of its own volition had already granted.

Then came the Fourteenth Amendment. The South would have accepted that too—three of its sections, despite the unprecedented character of the provisions; but the fourth section, imposing political disabilities on southern leaders, the very "wisest and best men" of the section, and at a critical time when such leaders were needed, as never before, for the work of rehabilitation—this section, the South, in honor to itself and the men penalized under it, who after all had but been the agents of the southern people, could not accept.

THE GREELEY CAMPAIGN

Congress, then becoming vindictive, had passed the Reconstruction Acts, which the South had no alternative but to oppose. These they opposed because they were palpably unconstitutional, demonstrably inexpedient, and cruelly unjust and fatal to southern society. But even so, the South was willing to intrust the decision as to these Acts to the courts of the very government enacting the legislation, but Congress blocked this appeal and decision.

Where then, in this record, exclaimed Hill, is the intractability, the unwillingness to accept the results of the war imputed to the South by its enemies? Had it not accepted every condition, every term imposed upon it, except that it voluntarily disfranchise its own intelligence and leadership, or permit negroes and strangers to accomplish this disfranchisement?

But negroes and adventurers, with military backing, had gone ahead with the execution of this plan; and with what results? Hill enumerated the results as follows: (1) Confidence in northern pledges and constitutional justice is broken in the South. (2) Capital and immigrants and all material improvements are checked in the South. (3) Property has depreciated one-fourth of its value since 1866, and production has lessened one hundred million annually. (4) These effects are increasing and are threatening the destruction of southern industry and prosperity. (5) Society is demoralized, laws are utterly inefficient, property is insecure, and life and innocence are in perpetual hazard.

Now then, this being so, the question becomes: Shall this condition be perpetuated? The Chicago (Republican) platform says yes; the New York (Democratic) platform says no. Hill then addressed himself in an impassioned argument to northern men that in the conservation of their own interest they put an end to this costly, destructive system, which but overtaxed the whole nation for a mistaken cause, founded on misrepresentation and sectional hatred. He concluded his speech with a passionate appeal for fraternity, for peace, for sympathetic understanding, and with a most eloquent tribute to the virtues and glories of American Constitutional government:

> Flag of our Union, wave on, wave ever! But wave over *freemen* not *subjects;* over *States*, not *Provinces;* over Union of *equals*, not of *lords* and *vassals;* over a land of law, of liberty, and of peace, and not of anarchy, oppression and strife.

It is impossible to determine just what effect, whether for good or bad, Hill exerted on the outcome of the campaign by his epistolary activity in New York. The press of Georgia and the country seem to have differed widely at the time, on this subject. Again, the Conservative press, for the most part, praised him. One editor remarked: "His letters appearing in the Tribune form one of the most powerful political documents of the campaign."[70] Another said he was proving a champion who understood his people's cause and was silencing the heretofore unanswered slanders of the *Tribune*.[71] The New York correspondent of an Augusta paper wrote: "The gratitude of the southern people is richly due Mr. H. for his efforts here in their behalf," and the correspondent follows up his own views with some

[70] *New Orleans Picayune*, quoted by *Augusta Constitutionalist*, October 22, 1868.

[71] *Columbus Sun*, October 9, 1868.

commendatory remarks on Hill's writings, from the *New York Herald*.[72]

As might be expected, the Republican journals of Georgia were very depreciating, even scurrilous, regarding Hill's letters and other activity in the North. Says one editorial gentleman:

> Ben Hill can no more keep his pen or tongue quiet than a victim of St. Vitus dance can hold himself still. Having recently proceeded to New York and possibly finding the Democrats indisposed to hear him "orate," in order to gratify his uncontrollable penchant for seeing his name and productions in print, Crazy Ben played strategy on Horace Greeley and wrote a letter to his *Tribune*.[73]

The *New York Sun* is quoted by a Georgia Republican paper as saying:

> Instead of delivering speeches from the rostrum to northern audiences, Mr. Hill of Georgia has taken to writing long epistles to all the newspapers. In this way he has favored the *Times*, *Herald* and *Tribune*. . . . . The Democratic leaders may prevent Mr. Hill from injuring their cause by his speeches, but they cannot prevent him from injuring it through the newspapers.[74]

One Conservative editor probably came nearer the truth than either the enthusiastic admirers of Hill or his detractors. He thought the efforts of Hill "to enlighten the Radicals and Puritans praiseworthy and patriotic," but feared that, considering the northern state of mind, it was "a useless waste of labor and time."[75] For these were days

---

[72] *Augusta Chronicle and Sentinel*, October 14, 1868, article signed "Tyrone Powers."

[73] *Augusta National Republican*, September 28, 1868. For similar views see the same paper, September 29, October 2, 11, 17, 21, 1868.

[74] *Ibid.*, October 21, 1868.

[75] *Augusta Chronicle and Sentinel*, October 6, 1868.

of prejudice and passion; and until prejudice and passion should burn or wear themselves out to some degree, logic and reason, and perchance, justice, too, must wait another day for a hearing.

The elections of 1868 came in November, and the "glorious tramp of the Democracy," which Hill had heard so distinctly in July, had become scarcely audible. Grant and the Republicans won 214 votes in the electoral college to 80 for Seymour and the Democracy. Georgia, however, was carried for Seymour and Blair, a result which the Republicans ungenerously attributed to "organized assassination."[76]

[76] Rhodes, VI, 306-7 gives the vote and circumstances connected with the election.

CHAPTER X

HILL'S CHANGE OF 1870

In order to understand the next step in Hill's political career, which seemed to reverse his whole Reconstruction course and came near resulting in his complete political eclipse, it is necessary to review briefly the course of Reconstruction in Georgia from the national elections of November, 1868, to the state election in Georgia of December, 1870. During this period it was Georgia's fate to undergo a third "reconstruction" process, and to experience a third régime of military rule.[1]

Bullock, the Republican governor of the state, addressed the Congress of the United States on December 7, 1868, declaring that the state of Georgia had not complied with the laws of Congress and that there was in its borders "no adequate protection for life and property, the maintenance of peace and good order, and free expression of political opinion." He demanded Congressional interference and suggested the remission of the state to military rule.[2] The last session of the Fortieth Congress, to which Bullock appealed, took no action, although in the House the matter

---

[1] This entire subject is admirably covered by Miss Thompson, pp. 255–70, and by Wooley, pp. 63–68; see also Avery, pp. 407–44.

[2] *House Journal* (Georgia), 1869, pp. 5–7. Bullock was moved to this action because he had failed to secure control of the Assembly elected in 1868. The governor realized that he possessed talking-points with the Radicals in Congress, such as the Seymour victory in Georgia and the expulsion of the negro members from the Georgia Assembly in September.

was referred to the Committee on Reconstruction, which took voluminous testimony on conditions.[3]

Meanwhile, the Georgia Assembly provided Bullock with additional ammunition, when in March, 1869, it voted down ratification of the Fifteenth Amendment.[4] The second session of the Forty-first Congress, therefore, quickly took up the Georgia case and passed on December 22, 1869, the Georgia bill remanding the state to military rule, declaring the existing state government provisional, and requiring the adoption of the Fifteenth Amendment as a further condition precedent to the full admission of the state to the Union.[5]

Under the terms of the bill, Bullock, with General Terry as coadjutor, proceeded to get the Georgia Assembly into a proper condition of Radicalism. The process is known in Georgia history as "Terry's purge." Some thirty-two of the expelled negro members were reseated, and some twenty-four Democrats or Conservatives replaced by Radicals. The entire complexion of the Assembly was thus altered.[6] This purged Assembly, now amenable to Bullock's

---

[3] *House Miscellaneous Reports*, 40 C., 3 S., No. 52, gives the testimony and report of the committee on Georgia.

[4] *House Journal*, 1869, p. 610; *Senate Journal*, 1869, p. 806. It seems probable that Bullock's partisans engineered the defeat of the amendment in order to increase the likelihood of congressional interference in their behalf (see Thompson, p. 261; Avery, pp. 410–12). In other ways during these months Bullock frustrated amicable settlement of pending disputes, as, for example, vetoing a resolution to have the negro-eligibility question referred to the courts. He preferred to keep them open sores.

[5] *U.S. Statute at Large*, 41 C., 2 S., Vol. XVI, pp. 59–60.

[6] For entire procedure, see Thompson, pp. 262–64; Wooley, pp. 74–79.

control, then ratified the Fifteenth Amendment on February 2, 1870.[7]

But Bullock and the Radicals did not yet feel safe, since the terms of the Assembly, so constituted, expired in December, 1870. Hence there followed what is known in Georgia history as the "prolongation scheme." An appeal was made to Butler and other Radicals in Congress to have the existing Assembly in Georgia "prolonged" for two years by Act of Congress. Bullock himself went to Washington and conducted a vigorous lobby for prolongation, which was subsequently the subject of Congressional investigation and pronounced corrupt.[8] However, the governor's scheme and Butler's parliamentary leadership met defeat in the Act of July 15, 1870, which declared Georgia entitled to admission to the Union and confirmed the right of the people of the state to an election for the General Assembly "as provided for in the Constitution."[9]

Bullock then transferred his ingenious efforts to Georgia and almost succeeded in forcing through the General Assembly a bill postponing the election due in December.[10] As a last stratagem to stave off defeat, he succeeded in hav-

[7] *Acts of the General Assembly*, 1870, pp. 492-93.

[8] For Butler's views favoring prolongation, see *Congressional Globe*, 41 C., 2 S., p. 1704; for Senator Wilson's statement: "Law or no law, we want to keep this [Bullock] state government in power, see, *ibid.*, p. 2061. For the report on the Bullock lobby, see Rhodes, VI, p. 403, quoting Rep. No. 175, 41 C., 2 S.

[9] *U.S. Statutes at Large*, 41 C., 2 S., Vol. XVI, pp. 363-64. Senators Trumbull, Schurz, and Edmunds seem to have been most active in opposing the prolongation measure. See *Congressional Globe*, 41 C., 2 S., pp. 1928, 1955-58, 2061 ff., for their speeches.

[10] *House Journal*, 1870, p. 343.

ing two special election laws passed, which were devised to give the Radicals every advantage in the coming December election which now loomed as inevitable.[11]

At this juncture Hill stepped back into the political picture from which he had almost effaced himself since the defeat of 1868. He published an address to the people of Georgia on the pending election for the General Assembly in December, which proved to be a knock-out blow to the majority of his old party associates, and which seemed to align him with elements for whom, for three years, he had exhausted a rich vocabulary in expressing infinite contempt and scorn.[12]

For the most part, as aforesaid, Hill had held aloof from the entire recent political drama since 1868. It is true he had published one additional "Note on the Situation" in December, 1869, in which he had advised a course of action in the expected contingency of the state being remanded to military rule.[13] He had urged the peaceful acceptance of the proposed measures, and discovered some compensation for what was seen as an inevitable development in the fact that the Georgia Assembly would thereby be spared from the voluntary humiliating step which it seemed about to take in regard to the expelled negroes, and its own white members, alleged to be ineligible under the

[11] *Acts of the General Assembly*, 1870, p. 431.

[12] The address, dated December 8, first appeared in the *Augusta Chronicle and Sentinel*, December 11. It is printed in Hill, *Life of Hill*, pp. 55-59.

[13] In *Augusta Chronicle and Sentinel*, December 21, 1869. The Georgia bill remanding the state to military rule was passed on the next day, December 22 (*supra.*, p. 202).

Fourteenth Amendment. The "Note" also contained a plea for kindness and justice toward the negro race, who are not the "authors of our wrongs." It concluded with an urgent plea for "quiet dignity and indifference" toward the whole iniquitous proceeding. This letter elicited from the *St. Louis Times* the following approbation: "The fifteen column speech by a carpet-bag congressman could not combine more practical wisdom and good sense than the Hon. B. H. Hill utters to the people of Georgia in four words: Do Nothing; Say Nothing."[14]

Hill had quietly looked on at the ratification of the Fifteenth Amendment by the "purged" Assembly, and the subsequent promulgation of this amendment, as a part of the organic law of the land on March 30, 1870.[15] He watched the failure of Bullock's scheme in Congress in July, 1870, and the subsequent desperate efforts of the Bullock Assembly to throw the election that was due in December, 1870, to the Republicans. At this juncture, December 8, he made the momentous decision to advise the Georgia people, in a temper different from his previous utterances, and in terms adapted to the present order, changed since the days of his stout-hearted appeals for resistance in 1867 and 1868, when the Congressional acts and the last two war amendments were only pending issues.[16] This address, in conjunction with certain other acts of Hill of approximately the same time, brought it

[14] In *Augusta Chronicle and Sentinel*, January 20, 1870.

[15] See Rhodes, VI, 404–5.

[16] See the address in *Augusta Chronicle and Sentinel*, December 11, 1870, or Hill, *Life of Hill*, pp. 55–59.

about that, from being one of the most popular men in the state, he became one of the most execrated.[17]

Hill began this surprising and forceful letter by reviewing his own political career as a leader of minorities, and stated that his past course, though ineffectual, had proven to him "a wellspring of joy through all the horrors of the past" because he had the consciousness that he had opposed the entire revolution through the three stages of "Secession, Coercion and Reconstruction."

But the revolution, "at least in its work of violence," is at an end; and what are the results? Hill finds them summed up in the war amendments. To the superficial view, these amendments have only established the "freedom, civil equality and political equality of the races" (excepting that some southern whites are deprived of political equality under the Fourteenth Amendment). But the amendments mean more; they mean, on closer examination, that the United States government has become national, not federal, "for jurisdiction over the civil and political status of all races in all the states will be held to have been transferred by these amendments from the states severally to the general government." And "These powers being conferred, it will be difficult to determine what power has not been conferred."

And there can be no doubt that these amendments "are in fact, and will be held in law, fixed parts of the Constitution." It is idle to imagine otherwise. Because, if it be urged that the Supreme Court will interfere and declare the ratifications "null and void" as forced, or usurpatory,

[17] Avery, p. 455. Numerous other citations will appear later in the text. See below, pp. 209-15.

Hill replies that it cannot be so, because the judicial power is only one to construe the Constitution; and these amendments having been proclaimed by the power having jurisdiction, namely, the political power, "the judicial power can have no jurisdiction to review or reverse that proclamation, but can only decide what the amendments so proclaimed mean."

But can usurpation become law? Hill answers, yes—and it was on this point that his critics were most caustic—"usurpation the most glaring, succeeding becomes law." Indeed Hill goes farther and says: "successful usurpation is the strongest expression of power; and law itself, in its last analysis, is only power."

The only remedy for usurpation is the sword. The South is unable, and the North unwilling, to apply this remedy.

> Conceding then that these amendments were usurpations, they were successful, and have become law—fundamental law. . . . . It may have been criminal—it was criminal—to aid in committing a usurpation; it is crime itself to break the law. And thus are we bound.

But, it may be argued, a reaction in the North will "obliterate these amendments." Hill demonstrates the improbability, even impossibility of any such development. Because the North, he says, cares little for the federative principle at best, believes that states rights was the cause of the war, is predisposed toward a strong national government for economic reasons, and, finally, is confident that the great philanthropic and religious fruits of the war in producing negro equality can only be safeguarded by the amendments.

What, then, are a few immediate and pressing duties resulting from the foregoing premises? He answers: First, to obey the Constitution and laws as they exist. No citizen is justified in refusing obedience to laws merely because he, personally, does not favor them. Second, to render "ready protection and cheerful assistance to the colored man" in the exercise of his rights, whatever the individual opinion held of his preparedness for these rights. Third, the time has arrived to discontinue divisions on "the principles and events which led to our present condition." Rather "let us cease all quarrelling over the past and all threatenings for the future" and seek to bring back prosperity and good will among our people.

The concluding paragraph of this letter created bitter resentment among the irreconcilable Bourbons of the Democratic party:

> Touching the pending election, I will add but one suggestion. It is of secondary importance whom else you choose for your General Assembly; but it is of first importance that you choose honest men. We are suffering for wise and honest legislation unless you elect members whom *feed lobbyists* cannot buy. A black man who cannot be bought is better than a white man who can and a Republican who cannot be bought is better than a Democrat who can. . . . .

A careful reading of this letter of Hill's will reveal no approving word of the amendments or the Reconstruction Acts. His advice may be reduced to the one single proposition: "Reconstruction is an accomplished fact; let us recognize it as such and turn our energies to other things." While on careful analysis it is difficult to discover any express inconsistency in Hill's previous course and the letter of December 8, contemporary opinion made no careful analysis, and the veritable floodgates of abuse were loosed upon him. Every unhandsome motive was ascribed to him, and the vocabulary of abuse was exhausted in reviling him who had been the hero of the state.

The *Augusta Constitutionalist*, an influential journal, grudgingly announced that it would print the letter of December 8 only as an "act of courtesy to a distinguished gentleman."[18] Hill had only sent the letter to the *Augusta Chronicle and Sentinel* so the editor of the *Constitutionalist* might have spared his pains. The *Constitutionalist* published the letter, with further disparaging remarks, the next day. The editor wrote: "as compared with the resonant and sublime utterance of the former 'Notes' it resembles the cold, cold drizzle following the thunder storm, or rather the scream of Mercury after the song of Apollo." He expressed the further view that Hill's advice was untimely, would work mischief to the Democratic party, and would confirm Hill's enemies in their opinion that "he is prudent when he ought to be bold, and bold when he ought to be prudent."[19]

The Conservative Georgia press, which had praised Hill so long, was a little slow to impute to him treachery and Radicalism, which eventually was freely charged; but from the first it deprecated the address of December 8 and attacked several of the positions assumed in it. Especially prominent was the note of concern as to its effect on the "harmony of opposition to Radicalism, which Mr. Hill had fought for years."[20] Two points in the address

[18] *Augusta Constitutionalist*, December 13, 1870.
[19] *Ibid.*, December 14, 1870.
[20] *La Grange Reporter*, December 23, 1870.

were challenged: first, that the amendments were of such force and finality as to be beyond recall, and second, that usurpation could in time become valid law. The first was questioned from a standpoint of fact; and on the second point, editorial gentlemen found an opportunity to air their moral indignation.

It was denied that the amendments were so irrevocably fixed in the Constitution as Hill represented, and it was said that fidelity to principle and honor would require that the southern states continue to do everything possible to secure the repeal of the obnoxious laws.[21] Considerable righteous scorn was expended on the portion of the address which dealt with successful usurpation and force as the origin of many governments, and as creating valid law. This was denied categorically, and a degree of moral obliquity was imputed to Hill for having discovered such a principle in his studies.[22]

Judge Linton Stephens, especially, attacked Hill's view that the amendments had become valid law though usurpa-

[21] For this view, see the following papers: *Savannah Morning News*, December 13, 1870; *Augusta Constitutionalist*, December 14, 1870; *Atlanta Intelligencer*, December 14, 1870; in *Brown Scrap Books; Columbus Sun and Times*, December 16, 1870; *Augusta Chronicle and Sentinel*, December 14, 1870; *La Grange Reporter*, December 16, 1870. It may be noted that all these papers, except the *Constitutionalist*, had been ardent admirers of Hill since 1867; the *Constitutionalist*, whose hero was Alexander Stephens, had been a lukewarm friend of Hill's.

[22] See *Savannah Morning News*, December 14, 1870; *Augusta Constitutionalist*, December 17, 1870; Reed, "Reminiscences of Ben Hill," *South Atlantic Quarterly*, V (April, 1906), 143-44; speech of Linton Stephens at Macon, January 23, 1871 in Waddell, pp. 336-38, and also printed in *Augusta Chronicle and Sentinel*, February 4, 1871.

tions in origin. He sarcastically alluded to Hill as a "new Daniel" come to judgment in Georgia. Stephens had been arrested in Sparta, Georgia, for a political offense and, on trial before a United States commissioner in Macon, had made his defense with a political speech, in which he attached the validity of the Fourteenth and Fifteenth amendments. It was on this occasion that the sarcastic allusion to Hill was made.[23]

Stephens' allusion to Hill and attack on his views was so pointed that they elicited a reply. The reply is also very sarcastic. Hill showed the absurdity of Stephens' position in expecting Judge Swayze (if he had expected, as he pretended) to be governed by Stephens' own interpretation of the invalidity of the amendments, when every department of every government, state and national, had declared the amendments of force.

He then sarcastically reviewed Stephens' proposed plan to get rid of the amendments by electing a Democratic president who would withdraw all troops and declare all Reconstruction legislation a nullity. Hill declared that Stephens would not even be able to find a candidate who would promise to execute this plan. Regarding Stephens' proffer of himself for martyrdom in the existing situation, Hill wrote satirically: "He is ready for the sacrifice, feels honored in being the victim. How these words would have cheered me once. Too late! Nearly four years after date!" This latter thrust was a covert taunt at Stephens for his

[23] For the Stephens arrest and trial, see Waddell, pp. 327-46. Stephens was arrested for interference with the December election but was subsequently released.

studied silence in the tumultuous struggles of 1867 and 1868.[24]

The Radical or Republican press of the state naturally acclaimed Hill's new position with approval and even enthusiasm.[25] It demonstrated a tendency to claim him as a convert to the Republican party, and thereby proved a source of embarrassment to him and of vindictive delight to the more hostile Conservative editors.[26]

The most enthusiastic and loyal of Hill's former supporters among the Conservative editors seemed, as it were, to avert their faces more in sorrow than in anger, that human frailty should have caused the fall of so great a man in Israel. Of this sort of comment, the following is typical: "We can only avert our face, draw closer around us the mantle of purer patriotism, and exclaim with lips warm with the glow of affection, *Et tu Brute!*"[27]

The critics of Hill's address of December 8 soon advanced to the charge of treachery; and in late December and early January following, the press was full of the accusation. An editor of a small-town paper, the *Warren Clipper*, seems to have initiated the new stage of the con-

---

[24] Hill's letter in reply to Stephens' speech at Macon is in the *Augusta Chronicle and Sentinel*, March 9, 1871. The same paper had earlier printed Stephens' Macon speech.

[25] The *Atlanta New Era* declared: "Mr. Hill is now to all intents and purposes with the Union Republican party of Georgia. He can be nowhere else since he is not a Democrat now any more than he was in 1850 and 1860" (quoted in *Augusta Constitutionalist*, December 17, 1870). See also, *Savannah Daily Republican*, December 13, 1870; *Augusta Constitutionalist*, December 15, 1870; *Savannah Morning News*, December 19, 1870.

[26] *Augusta Constitutionalist*, December 17, 1870.

[27] *Columbus Sun and Times*, December 20, 1870.

troversy: "Ben Hill and the banished Israelites are parallel cases judging from a private letter written by Ben to certain prominent Radicals. So sayeth the rumor."[28] The editor of the *Atlanta Constitution*, in reprinting this innuendo, stated that it was incumbent on Editor McGregor to prove his insinuations. The doughty editor responded that if the *Constitution* would claim to be the mouthpiece of Hill, he would undertake to supply the proof. The editor of the *Constitution* disavowed such a rôle but expressed an interest in fair play.[29]

Meantime Hill had written an indignant denial of having "cottoned to the Radicals" or of having had any political correspondence with any of them.[30] This brought from Editor McGregor the publication of several affidavits, in which it was set forth by several notorious Radicals of the eastern part of the state that in conversation and by letter to the persons making the affidavits, Hill had made known the position assumed in his address shortly previous to its publication and had expressed the sentiment that the "salvation of the country depended on the re-election of General Grant to the Presidency in 1872, or words to that effect."

These affidavits are couched in the vaguest terms and embrace much hearsay evidence. They do not make convincing reading, and were, moreover, made by Radicals of notorious character, recently defeated in local politics,

[28] Reproduced in *Columbus Sun and Times*, December 30, 1870.

[29] From the account in the *Sun and Times*, December 30, 1870.

[30] Published in the *Constitution*, reproduced in *Sun and Times*, December 31, 1870.

whose veracity on any other subject would never have been accredited by Conservatives.[31] In this case, incensed Conservatives were glad enough to believe any report derogatory to the new "apostate." Hill dismissed the charges with a categorical denial.

Hill, moreover, had not gone without making other defense, although he seems to have anticipated the storm and accepted calumny with more than his usual equanimity. In an interview with Colonel John R. Hart of the *Constitution*, he offered an explanation of his address. Colonel Hart asked: "What is the difference between your position now, and the position of Governor Brown in 1867." Hill replied: "Just the same as that between two sons, one of whom helps assassins to slay his father and the other, after exposing life and all to prevent the slaughter and fails, simply and sadly recognizes the fact that he is dead, and decently buries him, and honestly goes to work for the family. Is there no difference between parricide and filial love?"[32]

Indeed, the taunt that Hill had, by his address of December, assumed the identical position that the villified Brown had occupied in 1867, had rung through the press. It was thus that Hill attempted to differentiate. His argument seems a little labored; it is at least plausible; but the impression is inescapable that the much maligned ex-

[31] The affidavits were printed in the *Constitution* from which they were copied in the *Columbus Sun and Times,* January 10, 1871, where I have examined them. I have also seen the entire correspondence relating to the McGregor charges in the *Augusta Constitutionalist* and the *Savannah Morning News* of approximately the same dates.

[32] Reprinted in *Columbus Sun and Times,* January 21, 1871.

governor had merely anticipated Hill's judgment by three or more years and had displayed the keener foresight, whatever motives may have entered into his calculations. Hill was not a stranger to a bit of sophistry or casuistry, and his pride of opinion made it difficult for him to admit inconsistency.[33]

[33] His full defense occurs in a speech before the Georgia Assembly, January 20, 1877, printed in Hill, *Life of Hill*, pp. 473-93, especially, pp. 489-90.

CHAPTER XI

THE STATE-ROAD LEASE AND THE DELANO BANQUET

Second only to the address of December, 1870, in the caustic criticism that it evoked and in the ungenerous motives imputed to him, was Hill's participation in the lease of the state railroad which was awarded on December 27, pursuant to an act of the Georgia Assembly.[1]

Choleric, bibulous Bob Toombs wrote to Alexander Stephens on December 30: "When I saw Ben Hill's letter going over to the Rads, I stated to more than a dozen gentlemen before I had ever heard one word, that his price was a share in the state road."[2] Toombs, ordinarily, at this stage in his embittered life, would not have been taken very seriously, but in this particular instance he but voiced a sentiment entertained rather generally in the state.

The state-owned Western and Atlantic Railroad had long been a problem to state legislators.[3] Since 1867 it had proven a great source of expense to the state, and it was notoriously exploited and manipulated by Bullock appointees in the interest of graft and political patronage.[4]

---

[1] Act approved, October 24, 1870. See *Acts of the General Assembly*, 1870, pp. 423-27.

[2] Phillips (ed.), *Toombs, Stephens, Cobb Correspondence*, p. 712.

[3] The road had entered into the gubernatorial canvass between Hill and Brown as far back as 1857. See above, p. 30.

[4] For a full discussion of the mismanagement and history of the state road from 1867 to 1870, see Thompson, pp. 238-45. Miss Thompson gives a complete table of figures, showing gross earnings, expenses, amount paid

In the fall of 1870, Foster Blodgett, the Republican superintendent, was asking for an additional appropriation of $500,000 for the road from the General Assembly; and it was currently believed that Blodgett was deliberately running down the value of the road in order that he might buy it in cheap.[5] Moreover, public sentiment in the state had now come to demand either the sale or the lease of the road.[6]

The bill providing for the lease was introduced by a Democratic representative, Hon. Dunlap Scott, and was passed by a Republican Assembly. Under the terms of the bill the governor was authorized to lease the road for a period of twenty years, at not less than $25,000 monthly rental. The bill required that ample bond and security must be given by the leasing company, the bond being placed at $8,000,000; and it was stipulated that the lessees, a majority of whom must be bona fide citizens of Georgia, must be worth in their own property, above all indebtedness, at least $500,000.[7] These conditions were imposed to safeguard the interests of the state and prevent the lease from being awarded to irresponsible persons who might exploit the road and then throw it back on the state.[8]

Miss Thompson thinks that the passage of this bill by

---

to state treasury, and sundry other information (p. 244). On this subject, see also, Fielder, pp. 480-84; Avery, pp. 489-51. Space does not permit a treatment of the really appalling and almost picturesque exploitation of the road.

[5] Fielder, p. 481.

[6] Thompson, p. 245.

[7] *Acts of the General Assembly*, 1870, pp. 423-27.

[8] Fielder, p. 483.

a Republican Assembly reveals "corruption" on the face of it, and she attributes this corruption to Democrats and those interested in the lease.[9] Without attacking this position, it may be said that one of the most severe critics of the lease, Judge A. R. Wright, testified before the Ku Klux Committee that the lease was not a "party question," but also claimed that the Democrats had bolted to the Republicans—so attributing the corruption to the Republican party, who Miss Thompson thinks had to be corrupted in order to pass such a "self denying ordinance."[10] There is no evidence of corruption in the passage of the Lease Act; it was merely in response to an insistent and awakened public opinion.[11]

The fairness of the award of the lease of the state road to the so-called "Brown Company" on December 27, 1870, presents one of the most complicated and controversial questions in Georgia history. Hill was so prominently involved in the entire transaction, and a proper interpretation of the lease, therefore, being so essential to an adequate estimate of Hill, that the subject becomes a matter of some pertinence to this study.

When the Lease Act was pending, it was known that Brown was organizing a company to bid for the lease. So irreproachable appeared the whole transaction at this time that the impeccable Alexander Stephens wrote Brown a letter saying that he would like to be a member of the company and would take an interest "to the extent of his prop-

---

[9] Thompson, p. 246.

[10] July 13, 1871. *Ku Klux Report*, Pt. VII, p. 111.

[11] For the moment, this waives the fairness of the *award* of the lease. The statement in the text relates to the *passage* of the act.

erty."[12] It is not likely that Stephens, who sensed the popular mind with almost infallible foresight, would have desired connection with a lease, which, as has been alleged, could only be put through the Assembly by corrupt means.[13]

Brown's company included, among others, the rather notorious H. I. Kimball of Atlanta;[14] and also a gentleman of quite another character and background, John P. King, the constructive and respected president of the Georgia Railroad.[15] When news of King's connection with the Brown company got abroad, the railroads radiating out of Macon, in central Georgia, feared lest a lease awarded to a company in which the president of the Georgia Railroad, serving another section of the state, figured so prominently, would operate to their own hurt. The officials of these roads appealed to Hill to co-operate with them in organizing a rival company or in securing representation in the Brown Company.[16]

Hill, thereupon, wrote an interesting letter to King, in which he attempted tentatively to feel him out. He advised King that he (Hill) had approved the Lease Act, in part because he had heard that King would "organize the

[12] Johnson and Browne, p. 502; letter of Brown to Stephens in *Atlanta Constitution*, January 11, 1871.

[13] Miss Thompson's views (*supra*., pp. 217 f.).

[14] Kimball was popularly known as "Bullock's man Friday," but the relation may well have been reversed. Kimball built and sold opera houses, palatial hotels, and governor's mansions, when he was not involved in building railroads by means of fraudulently employed state aid (see Thompson, pp. 226-38).

[15] *Ibid.*, p. 247.

[16] *Ibid.*

Company." (Hill was not above flattery on occasion.) He then expressed concern about the personnel of the leasing company, because "if the company shall excite odium the odium will attach to the lease itself." Especially Hill warned King against a lease in which "your road and one in Tennessee" will be "sole endorsers and chief beneficiaries." "Let me beg you not to permit this," he importuned King. Another warning extended the Georgia Railroad president was that Brown as chief justice should not participate in the lease.[17] "As an individual I would not say one word against Governor Brown as a lessee..... But as a Chief Justice there is every objection to his connection with the lease."[18]

King's response to this letter, in the words of Hill, was "fully satisfactory and just such as I expected from one of the most useful and honorable men in this or any other state."[19] As a result, negotiations were opened for a fusion between the so-called "Brown group," including King and Kimball, and the "Hill group." In the meanwhile the Macon group of railroad men had interested the president of the Pennsylvania Railroad, Thomas A. Scott, and Simon

[17] In 1868 Brown had failed of election as United States Senator by the General Assembly, which Bullock could not control. Bullock had then appointed him chief justice of Georgia (see Avery, pp. 298, 399); the Conservatives represented this as a reward for political services.

[18] This letter, written November 30, 1870, was not intended for publication, but after the uproar about the state-road lease, Hill sent it to the *Augusta Chronicle and Sentinel* for publication. It is found in the issue of January 20, 1871. Hill says it is sent "to save some kind fellow the trouble of getting foolish affidavits from some other kind fellows about some foolish things they heard about it, or thought they saw in it."

[19] *Augusta Chronicle and Sentinel*, January 20, 1871.

Cameron, and John S. Delano, who might be expected to bring large capitalistic backing, and perchance, some political influence, to bear.[20] In referring to this increased personnel of the proposed lessees, Hill remarked that he had "no right to dictate all the lessees."[21] But since the company to lease the road was strictly a business corporation, there seem to have been no grounds for excluding the financial railroad backing represented by these men, other than sectional prejudice and entirely gratuitous suspicion.

The fusion between the Hill and Brown groups was effected just before the last day set for the reception of bids under the Act. Brown resigned as chief justice, this being one of the conditions stipulated by Hill,[22] and was named president of the Company.[23] The company made a bid of $25,000 monthly rental, the minimum, under the Act; offered an imposing array of securities in the shape of railroads and banking companies; and showed that they were worth, above individual indebtedness, some $4,000,000.[24]

In the meanwhile a rival company, known as the "Seago-Blodgett Company," representing local Atlanta men for the most part, had put in a bid of $36,500 monthly rental; offered as securities three Georgia railroad companies; and showed they were worth $950,000 above in-

[20] *W. and A. Lease Committee, 1872*, pp. 7 ff.

[21] *Augusta Chronicle and Sentinel*, January 20, 1871.

[22] *Ibid.*

[23] Avery, p. 456.

[24] The list of securities is printed by Fielder, p. 484. It included nine railroad and railroad-and-banking companies, seven of which were in Georgia.

debtedness.[25] However, the presidents of these companies offered as security—the Central Railroad and Banking Company, the Macon and Western Railroad Company, and the Southwestern Railroad Company—all happening to be in Atlanta when the bid was made public, at once notified Governor Bullock in writing that their companies were offered without authority, and repudiated the 'action.[26]

The governor, on December 27, awarded the lease to the Brown Company, and the state immediately resounded with cries of corruption and unfairness. The investigation of the writer has convinced him that these charges were largely due to the prejudice existing against the personnel of the leasing company. Brown, Kimball, Delano, and Cameron had been *personae non gratae* for years in Georgia; and Hill, the most recent object of obloquy in Georgia, had shared all their odium since the address of December 8.

The coincidence in time of Hill's address with his participation in the state-road lease is rather striking, and it is not surprising that the coincidence gave rise to ungenerous suppositions and even definite charges by a press accustomed to fierce partisanship. The actions, taken together, do indicate that Hill is facing about, that he is following the advice which he has given to the Georgia people, and is directing his energies toward other matters than the old Reconstruction issues. More than this they do not signify. He had not turned Radical, nor had he participated in corrupting an Assembly or a governor.

[25] Fielder, pp. 483-84.

[26] *Ibid.* See, also, letter of Brown to A. H. Stephens in *Atlanta Constitution,* January 11, 1871.

THE STATE-ROAD LEASE

Governor Bullock awarded the lease to the Brown Company because, on examination, there was no alternative. The company headed by Brown possessed a superior financial standing; it had incontestable assets and authenticated securities; it numbered in its personnel, experienced and successful railroad men who could be expected to make a going concern of the depreciated state road. As against these advantages, the Seago-Blodgett Company had offered a higher rental of $36,500, which experienced railroad men said was too high a rent and made the venture a gamble;[27] and the security offered by this company was, at the very least, extremely doubtful; and the total assets of the company did not equal one-quarter of those of its successful rival.[28] The public mind seemed only aware of the difference in the monthly rental. And yet under the terms of the Act, the rental was only one feature. Consideration had to be had for the substantiality of the company awarded the lease. On this score there was no ground for debate, Governor Brown claimed, indeed, that Bullock only awarded the lease reluctantly; that when the first security tendered by the Seago-Blodgett Company proved unauthorized, Bullock, contrary to the law, offered another opportunity to the Seago-Blodgett combination to provide

[27] President John P. King and Superintendent Cole of the Georgia Railroad in the *Augusta Chronicle and Sentinel,* May 12, 1871.

[28] These assertions are based largely on an examination of the testimony before the W. and A. Lease Committee of the General Assembly in 1872, and on an hour's conversation with Mr. Sam Small, the veteran newspaper writer and student of Georgia history for the last half-century. Mr. Small was the stenographer who took the proceedings before the Lease Committee. He tells me (conversation, April 2, 1927) that the Committee unearthed no real evidence of fraud or unfairness. For the contrary majority report of the Committee, see below, pp. 233-34.

adequate security, which the company could not, or did not, do.[29] Hill, in covering this same point, remarked that if Bullock had not awarded the lease to the successful company, the present critics of the lease would now be demanding the governor's impeachment.[30] The law ordered the lease, and the Brown Company was the only company meeting the conditions of the Act.

Alexander Stephens contributed much to the notoriety and odium attached to the state-road lease when he withdrew from the leasing company, offering his stock to the state.[31] He took this action as soon as the unpopularity of the lease became evident, and without consulting with Governor Brown, whom he had solicited for a share in the leasing company. Governor Brown took Stephens rather severely to task for such summary action, without an investigation or single inquiry regarding the transaction.[32] The conclusion is inescapable that Stephens had sensed the popular resentment and was only concerned in pharisaicly clearing himself, even if possible injustice and damage resulted thereby to his late colleagues.[33]

[29] *Atlanta Constitution,* January 11, 1871, in *Brown Scrap Books.*

[30] In *Augusta Chronicle and Sentinel,* May 25, 1871.

[31] Johnston and Browne, p. 502.

[32] Brown to Stephens, published in *Atlanta Constitution,* January 11, 1871, in *Brown Scrap Books.*

[33] Mr. Small calls Stephens' act a "political gesture." Stephens claimed that after the lease was awarded he came to suspect unfairness; but by his own statement he acted without inquiry or investigation (see Johnston and Brown, p. 502).

Stephens wrote a letter of explanation to the *Augusta Chronicle and Sentinel;* published January 6, 1871. The editor found the letter "unsatisfactory."

THE STATE-ROAD LEASE

Hill was not so quiescent under the charges of corruption in connection with the state-road lease as he had been regarding the assaults on his address of December 8, 1870. He made several vigorous defenses of the lease.[34] His fight at the Georgia Railroad Convention in Augusta, May 11 and 12, 1871, and his six papers, reviewing the majority report of the legislative Committee on the State Road Lease, in the summer of 1872, require some attention.

At the annual convention of the stockholders of the Georgia Railroad Company, at Augusta, the chief business proved to be a fight over ratification of the action of the directors of the company in offering the road as a security for the lease of the state road. Several days before the meeting, Toombs had purchased stock in the Georgia Railroad Company in order to be present and lead the fight against the action of the president and directors. Toombs was also, it may be added, the paid attorney of the defeated Seago-Blodgett Company.[35] Toombs was assisted in the fight against the lease by Hill's old political antagonist, Linton Stephens, who formulated the resolutions of protest against the action of the president and directors.[36]

[34] He wrote letters to the *Augusta Chronicle and Sentinel* which were printed in that paper January 20 and May 25, 1871. In these letters he reviewed the whole history of the lease, as set forth in the text, and proved to his own satisfaction, at least, its entire fairness, and beneficiary character to the state of Georgia.

[35] Remarks of Hill, John P. King, and others in the convention and undisputed; in *Augusta Chronicle and Sentinel*, May 12 and 13, 1871.

[36] The entire proceedings of this convention are reported in the *Augusta Chronicle and Sentinel*, May 12 and 13, 1871, and consume the greater part of the papers for those dates. The account in the text, with quotation, is taken from these reports. The newspaper account is captioned, "Toombs, Hill, Stephens and King—A Battle of Giants."

Debating on Stephens's resolutions, Mr. Mark A. Cooper, a prominent and successful business man of the state, favored indorsement of the directors' action. He asserted the lease would be of great value to all concerned; that "certain parties were so much opposed because they wished it broken up that they might get it themselves"; that he (Cooper) had repeatedly tried to lease the road, but failed for lack of security.[37]

Colonel E. W. Cole, the superintendent of the Georgia Railroad, stated that he favored indorsement not for any personal reason but "because he had a pride in railways and wished to build up a great line from the West into Georgia, and the people of Georgia would be the beneficiaries." The connections afforded the Georgia Railroad through the lease would aid this project; moreover, he had seen enough of political management of the state road for the last fifteen years to wish it abolished.

Colonel King and Toombs engaged in a hot debate on the convention floor, Toombs, as usual losing his temper; while King, a railroad man by profession, argued the fairness of the rental, the probable earnings of the state road, and the advantages accruing to the state from the freight facilities which the lease company, through its extensive railroad connections, could provide.

Hill went over the whole question of the lease from its inception, but made his strongest showing on the benefits which the lease would bring to the state treasury, to the Georgia Rialroad, and to the people of the state generally. He explained the eagerness of the directors of the Georgia

[37] For references to Cooper's position in Georgia, see Fielder, pp. 55, 82, 92.

THE STATE-ROAD LEASE

Railroad and of other railroad companies to consummate the lease, by quoting from a former report of President King's which showed that the increase in business for the railroads in Georgia in the last year had been largely in freight which had western connections. He continued:

> This business was greatly threatened by the dilapidated condition and inefficient management of the State-Road, and without some change would soon have been lost or greatly reduced—hence the zeal with which all connecting Roads offered every facility to consummate a lease to a private company, by which it is believed the danger to this important business will be averted.[38] . . . . The policy of leasing having been wisely adopted by the state, the policies of the Roads in offering their companies as security, to which there is no possible risk, I think equally wise. This gives them some claim to overlook the management of the Road, in which they, as well as the citizens, are so much interested.

The debate continued two days and finally concluded with a successful motion to table Stephens' resolutions of protest. John P. King was again elected president. Both sides claimed a victory, but the practical victory undoubtedly lay with Hill and King, as the action of the directors was not repudiated and therefore stood.[39]

It remains to examine the legislative investigation of the state-road lease, for which a committee was appointed by the General Assembly in December, 1871. This committee took voluminous testimony and made its report in July, 1872.[40] The majority report was adverse to the leas-

---

[38] The W. and A., the state-road, connected Atlanta and Chattanooga, and at this time was about the only western connection for the group of railroads radiating out of Atlanta and Macon.

[39] See Hill's letter to *Augusta Chronicle and Sentinel*, May 25, 1871, setting forth reasons for claiming a victory at Augusta.

[40] Fielder, p. 482.

ing company, saying: "The present lease of the Western and Atlantic R. R. obtained from Rufus B. Bullock, Governor of the State of Georgia, on the 27th day of December, 1870, was unfairly obtained."[41]

The testimony taken by the lease committee is conflicting and confusing. Much of it was given by interested and prejudiced parties; and in at least one case, an entirely innocent party gave testimony which seemed very damaging to the fairness of the lease, until it was explained, and then the witness giving the damaging testimony admitted the entire plausibility of the explanation.[42]

The majority report of the committee turned upon the testimony of Captain Andrew J. White, a member of the successful lease company.[43] Captain White testified that he had heard Kimball say that some of the lessees owed their seats to sums paid to "outsiders," and White admitted that he took this as a reference to Bullock and paid lobbyists before the Georgia Assembly. The lease committee adopted this construction and made its unfavorable report. There were other features connected with the lease which received adverse comment from the committee, but the reference to the money, approximately $50,000 "paid to outsiders," is the only plausible evidence of corruption, the

[41] See *House Journal*, 1871, Appendix.

[42] Miss Thompson (pp. 251–54), reviews the testimony and puts the most damaging construction upon it. She seems to credit all the assertions of the bitter enemies of Bullock and Kimball, and especially the utterances of A. L. Harris, who admittedly was a disappointed office-seeker on the road, and one with no great reputation for probity. See Avery, pp. 427–34.

[43] *Joint Committee on the Lease of the W. and A. R. R., 1872*, pp. 34 ff.

THE STATE-ROAD LEASE

other matters being legal questions about which honest men might differ and did differ.[44]

Hill wrote six letters to the *Atlanta Constitution* reviewing the majority report of the investigating committee and successfully refuting their conclusions.[45] In his third letter he took up the testimony of Captain White.[46] He established the fact that, while White was not present, Brown and Kimball had demanded that the Hill group pay over a large sum of money to aid in paying off certain claims to members of the original Brown Company who were excluded from the final company to make room for the Hill group. This the Hill group had refused to do. But the claims were paid off anyway, and it was reference to the sum so expended, approximately $50,000, to "outsiders" that White and the Committee had mistaken for a payment to Bullock and lobbyists. Hill included in his paper an admission by White that he had made the wrong inference.[47]

After a vigorous debate in the Assembly in July, 1872, both houses, by large majorities, voted to sustain the lease, thus expressing their dissent from the report of their own

[44] Hill answered successfully these legal objections to the lease award, viz., that the directors offering their corporations as securities had acted *ultra vires,* and that the successful lease company had illegally choked out competition in the bid. See his letters reviewing the majority report on the state-road lease, Letters No. 1 and 2 in *Atlanta Constitution,* July 30 and 31, 1872.

[45] This statement is based on the fact that a Democratic Assembly failed to sustain its own committee's report and the further fact that a careful reading of the press of the period discloses no effort to refute Hill's argument.

[46] *Atlanta Constitution,* August 2, 1872.

[47] This is the $50,000 which Miss Thompson says (p. 246 n.), "was never satisfactorily explained."

committee and confirming the fairness and validity of the state-road lease.[48]

The third action of Hill in 1870 that outlawed him temporarily from the Georgia Democratic party was his attendance on and speech at a banquet tendered Secretary of the Interior Delano, Simon Cameron, and others by Governor Bullock on December 28 in Atlanta. The scorn and vituperation of the Georgia Conservative press burst all bounds at this new and most shameful evidence of Hill's degradation.[49] The following is but a typical editorial comment, indeed hardly as scurrilous as the most:

> Bullock's slander-mill, the Atlanta Era, gives a full report of the hobnobbing and speechifying at the Bullock-Kimball banquet given a few nights since in honor of Secretary Delano, and at which Hon. Ben Hill, ex-Governor Joe Brown, Foster Blodgett and others were present. Whether the party dined heartily or not, there is no reason to doubt that they must heartily despise each other. Ben Hill eating and drinking at the same table with Bullock! Ben must have the stomach of an ostrich.[50]

At the banquet Hill was called upon to respond to a toast offered to "Georgia" by Secretary Delano, and in reply made a speech which greatly outraged the Conserva-

---

[48] *House Journal*, 1872, p. 369, and *Senate Journal*, 1872, pp. 296-97; see, also, Fielder, p. 482.

[49] A citation of such references to this occasion would exhaust a catalog of the Georgia Conservative press for the period. Besides the quotation in the text, reference may be made to the *Augusta Chronicle and Sentinel*, December 29 and 31, 1870; *Columbus Sun and Times*, December 30, 1870. Every opprobrious and sarcastic epithet was used in describing the personnel of the banquet, and every sinister motive imputed to Hill for his attendance.

[50] From the *Savannah Morning News* in the *Columbus Sun and Times*, January 7, 1871.

THE STATE-ROAD LEASE

tives. After admitting that his love and service of the state certainly, "in one respect," made him "the proper person to respond to the toast," he reviewed briefly the history of the Reconstruction ordeal and his own political career. In the course of his remarks, he said:

> I am back where I was ten years ago upon the platform of the Constitution and the enforcement of the law. Some people say that I have come to be a radical. That is a terrible mistake. That can never be, never, never. Some people say that I am not a good Democrat. If I ever was a Democrat I can honestly say that I did not *go to be*. (Applause) I was not a Democrat certainly from choice, and if a Democrat at all, I was a Democrat from necessity. People talk about my having changed. I have not changed a single sentiment you ever heard me express, not one; but times change; circumstances change; issues change; necessities change; and we should adapt ourselves to them if we expect to prosper. (Applause)[51]

Hill eventually weathered the storm of abuse that swept over him on account of the banquet episode, and some years later Henry W. Grady reported that Hill told him he regarded his course in connection with this banquet as "the most patriotic and bravest act of my life."[52] The reason for this view will appear in what follows.

Hill's own explanation of his entire course in 1870 and 1871, embracing the address of December 8, 1870, and the Delano banquet, is found in several places, and, judging by the political honors which were bestowed upon him in a few years by the white Democracy of the state, came to

---

[51] Quoted in *Columbus Sun and Times*, January 10, 1871; also found in Hill, *Life of Hill*, p. 63. For Hill's expressions of the same sentiments on his Democracy and party affiliations, see *Ku Klux Report*, Pt. VII, pp. 760, 763.

[52] In *Atlanta Constitution*, August 17, 1882.

be accepted as the true explanation.[53] In substance the explanation is about as follows:

By the fall of 1870 he had come to realize that it was vain to hope for relief from the Reconstruction measures at the hands of the northern Democracy. In 1870 he had made a trip North, one of several in the years 1867-70, and had found the northern Democracy "cold," despite his most impassioned appeals.[54]

In the meanwhile Bullock and the Radicals in Georgia were agitating for a prolongation of the existing Republican Assembly, and though defeated, in Congress in July, 1870, had not abandoned hope when the state elections in Georgia were coming on in December.[55] Hill affirmed that he "knew" the incoming Assembly would be Democratic, but the question was how to keep it so. Ample experience had demonstrated that adverse majorities did not restrain the Radical Congress when it had determined to act in a southern matter.[56]

Hill concluded that interference with the incoming Democratic Assembly and Democratic administration might be prevented if the Democracy of the state could be

[53] Among other places, in the following: speech before the Georgia General Assembly, January 20, 1877, printed in Hill, *Life of Hill*, pp. 473-93; in a long interview originally appearing in the *Atlanta Constitution*, reproduced in the *Columbus Sun and Times*, January 21, 1871; in another interview originally appearing in the *New York Sun*, reproduced in *Atlanta Herald*, May 31, 1874 (*Brown Scrap Books*); letter to the legislature, September 28, 1871, published in *Augusta Chronicle and Sentinel*, September 30, 1871.

[54] Interview published in *Atlanta Herald*, May 31, 1874, in *Brown Scrap Books*.

[55] *Supra*, pp. 203 f.

[56] Speech before Georgia Assembly, Hill, *Life of Hill*, p. 489.

prevailed on to affirm that "reconstruction was an accomplished fact."[57] He was the more ready to advise this position, because his recent trip North had convinced him that the National Democratic party would assume that identical position in 1872, in which opinion the event proved him correct. He had therefore issued his address of December 8 advocating this policy. He had expected to be abused by the Democrats "a little," but not so much as the sequel proved.[58]

At this juncture, while Bullock was playing his desperate game to retain control of Georgia, Secretary of the Interior Delano and other prominent northern men came to Atlanta while on a southern tour. Hill met Delano. Several friendly meetings followed. Hill found Delano a "courteous gentleman and not altogether unfriendly to the South." He determined to use him, if possible, to aid in the frustration of Bullock's designs.[59] Mr. Delano was surprised to discover that "all the respectable people in the South belonged to the Democratic party"; and Hill gave him his views, already detailed elsewhere, regarding the compulsion under which old Whigs and Union men had been driven into the Democratic party.[60]

A few days later Hill was surprised to receive an invitation to a banquet given by Bullock to Delano and others. He says he surmised at the time that Bullock had deliberately invited him thinking that he would play into the

[57] *Ibid.*

[58] *Ibid.*

[59] In *Atlanta Herald*, May 31, 1874, in *Brown Scrap Books*.

[60] For these views see above, p. 134. They were also given before Ku Klux Committee, *Ku Klux Report*, Pt. VII, pp. 760, 763.

Radicals' hands by such fiery intemperate utterances as he had once voiced. Secretary Delano urged him to accept; but, knowing it would be political suicide, Hill refused. After going home and thinking it over, he reconsidered. He would attend and deliberately incur the odium and criticism that would follow, in the hope of winning the support of Delano and the other influential northern Republicans with the administration at Washington, against Bullock and the Georgia rogues. He had already privately assured Delano that the incoming Georgia Assembly, if let alone, would, by its moderate course, vindicate its reliability and responsibility. He would make a public avowal that Reconstruction was "over" in Georgia, and make it in the very presence of the Radicals seeking to prolong and perpetuate the process.[61]

Consequently he went to the banquet and expressed these views; and as he went along, he saw that he had Delano's attention and support. "Thank God Reconstruction is over—over at last," he said; and Hill declares that he well remembered how Delano had nodded approval from the head of the table. "Right there I broke up Bullock's scheme of Reconstruction," Hill told the General Assembly in 1877.[62]

After the banquet, in subsequent interviews Hill persuaded Delano that the Georgia Assembly would "do nothing rash, and would not impeach Bullock on political grounds," as the latter had been representing to the Re-

---

[61] This narrative from the interview in the *Atlanta Herald*, May 31, 1874, in *Brown Scrap Books*.

[62] Speech before General Assembly, January 20, 1877, in Hill, *Life of Hill*, p. 490.

publicans at Washington. Delano left Atlanta, says Hill, with the promise that "he would do what he could to prevent further interference in Georgia."[63]

Hill also went to Washington in January, 1871,[64] and with Delano's aid, says he carried the day with Grant and prevented interference with the newly elected Democratic Assembly. For, when Morton and Butler, loath to give up the state of Georgia to the Democrats, called upon the president for information concerning the state, in the next Congress, the president merely sent them the *Journals* of the Georgia house and senate.[65] Hill said to the General Assembly in 1877:

People said I tricked Grant. I didn't. I tricked no man. I opposed Reconstruction, yet, when it was accomplished, I submitted. . . . . There was no trick in the matter. I thought I ought to save the legislature of Georgia, and save Georgia from further Radical domination. I believed that by taking that position in 1870 I could get into a position to do it. . . . . I won.[66]

When he went North in January, 1871, it was charged he was being considered for a place in Grant's cabinet; and even so sensible a paper as the *Chronicle and Sentinel* printed: "We believe it to be quite certain that Mr. B. H. Hill will be the next Attorney General."[67] When Hill reached Washington and was informed of the rumors of

[63] In *Atlanta Herald*, May 31, 1874, in *Brown Scrap Books*.

[64] *Columbus Sun and Times*, January 21, 1871, contains notice of his arrival in Washington.

[65] In *Atlanta Herald*, May 31, 1874, in *Brown Scrap Books*.

[66] Speech before General Assembly, January 20, 1877, in Hill, *Life of Hill*, p. 490.

[67] February 7, 1871. Akerman's resignation as attorney-general was expected.

this nature, he branded them all as unmitigated lies and said that nobody but a knave would say he was a Radical and nobody but a fool would believe it.[68] When no appointment was tendered Hill, his critics took refuge in the view that "Cameron and Delano have probably failed to persuade the President to call Ben Hill into the Cabinet."[69] When Hill returned to Georgia, he wrote a letter of mild protest to the *Chronicle and Sentinel,* which had formerly been his chief champion, against the publication of such "unfounded charges for which the paper can have no scintilla of evidence."[70]

In September, 1871, Hill took one more step that seemed to the Conservatives an act of effrontery and presumption. He wrote a very long public letter to the Georgia General Assembly elected in the last December, but not due to convene until the first of November, 1871.[71] In this letter he explained his actions of 1870, took occasion to repeat the arguments for the state-road lease, and concluded with a plea to the General Assembly for moderation in its forthcoming session.[72]

He especially urged that the members of the General Assembly in their forthcoming session should vindicate the representations that had been made to Washington that the Democratic party in Georgia, if left alone, would deal justly with all classes and that they would by their legis-

[68] *Augusta Chronicle and Sentinel,* January 26, 1871, quoting its Washington correspondent.

[69] *Savannah Morning News,* February 8, 1871.

[70] Published in the issue of March 9, 1871, with the editor's viewpoint.

[71] Thompson, p. 271.

[72] Letter found in *Augusta Chronicle and Sentinel,* September 30, 1871

lation recognize that the Reconstruction amendments were of force. He begged the Assembly to disappoint and refute the enemies of self-government in Georgia by taking no action that could be construed as an attempt to nullify existing laws and federal amendments.

The Conservatives raged at Hill's presumption in thus advising the Assembly. "Was there ever such a display of unblushing effrontery, egotism and vanity," was the query from one editorial sanctum;[73] and later the same editor saw in the letter an evidence that the "legislative ring" was ready to go to work, and that a conspiracy existed to save Bullock from impeachment, and the state-road lease from interference by the Assembly.[74]

Hill kept calm through the storm and merely claimed that in addressing the Assembly in this way, he was fulfilling his promises made to Delano that he would use all his influence to see that a Democratic legislature, if left alone, would recognize the amendments to the Constitution of the United States and would not interfere with the rights of the negroes or the Union men in the state.[75]

On November 1, 1871, the first Georgia Democratic Assembly since the war came together, and in the main were governed by Hill's advice, however much its author was reviled by some of its members.[76] On October 23, seeing inevitable defeat and probable impeachment ahead of

[73] *Savannah Morning News,* October 2, 1871.

[74] *Ibid.,* October 26, 1871. See the same paper, October 24, for adverse criticisms on the letter from other Georgia papers.

[75] *Atlanta Herald,* May 31, 1874, in *Brown Scrap Books.*

[76] For the personnel and work of this Assembly, see Avery, pp. 464-67; see also, Thompson, pp. 271-74.

him, Governor Bullock had secretly filed his resignation to take effect on October 30. Before the resignation had become public, he had furtively left the state; and in elections of December, 1871, James M. Smith, a Democrat, was elected governor of Georgia. With his inauguration on January 12, 1872, the last vestige of Republican governmental control passed away in the state.[77]

Georgia was one of the first southern states to regain self-government, and Ben Hill had played no small part in consummating that result.

[77] For Bullock's mode of departure, see Avery, pp. 460–61; for Smith's election and inauguration, see *ibid.*, pp. 467–70, also Thompson, p. 272.

CHAPTER XII

POLITICAL PROSCRIPTION

Hill was almost politically proscribed in Georgia by the Democracy from 1871 until 1875. The Georgia historian, Avery, writes:

For years Mr. Hill walked through the valley of the shadows. He was lampooned, abused and howled at. He was called Radical; accused of selling out to the Republicans; of changing politics with a view to election to the Senate, by a Republican legislature; and a thousand other hard criminations. For years he fought against public odium as Governor Brown had done. It looked as if he was politically shelved. His best friends turned upon him. His ordeal was not altogether as severe as Governor Brown's, but it was a harsh one, and his recovery was a striking instance of political vitality.[1]

On July 31, 1871, at the State University Hill delivered a speech before the University Alumni Society, which struck a new note for southern orators, and which, at the time, evoked harsh criticism from the Conservative press, now accustomed to impugn his every motive and challenge his every assertion.[2] In this speech Hill took a very advanced position on the problems and duties facing the defeated South. While professing to honor and glory in the heritage of the South, and in no wise to "under rate Southern civilization in the production of an elegant select so-

[1] Avery, p. 455. It will be observed that this experience had been forecast in the newspaper criticism quoted in chapter xi.

[2] The address is printed in Hill, *Life of Hill*, pp. 334-49. It was also printed in the state press at the time.

ciety, and of the most superior individualism,"[3] Hill dared to point out that the pressing urge on the South was to look ahead and meet the challenge of the future. The South should rather consider not "what their fathers were, but whether and what their children shall be."[4]

Leaving the "fascination of rhetoric and the cultured figures of oratory" to other speakers, Hill addressed himself to a most earnest analysis of the defects of southern civilization and to suggestions as to future policies and development. In the light of the present-day industrialized, and still rapidly industrializing, South, this speech of 1871 seems almost prophetic. Hill had essayed the rôle of a pioneer in ideas, even if, a half-century later, his utterances sound commonplace enough.[5]

He began his speech with a brief survey of the unsurpassed and, indeed, inexhaustible natural advantages possessed by the section, in climate, soil, minerals, harbors, and raw materials. How had it come about that other sections and countries, lacking many of these assets, had yet passed the South "in population, wealth and power?" Hill finds the answer in slavery, which like the Lernean Hydra had multiplied its evils, and cursed the South so long. He professed to waive all questions connected with the moral

[3] Letter, explaining the address, written to the *Atlanta Constitution*, August 3, 1871, reproduced in *Augusta Chronicle and Sentinel*, August 10, 1871.

[4] Hill, *Life of Hill*, p. 336.

[5] I am not unaware that there had been sporadic efforts in the South since about 1830, by isolated individuals, to promote industrial development. Such efforts, however, had hardly disturbed the surface of the southern complacency; and I think Hill's rôle may be designated that of a pioneer.

and political aspects of slavery, and confined himself to a most searching and convincing analysis of its disastrous economic effects.

> I only propose to show that slavery affected and most deleteriously affected the Southern States and people in general scientific, physical and educational progress, and especially in *material* and commercial development, and as a consequence delayed their growth in population, wealth, and physical power.[6]

This alleged "apostate" to his people then stood up and told them that the proud South had contributed and was contributing nothing to that "wonderful progress of modern civilization" which had as its chief interests and manifestations "the extension of educational facilities to the masses of the people," "the elevation and advancement of strictly industrial pursuits," "the establishment of scientific, mechanical and polytechnic schools," and "discoveries made and results wrought by educated and enlightened industries." And he attributed southern deficiencies to the evils of that "peculiar," that "domestic institution" which most of his auditors had always heard praised and defended as the crowning glory of southern civilization. Here was, indeed, a new note; and it is very probable that some of his fellow-alumni were alternately moved by amazement and indignation at such new-fangled heresy from an ex-Confederate Senator.

Hill's analysis of the disastrous effects exerted by negro slave labor on the southern mind, and on southern society and accomplishments, was particularly keen; but space forbids its repetition. At its conclusion, in a burst of eloquence, he compared southern genius to Prometheus

[6] Hill, *Life of Hill*, p. 337.

chained to the solid rock of slavery, and rejoiced that finally this genius was loosed. "Tis LOOSED! We inquire not how, whether by fate or by folly; whether in right or in hate; we thank thee God, for the *fact*—'tis LOOSED!"[7]

These views of the disastrous effects of slave economy on the South are common enough now, even among southerners. But to appreciate Hill's daring and his advanced thought, it only need be recalled that he was speaking to a group of ex-slavocrats, and within a scant six years after they had failed to establish a great nation, whose "cornerstone" should be the "peculiar institution."

But now that the South was at length loosed from its slave chains and still possessed its natural advantages and potential wealth, what of the future? He pleaded that educational facilities be improved; that "furnaces and foundries, studios and workshops" be constructed in the land and be used to demonstrate to southern people the honor and rewards of labor; that the negro be educated for usefulness; that the natural resources of soil and mineral and water power, which had so long been neglected, be utilized and developed to capacity. When the South aggressively and earnestly shall have turned its attention to these accomplishments:

> Then population will also flow in from other states and countries and in a form not to displace or dominate over us, but only to add to our strength. Then wealth will increase, homes will multiply, power become a fact and not a theory, and then, and not til then, we shall see and feel, taking bodily shape and form, those tantalizing, perplexing myths after which we have so long vainly grasped—state rights—state sovereignty—and state independence![8]

[7] *Ibid.*, p. 342.   [8] *Ibid.*, p. 343.

In the course of his argument for the new policies and issues which he advocated, Hill took occasion frequently to employ Massachusetts, Connecticut, and other northern states for purposes of comparison with Georgia in the matter of natural resources and the use made of them. Needless to say, this comparison was always disadvantageous to Georgia; and southern Conservatives, who had always been told by their orators that no good thing could come out of abolitionist New England, were aghast and indignant at what they construed as treachery to their own section and base truckling to northern Radicals.[9]

Despite the unorthodoxy of Hill's address, the Alumni Society displayed sufficient fairness to request from him, by resolution, a copy of the address for publication, which request was readily granted.[10]

The following comment on the address is not unrepresentative of a good deal that appeared in the press:

> The soundness of abolition principles and the superiority of Yankee civilization were his main topics of discourse. The superior insight of the Radical party into the true policy of the country was made very manifest and our own errors exposed in a masterly way.[11]

And another:

> He should have proposed a toast to: "The Republican Party—wiser in counsel and stronger in action—understand our interests better than ourselves. We apologize to them for our stupid opposition in the past. We return thanks for the services rendered to us

---

[9] *Augusta Chronicle and Sentinel*, August 24, 1871.

[10] The correspondence regarding its publication, between the secretary of the Society and Hill, is printed in Hill, *Life of Hill*, p. 334.

[11] *Augusta Chronicle and Sentinel*, August 24, 1871.

against our will. Henceforth be their policy, our policy—their civilization, our civilization. Let us have but one cause, one party—Above all—one purse."[12]

No word regarding party or politics had appeared in the address. It was as unpolitical as could be imagined, concerning itself largely with economic questions. The intemperate and far-fetched allusions to political malice and design are but further commentaries of what blind chauvinism and political prejudice will produce in an otherwise reasonable and kindly people. So savage were the assaults on the Alumni speech that Hill wrote a letter to the editor of the *Constitution,* combating some of the "ludicrous statements" concerning it, and otherwise explaining his motive, purpose, and message.[13]

While the discussion regarding Hill's Alumni address was still agitating the state press, another controversy, in which he figured prominently, began to get under way. This concerned the so-called "New Departure" of the National Democratic party.

As early as June, 1871, insinuations and rumors regarding the New Departure appear in the state press. The *Savannah Morning News,* editorially, had suggested that Hill's recent "apostacy" might be a preparation for surrender of the Democracy to the Radicals "by means of the so-called New Departure." The editor went on to say that there was good reason to believe Hill had been in conference with leaders of the "N.D." in the North and had

[12] *Ibid.,* August 25, 1871.

[13] August 3, 1871. Published in Hill, *Life of Hill,* pp. 332–34; also found in *Augusta Chronicle and Sentinel,* August 10, 1871.

POLITICAL PROSCRIPTION

probably received promises of "outside support" and "perhaps valuable considerations."[14]

In August the *Augusta Chronicle and Sentinel* printed a most scurrilous account of Hill's alleged designs respecting the New Departure under the caption, "Inauguration of a Third Party Movement in the South—How Ben Hill was Converted."[15] The article is absurd, transparent, and puerile, and is only significant in that it shows the extent of misrepresentation of which a partisan press could be guilty. The writer had collected and rehashed all the petty political backstairs gossip of the year and served it with seasoning of his own.

In August of this year, Hill first gave public expression to views favoring the New Departure, in a newspaper interview emanating from Monte Valle Springs, Tennessee, where he was resting.[16] He said at this time that the southern people wanted peace and were now willing to pass up the issues of war and Reconstruction; that Toombs, the two Stephens, and others of that ilk opposing the policy were southern Bourbons; that the Democracy should take new ground in the campaign of 1872, and by so doing would have some chance of success.

Perhaps it should be said in explanation of the so-called "New Departure" that since 1870 disaffection with-

[14] June 20, 1871. It may be recalled that Hill had gone North in 1870, before his address of December; and again in January, following the address. It was probably inevitable that only ungenerous motives should be attributed to him by a hostile press. See above, pp. 233, 235.

[15] August 9, 1871.

[16] Originally appearing in the *Knoxville Chronicle*, August 19, 1871; reproduced in *Augusta Chronicle and Sentinel*, September 10, 1871.

in the Republican ranks had been rife, due to the low political morality of Grant's administration. In Missouri this disaffection had already lost the state to the Administration party. Also since 1870 it had been evident, as Hill pointed out in his address of December, 1870,[17] that the northern Democracy were ready to recede from their position of 1868 on the nullity and invalidity of the Reconstruction laws in the South. Here, then, was an opportunity for a fusion or coalition. The Democracy would meet the disaffected or so-called "Liberal Republicans" half way on the southern question; together they would oppose the corrupt and domineering Radical Republicans in the South and in the nation. This was the New Departure, or the N. D., discussions of which occupied so much newspaper space in 1872, and which was the occasion of much crimination and recrimination in Georgia.[18]

Toombs and Linton and Alexander Stephens in Georgia bitterly opposed the New Departure, Judge Linton Stephens making a vigorous speech against the movement at the state capitol in Atlanta in June, 1872. He asserted that Greeley, whom the Liberal Republicans had nominated at Cincinnati in May,[19] was as bad if not worse than Grant in his radicalism and centralism, and that the only tenable position for the Democracy was to put out an independent Democratic ticket, bottomed, as in the past, on state rights. He asserted that otherwise he could not support the plat-

[17] *Supra.*, pp. 206 ff.

[18] For a full discussion of the development of the "New Departure" in the nation, see Rhodes, VII, 35–48; Oberholtzer, III, 1–68; for a treatment of the movement in Georgia, see Avery, pp. 501–2.

[19] Oberholtzer, III, 26; Rhodes, VII, 45.

POLITICAL PROSCRIPTION 247

form or the nominee of the forthcoming Baltimore Democratic Convention.[20]

On the next night Hill replied to Stephens in a speech which, at the time, was reported to have won the praise even of Toombs, who was a bitter opponent of the cause championed and who was on the platform to reply to Hill.[21] Hill sketched the history of the proposed coalition between Liberal Republicans headed by such men as Gratz Brown, Carl Schurz, and Frank Blair with the Democratic party.[22] The initiative of this movement on the Democratic side he attributed to "that great and noble man," Vallandigham, whose lifelong devotion to the Democratic party could not be questioned.[23]

The Liberal Republicans Hill represented as alarmed at the tendency in the Republican party, as exemplified in its Southern policy, "to subvert Republicanism and institute centralism in its stead." So these Liberal Republicans were willing, even anxious to co-operate with the similarly alarmed, but impotent, Democratic party. But could a common working-ground be gained? What concession was required of each side to the coalition? The Liberal Republicans, answered Hill, were willing to abandon their party, "in the zenith of its power"; while the Democracy was only called upon to recognize Reconstruction as an accomplished fact; not, be it noted, to approve it, but merely to reassure

[20] The speech is given in full in Waddell, pp. 368–83.

[21] Hill, *Life of Hill*, p. 350.

[22] Speech printed in Hill, *Life of Hill*, pp. 350–66.

[23] *Ibid.*, p. 354. Vallandigham was the "notorious copperhead," of the war period—a truly "stormy petrel" of Ohio politics. For his agency in the New Departure, see Oberholtzer, III, 4, 48.

the Liberal Republicans, who, condemning the Reconstruction policies themselves, yet feared that the process of undoing this policy might work a greater evil, in producing another revolution. "This was the only concession on earth any member of the Democratic party ever proposed to make."[24]

The Liberal Republican Convention at Cincinnati in May had extended the olive branch to the Democracy, said Hill, in effect, and had invited the co-operation of the Democracy; while the Radical party in convention at Philadelphia had thrown down the gauntlet of battle for a contest in which the issues would be "Federal bayonet supervision of state elections" and other odious policies of Radicalism. Would the Democracy fail the "gallant" men of the Liberal Republicans in their fight against "empire"?[25]

Hill then begged eloquently that the Georgia Democracy co-operate with the National party and assent to whatever policy the forthcoming Baltimore Convention of that party should adopt. He deprecated the tendency of some Democratic gentlemen to assert that they would support the party only on terms stipulated by themselves.[26] He suggested that such headstrong attitude and intolerant opinions had in the past done much hurt to the South. As

[24] Hill, *Life of Hill*, p. 352. It may be noted Hill is not entirely candid in this statement. Despite sophistry to the contrary, the Democracy had to concede something on the tariff issue (see Rhodes and Oberholtzer previously cited).

[25] Hill, *Life of Hill*, p. 355.

[26] This was a special stab at Linton Stephens, who had expressly stated he would support the party only if it put out an independent platform and nominees.

for himself, if he only consulted his prejudices and passions, he might also advocate extreme and impractical policies;[27] but his reason led him to the inevitable conclusion that the South would be best served if the Democratic party should accept the Cincinnati platform and nominees.[28]

Hill then applied himself to an apology for Horace Greeley, whom Stephens had bitterly attacked the night before. Admitting that Greeley would not have been his personal choice and that Greeley's past course had often met with his disapproval, he yet insisted that Greeley was a man of "independence and moral courage," who by his recent actions was doing much to undo or counteract previous errors; and he asserted that in his opinion any southern man could now vote for Horace Greeley without inconsistency.[29]

Moreover, Hill asserted, he was willing to support Greeley and his associates because of what they had already recently done for the South. They had secured a large measure of amnesty; they had opposed and minimized the "force bills"; and they had succeeded in strictly limiting the suspension of the writ of habeas corpus in the South.[30]

[27] His words were: "If I allow my prejudices and feelings to take possession of my judgment, I would every hour of my life pray God to spare me to the day that I could gather this whole record of Reconstruction infamy into one pile and make one grand bonfire of it" (Hill, *Life of Hill*, p. 357).

[28] The platform, among other planks, accepted Reconstruction as an "accomplished fact"; and the nominees were Greeley and Gratz Brown.

[29] Hill, *Life of Hill*, pp. 358-59.

[30] *Ibid.*, pp. 360-61.

Proceeding in the argument, Hill declared that only in agreeing to and supporting a movement which already had the support of the northern Democracy, was there any chance of success against Radicalism. Southern "ultraisms" had long embarrassed the true and lifelong Democrats of the North like Hendricks, Pendleton, Voorhees, and Seymour.[31] Let it not continue to do so. Let the South, in accepting this platform and those nominations, show the northern people "the highest possible evidence of our sincere desire to end sectional discord and have a cordial reunion." Southern support of a ticket headed by Greeley, and with such allies, would disarm northern demagogues, who could no longer maintain that the South sought to nullify all the results of the war and to restore slavery.[32]

And finally, the most important argument, said Hill: the election of Greeley, far more probable than that of a Democratic candidate on a separate ticket, would bring deliverance of the South from federal interference, and a return to the proper principles of republicanism.[33]

The New Departure came and went. Grant was overwhelmingly elected after a bitter national campaign, and whether Greeley would have realized the expectations of Hill and others remains a matter of conjecture. Georgia, however, was one of the six states in the nation casting its

[31] Hendricks was a Democratic Senator from Indiana; Pendleton, a prominent Democratic Congressman from Ohio, popularly ascribed with the authorship of the "Ohio Idea"; Voorhees, a Democratic Representative from Indiana at this time; and Seymour, a Democratic ex-governor of New York, defeated for the presidency by Grant in 1868.

[32] Hill, *Life of Hill*, p. 365.

[33] *Ibid.*, pp. 365-66.

electoral vote for the maligned *Tribune* editor.[34] Such Democrats in the South as had forced themselves "to eat boiled crow" had done so in vain.[35]

While the echoes of the New Departure acrimony were still alive in the state, speculation about the selection of a United States Senator by the Democratic Assembly, to succeed the Republican, Joshua Hill, started.[36] The election was to occur in January, 1873.[37] It seems to have been early accepted that the contest would be between Alexander Stephens, opposing the principles of the New Departure; Hill, advocating these principles; and General John B. Gordon, who had first indorsed Greeley and then pussyfooted to what was called the "Georgia Platform of 1870," a strictly Jeffersonian *pronunciamento*.[38]

As January advanced, interest in the Senatorial race became very warm throughout the state.[39] Hill, Stephens, and Gordon were all in Atlanta as the time for the election approached; and the friends of each were active in promoting the cause of their respective favorites. At the invitation of the Assembly the three leading candidates ad-

[34] Rhodes, VII, p. 61, gives the vote in the election. Grant received 272 electoral votes to 66 for Greeley.

[35] The *Nation* called Greeley "boiled crow," and it is said this gave rise to the expression to "eat crow" (see Rhodes, VII, p. 53).

[36] For Joshua Hill's election to the Senate in 1868, see Avery, p. 398; Thompson, p. 210. For Hill's difficult experience in securing admission, see Thompson, pp. 255, 267–79.

[37] *Savannah Daily Republican*, January 21, 1873; Johnston and Browne, pp. 517–18.

[38] Johnston and Browne, pp. 517–18.

[39] *Savannah Daily Advertiser*, January 17, 18, 1873; *Augusta Constitutionalist*, January 17, 19, 1873.

dressed the Assembly, Hill on the sixteenth, Gordon on the seventeenth, and Stephens on the eighteen of January.[40]

The prejudice against Hill was still running strong, and it is surprising that he should have had any hopes of election at this time.[41] He made a strong appearance before the Assembly on the night of January 16.[42] His address, in the main, proved to be an argument for a continuation of the fight against Radicalism and the contemporary "revolution" along the lines of the New Departure. Hill frankly let it be known that he proposed to continue that fight. When Gordon was subsequently elected, this led Alexander Stephens to say that, though defeated, he "had gained his main object which was to kill the New Departure in Georgia; and that he was content with the result."[43]

Hill, before the Assembly, asserted that the United States of America had experienced three revolutions: the revolution of 1776, a violent revolution; the revolution of 1787, a peaceful revolution; and the revolution begun in 1861, and still continuing, which had known both violent and peaceful stages. Some think, said Hill, of this last revolution only in terms of attempted secession, or of successful coercion, or of war and the specific Reconstruction Acts. As a matter of fact, these were mere incidents, secondary in importance and in significance to the real revolution, which was the complete overturning or "revolution" of the theory of American government—the utter subordi-

[40] *Savannah Daily Advertiser,* January 21, 1873.

[41] For adverse comment, see *Augusta Constitutionalist,* January 17, 19, 1873.

[42] Printed in Hill, *Life of Hill,* pp. 378-98.

[43] Johnston and Browne, p. 518.

nation and even threatened annihilation of state governments, leaving the federal government with absolute and unlimited powers.[44]

This, the true and significant revolution, had been begun, and in part accomplished, under the guise of necessity in war and the same necessity in preserving the fruits of the war. But there was no evidence that its perpetrators contemplated concluding it, now that peace had come and Reconstruction had been accomplished. On the contrary, the Republican party were demonstrating by their highhanded course in Louisiana, Mississippi, and South Carolina a determination to continue and extend "the revolution."[45]

Hill reminded the Assembly (of which reminder there was probably no need) that he had warned the people of Georgia as early as December, 1870, of the inevitable and sinister course the revolution was taking; but he was only misunderstood and traduced for his pains at the time.

But now, the course of "the revolution" being appreciated of all men, he would address himself to "the remedy." This remedy, he maintained, is not the Bourbon policy of denying the existence or validity of the war amendments, but will be found in applying the only true Constitutional construction to the interpretation of these

[44] For an expression of these same views in 1870, see above, pp. 206 ff.

[45] The most accessible and satisfactory general account of the events referred to in these states is found in Rhodes, VII, 99, 168–77, 155–61, 206–25. There are, of course, separate monographs dealing with Reconstruction in each state, of which James W. Garner, *Reconstruction in Mississippi* (New York, 1901), is the best. The others are: John R. Ficklen, *Reconstruction in Louisiana* (Baltimore, 1910); John S. Reynolds, *Reconstruction in South Carolina* (Columbia, South Carolina, 1905).

amendments, namely, that while prohibiting certain discriminatory acts to the states legislatures, they do not, at the same time, surrender the whole control and jurisdiction over local affairs to the federal government. He explained:

> I hold that the Fourteenth Amendment has not changed the right of the State to regulate its civil affairs, save only to qualify its exercise by saying you must not discriminate on account of color. I hold that the Fifteenth Amendment has not affected the right of the States on the subject of suffrage, except that in exercising the power they always had, they must not make a discrimination on account of color.[46]

And what a vastly different construction is this, Hill maintained, to that of the Grant party, who hold that the federal government is one of unlimited powers by virtue of these amendments, in the areas of local affairs dealt with by the amendments, and would therefore reduce the states to "mere provinces or proconsulates."

Greeley is then quoted to show that the New Departure, recently defeated, had been based on Hill's enunciated principles and on the mode of interpreting the amendments which he had suggested.[47] He then directed his argument to establish that only along lines of the New Departure could an end be put to the dangerous and subversive revolution still in process. He remonstrated with his so-called "Straight" friends and critics that in the pursuit of an ideal theory, like that of Calhoun, or of Jefferson, or of Clay, or of Webster, they not make the mistake of refusing to co-operate in achieving a clearly discerned goal, common to all these theories.

Hill, in this speech, also took occasion to bespeak con-

[46] Hill, *Life of Hill*, p. 389. [47] *Ibid.*, p. 389.

structive activity on the part of the Assembly, regarding the new educational, industrial, and commercial problems facing the state and the South, and admonished them that in prosecuting these new problems they could afford to allow war and Reconstruction passions and issues to die.[48]

Hill's speech elicited both praise and deprecation,[49] but it is not probable that it won him many votes in the Assembly. The election was hotly contested, the Assembly in joint session requiring seven ballots to reach a majority decision. Gordon and Stephens led from the first, and Hill came third, never registering more than thirty-five votes. On the seventh ballot, with "everybody at fever heat," Gordon polled a majority and was declared elected.[50]

Despite his political unpopularity, Hill was offered, if we may accept his own statement made to a correspondent of an Augusta paper, the position of chief justice of the Georgia Supreme Court, in February, 1873, by Governor James M. Smith, whom he had previously indorsed.[51] But he declined the position and went about the work of political recuperation.[52]

[48] These problems had been the subject of an address before the Alumni Society of the University of Georgia in July, 1871 (*supra*, p. 240).

[49] The Bourbon press, represented by the *Augusta Constitutionalist*, said the speech was "not considered as equal to his best efforts of argument and declamation," and otherwise depreciated it (see issue of January 17, 1873).

[50] *Savannah Daily Republican*, January 21, 1873, gives the details of the balloting (as does Avery, pp. 505-6) in a graphic account.

[51] Indorsement in *Savannah Morning News*, December 25, 1871.

[52] *Augusta Constitutionalist*, February 12, 1873, carries quite a story regarding this proffer to Hill and thinks the offer indicates an embarrassing paucity of available material.

In March, 1873, Hill made a forceful argument before Judge Erskine, a circuit federal judge sitting in Atlanta, regarding the right of the individual states to prescribe the qualifications for jurors, and the obligation resting on federal courts to accept only persons so qualified for jury service.[53] The speech was popularly designated as the speech on "The Purity of the Jury System,"[54] and it seems to usher in the barely perceptible turning-point in Hill's political fortunes. Even Bourbon newspapers praised the speech and the author for making it.[55]

As for the speech itself, it was in Hill's accustomed vein of close constitutional reasoning, and again reveals his profound knowledge of English and American constitutional law and history. His own summary of the argument may be utilized:

If, may it please your Honor, I have been fortunate in making myself understood, I have established by the argument the following propositions:

1. That it is neither unusual, nor unnatural, nor unwise, that the government of the Union should trust, confide in, and lean upon the government of the respective States in executing its functions in those States.

2. That from the beginning until now, the government of the Union has always left with the States, the exclusive legislation for the qualifications of jurors, as also did the Constitution itself the legislation for the qualification of voters.

3. That the acts of Congress now in force, expressly require the United States Courts, sitting in the respective States to empanel their juries exclusively of persons qualified as jurors by the laws of the States.

[53] Printed in Hill, *Life of Hill*, pp. 367-77.

[54] *Augusta Constitutionalist*, March 22, 1873.

[55] *Ibid.* Editor James Gardner had not said a kind word about Hill in two years, before this occasion.

POLITICAL PROSCRIPTION

4. That the order under review ignores and disregards these laws, and brings into this court persons to serve as jurors who have not been qualified as such by the laws of this State, and is therefore in contravention of the laws of the United States.[56]

Some months later the *Constitutionalist*, Hill's bitterest critic since 1870, is editorially defending him against certain disparaging remarks of a Savannah journal. The editor, after remarking on past differences, confesses that he regards Hill as "the most eloquent orator in the whole country, and one of the most gifted statesmen of the South." He further expressed the opinion that Hill could not long enact Achilles, but must soon be back in the arena of politics, and that the Democracy of Georgia would gladly welcome him back to the "true fold."[57] Such comment indicated that the clouds of political proscription were lifting just a little.

In 1874 Hill continued slowly to regain favor from that portion of the Democracy, alienated from him since 1870. During this year he was reconciled with Toombs. The occasion of the reconciliation was a dinner given to Zeb Vance, the stormy war governor of North Carolina, who was in Atlanta on a speaking trip. The press of the day carried a colorful account of the dinner and of the pleasantries which passed between Hill and Toombs.[58] During

[56] Hill, however, evidently had not succeeded in making himself "understood," as the court failed to sustain his position, thereby meeting "the just reprobation of the legal profession in Georgia," says the *Augusta Constitutionalist*, March 22, 1871.

[57] August 8, 1873.

[58] A long account of this dinner was written for the press by "one present." It appeared originally in the *Atlanta Herald*, from which it was reproduced in the *Augusta Chronicle and Sentinel*, August 14, 1874.

the evening Hill was called on for a speech and, after first declining, made a speech in which he reviewed the whole course of his own actions in 1870. At its conclusion, Toombs is quoted as saying: "I did think, Ben, you had gone and turned rascal, but now I see you were right."[59]

In the summer of 1874 the South became greatly agitated over the new Civil Rights bill, which had been passed by the Senate as a "sort of memorial" to the recently deceased Charles Sumner.[60] The intent of the bill, among other things, was to secure equal rights to negroes in public conveyances, inns, and places of entertainment.[61] Hill was represented by a northern newspaper correspondent as saying that the South looked to Grant for succor from this new blow, which would "disorganize southern society"; and that the South was willing to make Grant president for a third term if he would veto the bill. "We will be too grateful to parley about the traditions of the Republic, or the fear of a monarchy," Hill was quoted as having said.[62] The publication of this interview drew from Hill a speech in Athens, saying that Mr. Redfield had "misunderstood or misrepresented" him; that he would not favor Grant for a

[59] This quotation occurs in the *Herald* article. I have also personally heard accounts of this dinner from two persons who were present, Messrs. H. H. Cabaniss and D. M. Bain of Atlanta (conversation, April 2, 1926).

[60] The phrase is Rhodes' (VII, 154).

[61] Rhodes, VII, p. 154. Joe Brown wrote a long letter opposing the Civil Rights bill, as really a *social* rights bill. Brown urges the defeat of the Republicans in the fall elections to defeat this bill. He has been a Democrat since 1872. Brown's letter is found in the *Gainesville Eagle* (Georgia), September 11, 1874, in *Brown Scrap Books*.

[62] The correspondent was H. V. Redfield, writing for *Cincinnati Commercial*, July 21, 1874 (*Brown Scrap Books*).

POLITICAL PROSCRIPTION

third time, even if he should veto the proposed bill.[63] As is well known, the Civil Rights Act became law in 1875, but its salient clauses were all eventually ruled unconstitutional.[64]

Hill participated aggressively in the political campaign of the autumn of 1874 in Georgia, stumping several Congressional districts for the Democratic candidate. He especially labored in the Second District in southwest Georgia, where a Radical Congressman had held on since 1867. "If Whitely is beaten and the district [Second District] redeemed from Radical control," said the editor of the *Sentinel and Chronicle*, "this glorious result will be principally due to the exertions of Mr. Hill."[65] The editor further voiced a wish, which was becoming audible throughout the state, that "Hill were in Congress to make one speech on the Louisiana usurpation."[66]

On the twenty-sixth of this same month, October, Hill showed the Augusta editor how he could speak on the "Louisiana usurpation," for on that day in Augusta he delivered a flaming attack on Grant's course in Louisiana in maintaining the Kellogg state government by use of the military forces of the United States.[67] The ovation extended Hill on this occasion, which included a serenade at

[63] *Augusta Chronicle and Sentinel*, August 7, 1874.

[64] Rhodes, VII, 154.

[65] Whitely was beaten by the Democrat (see Avery, p. 511).

[66] October 3, 1874.

[67] For the McEvery-Kellogg imbroglio in Louisiana, see Rhodes, VII, 173–80; also Oberholtzer, pp. 233–39. Grant's proclamation affecting Louisiana of September, 1874, which especially outraged southern whites, is found in Richardson, VII, 309.

his hotel, after the speech, indicated that he was rapidly regaining popularity.[68]

After the Congressional elections in November, the *Newnan Herald* inquired rather sarcastically if it were not time that the Democratic press began abusing Ben Hill again, since "there will be no further need of him until 1876." An Augusta editor, in commenting on this sarcasm, agrees that there is much truth in its implications that Hill had always been used when there was work to do and then "dismissed not only without thanks, but with reproaches." For the recent Democratic successes in the state, said this commentator, Hill deserves more credit than any other man, and he is "entitled to the thanks and gratitude of the people of Georgia."[69]

Early in 1874, petitions began to come in to Hill that he stand for Congress from the Ninth District. At the time he was living in Athens in the Ninth District, though he had bought a house in Atlanta which was in another Congressional district; and of course his profession often detained him in Atlanta.[70] There was some local opposition to Hill's candidacy on this account, which, for the most part, was stimulated by other candidates in the District.[71]

[68] *Augusta Chronicle and Sentinel*, October 27, 1874, contains a synopsis of Hill's speech and a graphic account of the occasion.

[69] The editorial comment of the *Newnan Herald* is reproduced in the *Augusta Chronicle and Sentinel*, December 9, 1874. The comment on the *Herald's* sarcasm is that of the *Chronicle and Sentinel* editor in the same issue.

[70] Hill, *Life of Hill*, p. 65. Conversation with Hill's granddaughter, Mrs. Caroline H. McConnell.

[71] This opposition was especially voiced in the *Gainesville Eagle*, edited by a Congressional aspirant himself. See excerpts of this criticism in *Augusta Chronicle and Sentinel*, March 10, 1874.

POLITICAL PROSCRIPTION

At first there was some uneasiness in the Democratic press, as the demands that Hill stand for Congress increased, lest he should elect to stand as an Independent.[72] Hill soon put a stop to these fears, issuing a statement which was taken to mean he would not "stand" except as the nominee of the regular party convention.[73] The Democratic press then, for the most part, wished him success, the common opinion being that the "South stands sadly in need of his services on the floor of Congress."[74]

However, when the Ninth District Convention was held at Gainesville in August, it nominated Hon. Garnett McMillan on the forty-seventh ballot, Hill's name being withdrawn after the forty-sixth ballot.[75] There is good evidence that Hill was deeply disappointed at this outcome.[76] He had been beaten by Gordon for the Senate and by McMillan for the House. It seemed his talents were not to be employed in office for his state and section.[77]

But Garnett McMillan died in the following January, before taking his seat, and another opportunity opened up. Again there was a widespread indorsement of Hill as suc-

[72] *Ibid.*, February 26, 1874.

[73] In the *Athens Watchman*, reproduced in *Augusta Chronicle and Sentinel*, April 14, 1874.

[74] *Ibid.*

[75] In the *Athens Watchman*, reproduced in *Augusta Chronicle and Sentinel*, August 22, 1874.

[76] Henry W. Grady, writing in the *Atlanta Constitution*, August 17, 1882, gives this evidence.

[77] Hill had not held office since 1865, when he was Confederate States Senator. Indeed, most of his significant career until this time had been as a leader of minorities, out of political office.

cessor to McMillan.⁷⁸ Being invited to address the General Assembly at this time, Hill on January 20, 1875, increased the favorable sentiment that was setting in for him and demanding that the South have the benefit of his services in Congress.⁷⁹

Hill's friends were quite active as the second Democratic Convention of the Ninth District came together in April, 1875, to nominate a successor to Mr. McMillan. The Convention proved a record-breaker for a Congressional-district affair. It sat for eight days, casting more than four hundred ballots without a nomination. The fight was Hill against the field.⁸⁰ After vain endeavors to break the two-thirds rule, which Hill's "28" supporters would not consent to do, the opposition, which at the same time was the majority of the Convention, "recommended" Colonel J. B. Estes as the candidate and adjourned *sine die*.⁸¹

Hill's friends united in writing a public letter requesting that he take the stump as the real choice of the District, and arguing that he had been defeated by unfair tactics and that the unprecedented and unwarranted action of a

---

⁷⁸ *Augusta Chronicle and Sentinel*, January 24, 1875, quoted such indorsements and again adds its own; see also the issue for January 29 for same evidence.

⁷⁹ The speech is printed in Hill, *Life of Hill*, pp. 415-31. It was largely concerned with Constitutional problems growing out of the Louisiana situation. For favorable comment on it, see *Atlanta Constitution*, January 21, 22, and *Augusta Chronicle and Sentinel*, January 29, 1875.

⁸⁰ The Convention sat from April 14 to 22. *Augusta Chronicle and Sentinel* for these dates records the daily progress of the balloting and maneuvering.

⁸¹ *Ibid.*, April 24, 1875.

part of the Convention in presuming to "recommend" a candidate was manifestly of no force and not binding on the Democracy of the District.[82] In the meanwhile, Hill in Atlanta had been so crushed at the failure to nominate him on the first ballot in Gainesville that in the first moments of his disappointment he had said to Henry W. Grady: "I shall at once withdraw my name and never again allow it to go before the people."[83]

Other counsels prevailed. He took the stump in the Ninth District and easily outgeneraled his two rivals, Judge Estes, running as the "recommended" candidate, and Colonel W. P. Price, running as an avowed Independent. There was talk of collusion between Price, Estes, and the Republican candidate, Colonel J. B. Finley, who had withdrawn before the election. But the election on May 5 resulted in a large majority for Hill over both Price and Estes.[84]

In Atlanta, there seems to have been quite a celebration when it was known that Hill was elected to Congress. The opinion was commonly expressed that the South had at last sent a man to Congress competent to face her traducers and protect her interests.[85] Hill was asked to address an assembly of his friends at a sort of political jubilee in his honor. He did so on May 12, 1875, in a glowing

[82] Published in *Augusta Chronicle and Sentinel*, April 23, 1875.

[83] *Atlanta Constitution*, August 17, 1882.

[84] *Augusta Chronicle and Sentinel*, May 5, 6, 9, 11, 1875, carries the story of the election; the official vote: Hill, 6,381, Estes, 3,021, Price, 1,267, is given in the same paper of May 18, 1875.

[85] *Augusta Constitutionalist*, July 3, 1875.

speech in which he undertook to interpret the meaning of his recent election and to review once again grave problems facing the state and nation, which he had so often discussed. In this speech he pledged himself anew to the service of the Union and the Constitution.[86] The period of his political proscription was ended.

[86] Speech found in Hill, *Life of Hill*, pp. 432-41.

CHAPTER XIII

IN THE HOUSE—SOUTHERN CHAMPION

Hill's election to the Forty-fourth Congress, the first Democratic Congress since the Civil War, became the topic of editorial comment from all parts of the country.[1] The event at once was invested with peculiar significance. Hill had attracted nation-wide attention in his bold policies since the war, first in opposing the acceptance of Congressional Reconstruction, and then, when that became an accomplished fact and was recognized by Hill as such, in urging the South to unite on a new basis with the Liberal Republicans against the Radical administration of Grant.

It seems to have been rather generally accepted that Hill went to Congress, not as a mere representative of the Ninth District of Georgia, or indeed as a mere representative of Georgia itself, but as the "prospective champion of the South." And it was freely said that he would be the peer of any man in either house of Congress as an orator and debater.[2]

The Democratic press for the most part expressed it-

[1] *Augusta Constitutionalist*, July 3, 1875, quoting *Louisville Courier Journal;* and the same paper *(Augusta Constitutionalist)*, September 26, 1875, quoting the *Washington Chronicle*. The *Atlanta Constitution* for the months following the election is full of such evidence. See issues of May 8, 9, 11, 1875.

[2] F. H. Alfriend in *Louisville Courier Journal* reproduced in *Augusta Constitutionalist*, July 3, 1875. Also, Reed, "Reminiscences of Ben Hill," *South Atlantic Quarterly*, V (April, 1906), 145. Mr. Reed was a contemporary of Hill's, a writer, student, and amateur historian. See also testimony of *Columbus Times*, January 19, 1876.

self favorably; but there was not lacking a note of challenge and animosity in some of the Radical journals. For example, one Washington editor challenged Hill and other rebels, in a very sarcastic article, to come on up to Washington and prove that the people of the North were the "true rebels." A southern editor, in replying to this challenge, remarked that Hill would "come right along" and would probably disappoint extremists in "not tearing passion to tatters," while at the same time he would resurrect some salutary constitutional truths.[3]

Hill took his seat in the Forty-fourth Congress in December, 1875; and his leadership and prestige was at once recognized in his appointment to the powerful and important Committee of Ways and Means, a most unusual appointment for a man serving his first term in Congress.[4] He did not pitch into the Radicals at once, as his enemies had anticipated and as some of his friends had feared he would do. He pursued a moderate and co-operative course with northern Democrats, usually maintaining his views on Constitutional questions and on southern rights with force and restraint.[5] He easily established himself as the equal of any experienced debater on the floor of the House.

Hill's great opportunity, however, came rather early in the session, when James G. Blaine on January 10, 1876, in

[3] *Washington Chronicle,* quoted and answered by *Augusta Constitutionalist,* September 26, 1875.

[4] *Cong. Rec.,* 44 C., 1 S., p. 250. He was also appointed as one of the three regents for the Smithsonian Institute, *ibid.,* p. 216.

[5] These views are based on a reading of the Congressional Record for the first session of the Forty-fourth Congress. Also see an expression of his moderate course to be adopted by the Democracy, in *Columbus Sun and Times,* January 4, 1876.

IN THE HOUSE—SOUTHERN CHAMPION

speaking to H. R. No. 214, "to remove the disabilities imposed by the third section of the 14th Article of the Amendments to the Constitution of the United States,"[6] took occasion to deliver an intemperate and venomous attack on Jefferson Davis for his alleged responsibility for the so-called horrors of the Confederate war prison at Andersonville, Georgia.[7] It seems to have been generally admitted that Blaine's attack was a political maneuver in the approaching presidential campaign[8] and was designed, in the words of Garfield's most recent biographer, "to revive sectional feeling, and more especially to goad the southern brigadiers into language that should disclose their secessionist sympathies."[9]

Blaine, then, waved the "bloody shirt"; and whatever opinion may be entertained as to the statesmanship of this

---

[6] *Cong. Rec.*, 44 C., 1 S., p. 345.

[7] The "Andersonville atrocities" had long been the source of crimination and recrimination. It will be recalled that the Confederate officer, Captain Henry Wirz, commander at the Andersonville prison, had been executed in the first frenzy following the assassination of Lincoln (see Oberholtzer, I, 19–20). Many Federal prisoners had died at Andersonville in the last year of the war, due to a lack of medicines, which the whole South shared, due to the blockade of the coast. For a treatment of the Andersonville subject from a southern viewpoint, see Stephens, II, 501–10; from the moderate northern view, see James K. Hosmer, *Outcome of the Civil War*, pp. 240–48. Rhodes devotes a whole chapter in his fifth volume (chap. xxix) to the subject, succeeding in clarifying the admittedly "difficult" subject very little. Of course, there is, for a detailed study of the question, the famous Report No. 45, of the Committee of the House of Representatives on the "Treatment of Prisoners of War by Rebel Authorities," submitted in 1869, in a thoroughly *ex parte* spirit.

[8] Edward Stanwood, *James Gillespie Blaine*, p. 135.

[9] Theodore C. Smith, *Life and Letters of James Abram Garfield*, I, 593.

device,[10] it drew from Ben Hill a reply which could only have disappointed Blaine because of its force and effectiveness.

Blaine, in opposing amnesty for Jefferson Davis, had used the following language:

> I now assert deliberately before God, as my judge, knowing the full measure and import of my words that the cruelties of the Duke of Alva in the Low Countries, the massacre of St. Bartholomew, and the screws and tortures of the Spanish Inquisition did not approach in cruelty the atrocity of Andersonville."[11]

And for all this Jefferson Davis was represented as directly responsible.

Whether Hill should have taken up this gratuitous slur and challenge of Blaine long remained a subject of editorial debate in the South and the nation.[12] There is much to be said on both sides. Here was uttered, flung in his very face, a libelous calumny against Hill's former chief; and there is some evidence that Blaine, in staging his denunciation, singled out Hill, the former champion of Davis, from the Democratic representatives, and tossed the slur, as it were, directly at him, expecting to prod him into utterances which would damage the Democratic cause in the coming election.[13]

As Blaine spoke, uttering what was to Hill calumny after calumny, and baiting southern loyalists with as much

---

[10] Even Blaine's kinsman and biographer says: "The political expediency of his course, and the usefulness of the object which he had in view, are open to doubt" (Stanwood, p. 135).

[11] *Cong. Rec.*, 44 C., 1 S., p. 324.

[12] See below, pp. 280 ff.

[13] Hill, *Life of Hill*, p. 68.

IN THE HOUSE—SOUTHERN CHAMPION

invective as he could summon, Hill was visibly affected.[14] Radicals had grown accustomed to slandering southern leaders and the southern people, and no southern man or northern apologist had yet risen to answer them back. Hill well knew that he was regarded, whether correctly or not, as a sort of champion of the southern people. Also he knew that on this subject he was reasonably well informed, having been close to the Davis administration, and that Blaine lied in his throat, as he talked, whether from ignorance or malice.[15] Every instinct in his being summoned him to reply and disprove the Republican leader's slanders. On the other hand, there was the question of expediency to be considered. In defending the southern cause, the defeated Confederacy, on the very eve of a national election, would he not play into the hands of the Radicals, enabling them to focus attention on the eternal "southern question" and so avoid the embarrassing issues of political corruption that Grant's administration was steadily revealing.[16]

When Blaine concluded his remarks, Hill endeavored to get the floor to reply, but Representatives Cox of New York and Kelley of Pennsylvania received earlier recognition from the speaker. Each made short replies to Blaine, without attempting to cover the subject of his charges, as neither was competent to do.[17] Hill secured the floor just

[14] Statement of Mr. Sam Small, Hill's private secretary at the time, in conversation with the writer, April 2, 1927.

[15] For Hill's relations to Davis, see above, chaps. vi and vii.

[16] For the notorious corruption of the Grant administration, which greatly embarrassed the Republicans in the election of 1876, see Rhodes, VII, 65–109, 247–70; Oberholtzer, III, 69–89, 129–83.

[17] *Cong. Rec.*, 44 C., 1 S., pp. 328–29, 329–30.

before a motion to adjourn was carried, leaving him the opening hour on the morrow.[18]

The narrative of what follows, of the preparation for his famous reply to Blaine on January 11, which earned for him a national reputation, has been provided the writer by Mr. Sam Small, who at that time was a young man serving as secretary to Hill.[19] On entering his office after leaving the House, Mr. Small says, Hill was visibly excited, clinching his fists, and continually repeating: "If I only had the facts and figures in my possession which I know to exist, I would eat him up." Mr. Small inquired of him, "What facts?" Hill replied by enumerating the main heads of Blaine's attack. Small asked him when he would have to have the facts. Hill replied, "By tomorrow." Small then astonished Hill by saying that if he, Hill, would give him a note to Mr. Ainsworth R. Spofford, the Congressional Librarian, that he, Small, would deliver the facts and figures into Hill's hands by ten o'clock the next morning.

The consequence was that Small hired two stenographers, secured the assistance of the night watchman "for five dollars," gained access, with his working force, to the Library in the early evening, and at seven o'clock the next morning, after a continuous all-night session, had completed an abstract of the facts and data which went into Hill's famous reply to Blaine. At ten o'clock when Hill reached his office, he received this abstract; and on the same day

[18] *Ibid.*, p. 330.

[19] In conversation, April 2, 1927, with Mr. Small, at present an active and widely known newspaper writer of Atlanta and Washington.

IN THE HOUSE—SOUTHERN CHAMPION

delivered the speech which made him, for the time, the most talked-of man in Congressional circles.[20]

Despite some protestations from colleagues who feared the expediency of answering Blaine at this time, Hill had determined to make a reply; and in a very dramatic setting began his defense of Davis and the South on January 11.[21] Soon he had chained the attention of the House and was producing various emotions in its membership—relief and admiration among his Democratic colleagues, and uneasiness and "sheer wonder" among the Republicans.[22]

He began his reply to Blaine by remonstrating that he called the House to witness that "nothing could have been farther from the desires and purposes of those who with me, represent immediately the section of country which on yesterday was put on trial, than to reopen this discussion of the events of our unhappy past." However, "the gentleman from Maine," the acknowledged leader of the Republican party on this floor, had maliciously and gratuitously forced the discussion.[23]

[20] Anyone who knows Mr. Small will not confuse this first-hand recital of facts with that dubious historical source called "old men's recollections." Since there are doubtless many who do not know this alert, vigorous, and active gentleman, he or his friends will know how to pardon this explanation.

[21] Henry W. Grady in the *Atlanta Constitution*, January 13, 1876, gives an account of the speech, its setting and accompaniments, received from "one who was present." Also see article in *Augusta Chronicle and Sentinel*, quoted in Hill, *Life of Hill*, pp. 69-71.

[22] *Ibid.*

[23] The Blaine-Hill amnesty debate is found in the *Cong. Rec.*, 44 C., 1 S., pp. 345-51, 385-89, 404-8. Hill's main speech in reply to Blaine is printed in Hill, *Life of Hill*, pp. 440-62. The speech was printed as it ap-

The gentleman had made certain grave charges against Mr. Jefferson Davis, who, Hill is sure, requires no eulogy from himself, and whom, moreover, no censure from the "gentleman from Maine" could damage, nor any act or resolution of the House affect. But Hill had waited, certainly expecting, in view of the "high reputation of the gentleman from Maine," that he would substantiate such grave charges, deliberately made. And what was his "amazement," he said, to observe that the gentleman merely introduced in evidence a notoriously *ex parte* report of a House committee, made at a time when "passions were at their height" and when the party accused was deprived of the elementary "Anglo-Saxon right" of being heard in his own defense.

Hill then addressed himself to exposing the character of the famous report No. 45, which had stigmatized the Andersonville prison as a "den of horrors" and, without citing any definite proof, had incriminated Jefferson Davis in connection with the prison. He showed, among other things, that a very material document, a report of the Confederate prison physician, Dr. Jones, to the Confederate authorities, had been mutilated and otherwise made to suit the committee's purposes, and that Dr. Jones, himself, before the committee had protested that the report could not be made to bear the construction which the committee put upon it.[24]

He showed further that Captain Henry Wirz, the Con-

---

pears in the *Record*. I have personally compared the two, and there is no difference. For purposes of convenience, I am making citations to the copy in Hill, *Life of Hill*. The speech was also rather fully reported in the Georgia press of the time; see *Columbus Times*, January 13, 14, 15, 18, 1876.

[24] Hill, *Life of Hill*, pp. 444–45.

federate officer who had been executed because of his connection with the Andersonville prison,[25] had been offered commutation of his sentence if he would implicate Jefferson Davis. But on the very day of his execution, Wirz had said: "Mr. Schade, you know that I have always told you that I do not know anything about Jefferson Davis.[26] He had no connection with me as to what was done at Andersonville. I would not become a traitor against him or any one else even to save my life."[27] And yet what this unhappy officer would not allege to save his life, charged Hill, the "gentleman from Maine says to the country to keep himself and his party in power."[28]

But Hill would advance to the question of the "real facts about Andersonville." It would require too much space to follow the course of his entire argument, with its closely massed facts and figures, gathered by Mr. Small from the record, or to comment on the close reasoning with which he established conclusions from the facts. The contemporary testimony is beyond cavil, that his speech was powerful and irresistibly carried conviction to his auditors, Democratic and Republican.[29]

[25] See footnote 7, this chapter.

[26] Schade was counsel for Wirz, and made the report quoted by Hill. He was a northern and a Union man, according to Hill; and his report had never been contradicted.

[27] Hill, *Life of Hill*, p. 446. [28] *Ibid*.

[29] A mass of contemporary newspaper comment could be cited to substantiate this statement. Some of it will appear later (*infra.*, pp. 280 f.). In Hill, *Life of Hill*, pp. 69–71, is printed an article from the *Augusta Chronicle and Sentinel*, containing quotations from many of Hill's auditors, all sustantiating the statement in the text. Also see a long article, to the same effect in the *Chicago Times*, copied in *Augusta Constitutionalist*, January 16, 1876.

Hill established by evidence from northern sources, not only that the Federal prisoners at Andersonville were issued the same rations and other supplies that Confederate soldiers received, but that they were allowed to purchase outside articles with their own money, which, on account of its appreciated value, gave them a great advantage over southern soldiers. As for medicines, for lack of which many died, the Federal blockade of the southern coast had produced that situation, he said; and moreover, the lack also caused untold suffering among southern soldiers and non-combatants. There simply were no medicines. And surely the Confederate government or the southern people could not be held responsible for what was the direct result of the stringent war measures of the Federal government.

But he would show more. He then "regretfully" reviewed conditions in the northern prisons; and on the evidence of a Federal surgeon at the Elmira prison in New York State, which was published in the *New York World*, proved that the mortality among Confederate prisoners at Elmira was as great as among Federal prisoners at Andersonville.[30] He then produced the most startling facts of his entire speech, which did much to put an end to the loose and irresponsible talk about Andersonville "horrors" and similar representations, which had been a stock in trade for many Radicals.[31] Using the report of Secretary of War Stanton of July 19, 1866, he showed that of Federal prisoners of war in Confederate hands, 22,576 had died, while of Confederate prisoners in Federal hands, 26,436 had died; and from another report, of Surgeon General Barnes,

[30] Hill, *Life of Hill*, p. 449.   [31] *Columbus Times*, January 19, 1876.

IN THE HOUSE—SOUTHERN CHAMPION 275

he established that there had been approximately 500,000 more Federal prisoners than Confederate.[32] Hence the mortality in northern prisons had far exceeded that in the South, the proof of which was derivable from Federal official reports; and despite all of the gentleman from Maine's "researches into the Massacre of St. Batholomew and the Spanish Inquisition," he had not ascertained this simple fact from the archives of his own government.

But Hill would not stop here. He would establish the responsibility for the mortality at Andersonville, and it would be found not to rest on Jefferson Davis, the Confederate government, or the southern people. He then reviewed the history of the exchange of prisoners. In 1863 the Federal government had interrupted the existing cartel of exchange and refused to continue the policy of exchange. Desperate efforts were vainly made by the Confederate government to renew the cartel of exchange. Finally the Federal prisoners in the South themselves appealed to their government in resolutions begging for exchange. One of the resolutions, among the others which Hill read, states:

Resolved: That while allowing the Confederate authorities all due praise for the attentions paid to our prisoners, numbers of our men are daily consigned to early graves . . . . and this is not caused intentionally by the Confederate Government, but by the force of circumstances.[33]

But the Federal government was relentless. Knowing the straitened circumstances of the South, which must inevitably entail deprivation on Federal prisoners; having refused overtures for an exchange of prisoners man for

[32] Hill, *Life of Hill*, p. 450.
[33] *Ibid.*, p. 455.

man; and finally, in an offer made by the South, in the "name of Humanity" on any conditions; having refused, though begged by the Confederate government to do so, "to send surgeons of their own army to accompany their prisoners in the South, with full license and liberty to carry food, medicine and raiment, and every comfort that the prisoners might need," the Federal government now turned a deaf ear to the "touching appeal" of its own "heroes."[34]

And why? Hill would answer out of the mouths of their own high officials. He then cited official reports and other testimony to prove that Grant and Stanton had opposed the exchange of prisoners as a "bad military policy" under the existing circumstances. Here, then, was found the responsibility for the "unnamed graves," not only at Andersonville, but in many prisons, North and South. But, Hill asserted, he was not interested in inculpating others. As a matter of fact, the cruelty of war itself had been explanation enough for this and many other unhappy events of the past. But slander of the South and of Davis must stop.

Hill did not doubt, he said, that he was "the bearer of an unwelcome message to the gentleman from Maine and his party." But the honor of the South, and even common fairness and decency, demanded that a stop once and for all be put to gratuitous slurs on a patriotic people. He would put gentlemen on notice that hereafter slanderous assertions against his section and his people must be accompanied by proof or else he would brand them with the infamy they so richly deserved.

He then went on to deprecate in a restored Union such controversies as Blaine had forced upon the House; he

[34] *Ibid.*, p. 457.

IN THE HOUSE—SOUTHERN CHAMPION 277

begged that passions of war be allowed to die; he said it was "unworthy of statesmanship" to put obstacles in the way of pacification. He assured the House and the country, speaking for his section, that it cherished no revenge, harbored no enmity, and wished but to co-operate in the common service of a common country.

But there was a hint of iron in this earnest message of fraternity. The South, warned Hill, did not propose again to be jockeyed out of its true position, to be deprived again of the blessings of the Constitution and the Union:

> Sir, my message is this: There are no Confederates in this house; there are no Confederates anywhere; there are no Confederate schemes, ambitions, hopes, desires, or purposes here. But the South is here and here she proposes to remain. . . . . We are here: we are in the house of our fathers, our brothers are our companions, and we are at home to stay, thank God![35]

Hill concluded his speech with an earnest appeal to the Republican party for amity and a common service of the country:

> We ask you, gentlemen of the Republican party, to rise above all your animosities. Forget your own sins. Let us unite to repair the evils that distract and oppress the country. Let us turn our backs upon the past, and let it be said in the future that he shall be the greatest patriot, the truest patriot, the noblest patriot, who shall do most to repair the wrongs of the past, and promote the glories of the future.[36]

On the next day, January 12, James A. Garfield entered the debate, replying to Hill's reply to Blaine.[37] To some

---

[35] *Ibid.*, p. 459.   [36] *Ibid.*, p. 460.

[37] Garfield's reply is found in *Cong. Rec.*, 44 C., 1 S., pp. 382–89; it is also reproduced with other material affecting the debate, in Hinsdale (ed.), *Works of Garfield*, II, 218–45.

extent Garfield supported Blaine, but he spoke without the bitterness displayed by the latter. Garfield was determined, so he wrote, "to keep my temper under control and do two things. First show a kind and magnanimous spirit toward the South, and second to crush the speech of Hill."[38] In the opinion of the writer, after a careful reading of the speech, Garfield failed to accomplish his second purpose. On the next day Mr. Blaine replied to Hill, attempting, for partisan purposes, to translate Hill's speech into an attack on the North, but leaving unanswered "the weighty facts and strong arguments" which constituted the bulk of the speech.[39]

Respecting the true view of this unfortunate controversy, which all the evidence tends to show was prolonged by the Republicans for purely "party purposes,"[40] the conclusion of Mr. James K. Hosmer may be cited as the probable judicial verdict of the historian: "The statistics show no reason why the North should reproach the South. . . . . Certain it is that no deliberate intention existed in Richmond or Washington to inflict suffering on captives more than inevitably accompanied the confinement."[41]

Whatever the propriety or wisdom of Hill's participation in this debate, there can be no question, as one of his hostile critics expressed it, that he had gone to the front "at

[38] Smith, I, 594-95.

[39] *Columbus Times,* January 15, 1876, contains a review of the debate from the southern view, appraising the rôles of Hill, Blaine, Cox and Garfield.

[40] The biographers of both Blaine and Garfield admit that they were acting in a purely party spirit. For Blaine, see Stanwood, pp. 134-35; for Garfield, see Smith, I, 594-95.

[41] *Outcome of the Civil War,* pp. 247-48.

a stride."[42] And perhaps the most significant thing about the speech was that it marked Hill as the spokesman, the champion of his section.[43] The reaction in the country to Hill's acceptance of Blaine's challenge, and his stout reply, was of three kinds: some damned him; some praised his argument and execution, but doubted its expediency; and some saw in it an unadulterated triumph for Hill, the South, and justice.

The Radical press, mostly of the North, and a very few Democratic journals at the North were indignant and expressed very ungentle sentiments. The burden of the Radical criticism seemed to be the remarkable charge, considering the circumstances of the debate, that he had re-opened "the bloody chasm"; while the hostile Democratic press charged that he had fallen into Blaine's "trap."[44] Among the hostile criticisms the following is a fair sample:

Ben Hill, the living embodiment of Morton's bloody shirt, is the ablest Republican politician in the 44th Congress. Although elected a Democrat from the Atlanta (Georgia) district, he has done more than all the Blaines and Hoars in the Republican party to awaken the smouldering animosities of the war, and rally the rank and file of that party in the North under the banner of bigotry and hatred.[45]

[42] *Augusta Constitutionalist*, January 13, 1876.

[43] *Columbus Times*, January 19, 1876.

[44] *Savannah Morning News*, January 15, 20, 21, 22, 1876, carries a résumé of such northern criticism, quoting among others the *New York World*, the *New York Herald*, the *Washington Capitol*, the *Pittsburgh Commercial*, and the *Philadelphia Herald*.

[45] *Cincinnati Enquirer*, quoted in *Columbus Times*, April 11, 1876. The writer continues his scathing attack on Hill for a column and more, depicting him as the "Donkey Howitzer of the House," and sarcastically suggesting that Hill and Morton debate the war issues over the North "like two Kilkenny cats."

The prominence into which Hill sprang in his debate with Blaine drew down on him the penalty of the famous. He became the subject of newspaper stories over the North. The *Washington Chronicle* printed one ridiculous "war story" about "General Ben Hill" which purported to come from a Union man residing in Aurora, Illinois. The story said that General Ben Hill had led 500 Georgia and Alabama home guards against 80 Federal soldiers on April 23, 1865, and was repulsed, retreating "on a mule." Commenting on this story, a southern editor remarked that it was difficult to decide which to wonder at most, the "inventive capacity" of the story teller or the "credulity of the Washington paper."[46]

Among the critics of Hill, on the score of the inexpediency of his action, the most persistent in Georgia was his old political enemy the *Augusta Constitutionalist*. This paper is almost as venomous as the hostile northern press. "Had he been a man of true genius and not a political gladiator of much talent and eloquence, he would have avoided Blaine's trap," was the uncharitable verdict of the editor.[47]

A more charitable version was that of a northern Democratic correspondent who praised Hill's eloquence, logic, and argument extravagantly, but thought that his course was unwise and would be disastrous to the Democratic party in the coming elections. "Its facts are right, members agree" said this correspondent, "but the North don't want any such speeches." And again this writer, referring to

[46] The story and editorial comment thereon appear in the *Columbus Times,* January 28, 1876.

[47] January 15, 1876. For similar criticism, see the same paper for January 12, 13, 16, 20, 1876.

IN THE HOUSE—SOUTHERN CHAMPION

Hill, says: "Speaking for two hours, it is the testimony of the oldest members that no one in the present Congress has ever delivered a more significant and masterful argument."[48]

But as might be expected, there was a loud chorus of unqualified approval of the speech from a good part of the southern press. Said a Savannah paper, editorially: "In him [Hill] not only the people of the South, but the cause of the truth, right and justice found an able, eloquent and successful champion."[49]

A common opinion was expressed by the editor of the *Columbus Times:*

> Mr. Hill in this speech was but executing a trust confided to him by the people of Georgia. His election to Congress last year was not an event of interest and gratification to the voters of the 9th District alone. From all parts of the state . . . . there was a general call for a man of his ability and courage to meet the defamers of the South on the floor of Congress. He has performed his duty with prudence, moderation and forbearance, but at the same time he has performed it well.[50]

The same editor remarked that the critics of Hill's action overlooked the fact that the issue was forced upon him

---

[48] Washington correspondent of the *Chicago Times*, quoted in *Columbus Times*, January 19, 1876, and *Augusta Constitutionalist*, January 16, 1876. For further similar criticism on ground of expediency, see *Columbus Times*, January 20, 1876, reproducing a review of the debate from the *Washington Star* (Ind. Rep.); and *Augusta Constitutionalist*, January 16, 1876, for reproductions from *Washington World* and *Philadelphia Chronicle*.

[49] *Savannah Morning News*, January 12, 1876. This paper on January 4, carries an article from the *Nashville American*, approving Hill's course.

[50] January 19, 1876.

as a measure of self-defense and that Hill clearly evidenced that his attitude was not an aggressive, but rather a defensive, one, and assumed with much pain.[51] He had done well "to vindicate the Confederates and their government from the charge of brutality to their prisoners."[52]

One Georgia editor was responsible for the statement that the *London Times* had congratulated the South upon having in the halls of Congress a man like Hill, who had the "ability and courage to defend his section and establish the truth of history."[53] Contrary to much other expressed opinion, a Washington correspondent wrote the *Rome (Georgia) Courier*:

> Northern Democrats tell me that Hill's speech will help them in their fight; that it deprives the Radicals of their "Andersonville" ammunition, explodes a thousand calumnies, and places the South in a better light before the country than it has occupied since the war. Even Moderate Republicans on the floor of the House confessed themselves amazed at the facts that Mr. Hill exhibited.[54]

Hill's participation in the amnesty debate was far and away the most conspicuous feature of his service in the first session of the Forty-fourth Congress; but it did not exhaust his activity. As a member of the Committee on Ways and Means, he had an influential position in a Democratic Congress. He took a leading part in a debate to restore to the pension rôle of the war of 1812 certain names dropped, by a law of 1862, for "participation in rebellion."

[51] January 16, 1876.

[52] January 19, 1876. An issue of the same paper on January 28, reprinted editorial praise of Hill from the *Macon Telegraph* and the *Mobile Register*.

[53] *La Grange Reporter*, January 1, 1877.

[54] Quoted in *Columbus Times*, January 22, 1876.

Hill of course argued the restoration of such persons.[55] He took a conspicuous part in the debates over the Appropriation bill, especially opposing the provision in the bill for informers in the government Revenue Service, as "contrary to the spirit of American institutions" and apt to produce graft and corruption.[56]

Hill also drew attention to himself when he supported and voted for the Centennial bill, which provided for a national celebration in 1876. The bill was very unpopular among southerners, who saw no occasion for national rejoicing under the auspices of a Radical administration in 1876. Hill proved to be the only representative from Georgia to vote for the measure, and his vote evoked some sarcasm to the effect that it was "to offset his amnesty speech" and was "a sort of sop to Cerberus."[57] To any reader of Hill's speeches at this period, the slur is entirely gratuitous and unwarranted.[58]

[55] *Cong. Rec.*, 44 C., 1 S., pp. 1366-76.

[56] Hill also would have amended the clause in the bill reducing the salaries of Senators, so as to prevent it going into effect until the next Congress. For his many and widely scattered arguments on the appropriation bill, see *Cong. Rec.*, 44 C., 1 S., pp. 1958-59, 2055-56, 2397, 2400, 2431-36.

[57] *Augusta Constitutionalist*, January 27, 1876, always hostile to Hill, gives the vote on the bill, and disparaging comments.

[58] Aside from the narrative in the text, and leaving out of account private bills introduced and petitions submitted from his constituents, Hill figured in the following in this Congressional session: He offered H. R. No. 1437, "to amend the Revised Statutes relating to the Treasury Department" (*Cong. Rec.*, 44 C., 1 S., p. 588); he argued at some length H. R. No. 2685, "for the distribution of the unappropriated moneys of the Geneva Award" (*ibid.*, pp. 4405-6, 4408); joint resolution, H. R. No. 196, "to provide for the protection of the Texas frontier on the Lower Rio Grande" (*ibid.*, pp. 4621-42, 4712); H. R. No. 84, "extending the time for redemption of lands held for direct taxes" (he reported and explained this bill from the Ways and Means Committee) (*ibid.*, pp. 4856-57, 4946).

As the Congressional session progressed, there was some tendency on the part of the Radicals to goad Hill into another outbreak.[59] The word went around that Hill was "primed with a speech in defense of the right of secession," and his best friends were very nervous lest he provide the Radicals with more "thunder" for the coming campaign.[60] Hill denied that he had any intention of speaking on secession and denounced the report as a "Radical lie, absurd on the face of it."[61] He certainly gave no further occasion for criticism in this session, sitting "quietly in his seat," says a Washington newspaper correspondent, while the Radicals tried to arouse him.[62]

Hill's party regularity during this, his first year in Congress, was also a matter of grave concern to some of the Bourbon papers of Georgia. It was feared he might repeat his course of 1872 and advocate another coalition with anti-administration or Liberal Republicans. He was quoted as saying:

I think it will be a great pity and a lamentable disaster if the Democrats shall fail to make a platform and nomination entitling them to the support of the anti-administration people of all parties and factions, and in that event the Liberals [Republicans] will be very censurable if they shall refuse to act in hearty accord with the Democrats.[63]

[59] *Augusta Constitutionalist*, March 9, 1876, quoting various northern papers.

[60] *Savannah Morning News*, March 9, 1876. The editor begs Hill to make no such speech.

[61] *Augusta Constitutionalist*, April 6, 1876.

[62] *Baltimore Sun* quoted in *Savannah Morning News*, March 28, 1876.

[63] In an article signed "F. H. A." (Allfriend), published in the *Louisville Courier Journal*, reproduced in *Augusta Constitutionalist*, July 3, 1876.

This brought from Bourbon editors a harsh and warning note against "Greeleyism for 1876"—called by one editor, the "Trojan horse introduced among the Democracy."[64]

But after the experience of 1872 the Liberal Republicans of the North evinced no desire to re-enact the experiment; and the sequel proved them "censurable," in the words ascribed to Hill, since they elected to stand by the regular Republican organization, receiving some concessions at the Cincinnati Convention in 1876, which nominated Hayes.[65]

When the second session of the Forty-fourth Congress came together in December, 1876, it is not an exaggeration to say that the whole nation was agog over the famous Hayes-Tilden election dispute. While the many debatable and controversial questions connected with this dispute are not within the purview of this study, it is very germane to the study to disclose the significant rôle that Ben Hill played in the Congressional action which settled the dispute. The essential facts of the situation are well known. Samuel J. Tilden, the Democratic candidate, was conceded 184 electoral votes. Hayes had 166 votes undisputed. The 7 electoral votes of South Carolina, 4 of Florida, and 8 of Louisiana were in dispute. In order to be elected, Hayes must secure every one of these disputed votes; while the vote of any one of the three states would elect Tilden.[66]

The disputed vote in the three southern states had

[64] *Constitutionalist* editor, July 3, 1876.

[65] For this convention, see Rhodes, VII, 270–76; Oberholtzer, III, 264–68.

[66] Rhodes, VII, 291–93.

come about because of the anomalous political conditions prevailing. Rival governments—the Reconstruction Radical governments, still maintaining a precarious hold; and Southern white governments, Democratic, of course—had each sent in electoral tickets. The situation was without precedent, and there was no available authority on what course should be taken when the president of the Senate should come to count the electoral vote, as was his function under the Constitution. Should he rule on which set of votes should be counted, as was the Republican contention? If so, the result was foregone—the election of Hayes. The Twenty-second Joint Rule, requiring the consent of both houses to count a disputed electoral vote, had been abrogated; and moreover, under it, there would have been no chance of agreement, as the Senate was Republican and the House Democratic.[67]

In the meanwhile, since the election in November, both political parties had had representatives—"visiting statesmen" as they were, perhaps, euphemistically styled—on the ground in the disputed states; and the air was rather lurid with crimination and recrimination, respecting bribery, suborning, and cheating, charged by each party on the other.[68]

---

[67] The Twenty-second Joint Rule had been passed in 1865 to prevent Lincoln from using the electoral votes of the southern states reconstructed under his plan, which did not meet the approval of the Congress. The Rule was dropped in 1876 because the House was Democratic (see Bassett, pp. 598–99).

[68] This account, confessedly general, as seemed indicated in the circumstances, may be confirmed in any of the standard histories of the period. See Rhodes, VII, 291–312; Oberholtzer, III, 281–91; Dunning, pp. 309–22.

In this situation Congress met. There was much wild talk in the country about violence and war; and patriotic men viewed anxiously the danger of a renewal of fratricidal bloodshed.[69] After the organization of the Democratic House, with the election of Samuel J. Randall as speaker,[70] the House appointed and dispatched committees to Louisiana, Florida, and South Carolina to conduct investigations.[71] The Republican Senate also sent subcommittees to the states in dispute, ostensibly to aid in solving the tangle.[72] Such of the Congress as remained in Washington addressed themselves to working out a method by which the electoral count might take place in February. There was already at this time much talk of violence in the Democratic press; and some of the Democratic Congressmen, taking the cue from the excited public opinion of the country, were disposed to defy the Republicans and refuse to grant any concession in solving the tangle. It was said that the Republican party, possessing the administration and the military forces necessary to do its bidding, were clearly preparing to steal the election; and Democrats were urged to go to any extreme to defeat such a crime.[73]

Typical of the extreme utterances of Democratic leaders was Joe Brown's advice counseling resistance to Hayes'

[69] See Hill's remarks on this score in letter to A. B. Culberson, Atlanta, dated December 21, 1876, in *Atlanta Constitution*, December 24, 1876.

[70] *Cong. Rec.*, 44 C., 2 S., p. 6.

[71] *Ibid.*, pp. 11, 16, 17, 45.

[72] *Ibid.*, 44. C., 2 S., p. 373.

[73] President Grant, in addressing Congress, had said: "The country is agitated. Its industries are arrested, labor unemployed, capital idle, and enterprise paralyzed by reason of the doubt and anxiety prevailing over the situation" (see Richardson, VII, 424).

inauguration. He wrote: "Should the people of the United States submit patiently and peaceably to military usurpation on the present occasion, it is mere mockery to talk of the peaceful remedy of the ballot box in the near future." Brown urged "no weakness" and "no compromise" on the part of the Democracy. He asserted that a stiff resistance to the northern Republicans would demonstrate that'they loved their money bags too well to endanger their safety with another civil war.[74]

Hill, from the time Congress first assembled in December, had deprecated all talk of violence and had counseled moderation and prudence. His remarks delivered in a Democratic caucus in early December had evoked intemperate abuse from southern Bourbons, who accused him of contemplating another New Departure or even of having been "bought" by the Radicals.[75]

At the December caucus it seems Hill had had a heated colloquy with Representative Wood from New York, an extremist against electoral compromise. Hill took occasion to recall to Representative Wood and other northern Democrats what had happened to southern Democrats once before when they had hearkened unto advices of some northern Democrats and adopted extreme measures in 1861. Some of the same northern Democrats had then joined in subjugation of their southern brethren.[76] The re-

[74] Letter in *Atlanta Constitution*, December 31, 1876.

[75] Editorials in *Savannah Morning News*, December 18, 19, 20, 22, 1876, giving the views of the editor and quoting many similar views from Bourbon papers.

[76] The *Savannah Morning News*, December 18, 1876, gives a report of the caucus, which is said to have broken up "in confusion."

IN THE HOUSE—SOUTHERN CHAMPION 289

minder was, perhaps, unfortunate; and Hill was represented as attacking the northern Democracy.[77]

Hill had also given an interview to the *New York Herald* in December which outraged Bourbon extremists. He was quoted as expressing a preference for Hayes to Grant and "Grantism," and as interpreting the nomination of Hayes by the Cincinnati Convention as a "victory over the ultraisms of the Republican party." The interviewer further represented Hill as being "almost indifferent whether Hayes or Tilden is the next President, so long as the Southern States secure good local government."[78]

Misrepresentations of his true position, to Hill's way of thinking, caused him to write an open letter published in a Georgia paper giving his own explanation of his position. In this letter he wrote:

> None but cool men and patriots who love country more than office can avert the most horrible civil war that ever disgraced and destroyed liberty and humanity. And yet there never was less excuse for any war in the history of the world. Such a war if it comes will be the culmination of human crime in the dastardly destruction of human rights by a disgraceful scramble for office.[79]

He then went on to deny that he had defamed northern Democrats or been involved in any "bargaining" or other political negotiations with Hayes or any of the Republican politicians as his critics had alleged. He asserted that his

---

[77] Hill emphatically denied the published reports that he had "abused" the northern Democrats. See open letter to A. B. Culberson, dated December 21, 1876, in *Atlanta Constitution*, December 24.

[78] Interview reproduced in *Savannah Morning News*, December 18, 1876, with severe criticism.

[79] Letter to A. B. Culberson, dated December 21, 1876, in *Atlanta Constitution*, December 24, 1876.

whole desire was to preserve peace in the country, thereby protecting the Constitution, which would certainly be destroyed if the alternative to peace, namely, civil war, and the dictatorship of Grant should be brought about through the misguided zeal of honest but unwise Democrats.[80] He insisted, moreover, that his views and actions had met the approval of Tilden and the majority of the Democratic caucus. He closed his letter by begging for the confidence of his friends in his integrity, and in warning them against the misrepresentations of his enemies.

Respecting the effect of Hill's course in Washington, the correspondent of the *Atlanta Constitution* wrote that it was seriously disconcerting Grant, who had hoped for and expected extreme utterances which might afford the opportunity to inaugurate Hayes forcefully. This correspondent further said that Hill's course was "in perfect accord with the wishes of Mr. Tilden," and that "the men who denounce Mr. Hill had better wait for results."[81]

An Atlanta paper of early January, 1877, printed in parallel columns on the first page the utterances of Ben Hill and Joe Brown on the proper course to be pursued in the electoral dispute. The Brown pronouncements were captioned "Southern Fire"; Hill's views were headed "Cold Water." The contrasting sentiments were printed without comment.[82]

---

[80] See further views on what would happen if the Democrats refused to allow the electoral count to proceed (*infra.*, pp. 295 ff.).

[81] *Atlanta Constitution*, December 18, 1876. Of course the construction put upon Grant's position in this matter, by the correspondent quoted, carries no weight. It is quoted merely to illustrate Hill's course.

[82] *Atlanta Evening Telegram*, January 8, 1876, in *Brown Scrap Books*.

In the meanwhile Congress had made little progress toward a solution of the electoral count before the Christmas recess. On December 13 Garfield had written Hayes: "After my speech today . . . . as to the validity of the Joint Rules, *Hill* came to me and said: 'You are clearly right and I don't intend to follow our people in this sort of reckless warfare.' "[83] And in the same letter occurred the following significant passage, which is probably the first word presaging the definitive end of the Reconstruction period at the South:

Just what sort of assurance the Southern members want is not quite so clear. Let me say I do not think anybody should be the custodian of your policy, or have any power to commit or embarrass you in any way, but It would be a great help, if, in some discreet way, those Southern men who are dissatisfied with Tilden and his more *violent* followers, could know that the South was going to be treated with kind consideration by you.[84]

Had Garfield read the interview with Hill in which the latter had been quoted as being chiefly concerned in the whole electoral dispute, that "the Southern States should secure good local government"?[85] The seed planted by Garfield in this letter was to bear abundant harvest in the restoration of home rule at the South; and Hill had, it would seem, borne no inconsiderable part in pointing the way to planting.

The Electoral Commission bill, (S. No. 1153), "to provide for and regulate the counting of votes for President and Vice President, and the decisions of questions arising thereon for the term commencing March 4, 1877," came

[83] Smith, I, 624-25.
[84] *Ibid.* [85] *Supra.*, p. 289.

from a joint committee of the Congress on January 18.[86] It was vigorously debated in both houses, meeting the opposition of the extremists of both parties; but it was finally passed, and received the signature of the president on January 29.[87] The bill, as is well known, created an Electoral Commission, to consist of five members each from the House, the Senate, and the Supreme Court, with full powers to determine all contested questions.[88]

Hill championed the Electoral Commission bill as a mode of escape from the threatened *impasse*. He made an able speech.[89] He informed the speaker and the House that he supported the bill because it was "constitutional" and "wise" and "patriotic." He deprecated the expressed fear, on the part of some members, that the Commission appointed would be partisan, but rather believed that the Commission's decisions would be "unanimous on every important point," would be "respected by the Congress," and would "give peace to the country" and "satisfaction to the people."[90]

Hill took occasion to bring to the attention of the

[86] *Cong. Rec.*, 44 C., 2 S., pp. 713–14.   [87] *Ibid.*, p. 1081.

[88] Of the fifteen, it was expected that one, the fifteenth, would be an Independent in politics, Justice Davis; the other fourteen were divided equally between Democrats and Republicans. How this calculation went awry, and the fifteenth member, Justice Bradley, was also a Republican, is well known. The narrative is succinctly set forth by Rhodes, VII, 326–28.

[89] Speech in *Cong. Rec.*, 44 C., 1 S., pp. 1008–09.

[90] It is superfluous to remark that in none of these prophesies did Hill prove correct. That he should express such convictions is either a tribute to his own large and unsuspecting statesmanship or else was a gross misrepresentation for ulterior purposes. The writer inclines to the former view.

House at this time the "patriotism and manliness" which the South had demonstrated in this crisis. He spoke of the "forbearance, kindness, patience" shown in the South during the political storm that had been wracking the country over the Hayes-Tilden election, though every southerner had "believed earnestly that Tilden was elected, and that the only remaining rights of the long suffering section hinged on his inauguration." He concluded with this burning patriotic sentiment:

In the future let me express the hope that he alone will be viewed as the chief rebel, who after the passage of this measure of peace, shall first again whisper the word of sectional hate. Let him be regarded as the chief traitor who shall again seek to breed the horrors of sectional strife.

For myself I feel a pride in being able to say I can look upon every foot of soil upon the American continent and thank God it is part of my country. I can look upon every person upon this continent and say "this is my fellow citizen," and I can raise my vision to the uttermost boundaries of the Republic and say, 'my country, my whole country, blessed is he that blesseth thee, and cursed is he that curseth thee." (Applause)[91]

A northern statesman, writing of Hill's argument for the Electoral Commission, called it a "speech of unusual cogency." The speech throughout, he said, breathed "the true patriotic spirit." "His enthusiasm kindled a lambent flame charged with electric force."[92]

When the Electoral Commission proved a purely political junket, deciding every point and every vote on straight party lines,[93] the Democrats were inclined to be

---

[91] *Cong. Rec.*, 44 C., 2 S., p. 1009.

[92] S. S. Cox, *Three Decades of Federal Legislation*, p. 69.

[93] Rhodes, VII, 329-41; Oberholtzer, III, 303-14.

truculent. Many advocated the adoption of filibustering tactics to defeat the peaceful inauguration of Hayes. This could have been easily done under the circumstances.[94] That it was not done, bringing with it all the attendant evils sure to have followed in its train, is due very largely to Hill.[95]

By February 12 it was clearly evident that the Electoral Commission was acting and would continue to act in a partisan spirit.[96] The Democrats had been dissatisfied with the Commission since their first plans regarding Justice Davis had gone awry. With the announcement of the decisions regarding Florida, on February 12, a determined effort was made in a Democratic caucus of that date to adopt a definite program to defeat the electoral count by filibustering.[97]

Hill opposed the proposal in caucus with much force.[98] He cautioned that "those who take counsel of their passions are often honest, but rarely wise." He pleaded for calmness and control. He argued that the decision of the Electoral Commission, "right or wrong" (and he admitted

---

[94] The Commission made its final report, February 27. The inauguration was due March 4. The Democrats controlled the House and could have easily filibustered the intervening five days and prevented the inauguration. One Ohio Democrat said: "When fraud is law, filibustering is patriotism" (Rhodes, VII, 342).

[95] This statement, it is true, is based largely on Hill's own evidence, as the sequel will show, but his responsibility was openly avowed and criticized in the South; and the facts in the case were never attacked or denied.

[96] Rhodes, VII, p. 338.

[97] Rhodes, VII, p. 341, says the recalcitrant representatives were about sixty from the North and West.

[98] These "Remarks in Caucus" found in Hill, *Life of Hill*, pp. 75–77.

it seemed determined to count in Mr. Hayes), should be accepted and the proposed filibustering program abandoned. He would advance three reasons: first, the Constitution, to support which all were sworn, enjoined the duty of making the count; second, the Electoral Commission bill, however wicked the manner of its execution, was a law of this Congress; third, a contrary course, while it might prevent the peaceable inauguration of Hayes, would not secure the peaceable inauguration of Tilden. Hill then pointed out the sure sequel of the failure to inaugurate Hayes. It would produce a contingency not contemplated in the organic or statute law; and who could doubt that Grant, with the army at his back, would continue in power, and perhaps indefinitely? If the House should attempt to declare Tilden President by resolution, who could doubt that the charge of "revolution" would be made by the party in power? and bloody, terrible war would follow—a war, responsibility for which would be charged to the South and ex-Confederates of the Congress.

But suppose Hayes, though fraudulently counted in, should be inaugurated? Certainly the Republicans would have the presidency another four years; but it would be a "tenure of fraud," which "after four years of infamy will go out of power and out of respect forever." Certainly the Democratic party would lose the presidency for four years, but "we shall save the peace of the country and end the revolution of force which has brought upon the people so much suffering." And the self-sacrificing course of the Democracy, winning the confidence of the nation, "would surely sweep them into possession of the government four years hence."

Hill secured the pledges of some forty-two ex-Confederates who were members of the House, to oppose the filibustering scheme; and with the able support of the speaker, Randall, advocates of the opposition to the count were defeated.[99] This was the more easily accomplished because of developments of the twenty-sixth of February. On that day certain significant conferences took place in Washington. Congressman John Y. Brown, Democrat of Kentucky, with Senator John B. Gordon, Democrat of Georgia, at the former's initiative waited upon Congressman Charles Foster, representing Hayes's Ohio district. In substance, they requested of Congressman Foster, in return for their continued opposition to the effort to prevent the electoral count, that he provide some assurance in writing that Hayes would cease to support the fraudulent governments in Florida, Louisiana, and South Carolina and would, directly after his inauguration, withdraw the federal troops from those areas.

About midnight, February 26, Foster had a conference with other Democrats from southern states, who indorsed Brown's efforts at an understanding—a "capitol understanding," as the captious Joe Brown of Georgia designated it.[100]

On the next day, February 27, Foster delivered two letters to Brown, one signed by himself and the other by

[99] *New York Times,* June 10, 1878, in *Brown Scrap Books.*

[100] Joe Brown, under the nom de plume of "Citizen," in *Atlanta Constitution,* April 7, 15, 1877, wrote two letters fiercely attacking this "capitol understanding," and claiming that the "bargain" from the standpoint of the Democracy and the South, was too cheap, was unnecessary, and was unauthorized.

IN THE HOUSE—SOUTHERN CHAMPION

Stanley Matthews, a relative by marriage, and the confidential adviser to Hayes. These letters gave the required assurance in Hayes's name.[101] The execution of these promises ended what is known as the period of Reconstruction in the South.

Before this consummation, toward which he had rendered signal service, Hill had been promoted from the House to the Senate, by the General Assembly of Georgia.[102] Hill had no sooner been elected to the House in May, 1875, than the Liberal Democratic papers of the state began to advocate his election to the Senate to succeed the rather mediocre Senator Thomas M. Norwood, whose term would expire with the Forty-fourth Congress in March, 1877.[103] Innuendoes regarding Hill's Senatorial aspirations had often appeared in the criticism directed against him for his rôle in the amnesty debate in January, 1876, and the Hayes-Tilden dispute in December.[104]

Indeed, Hill made no secret of the fact that he wanted to go to the Senate. He professed to believe it to be the chamber in which he could render his greater service. Further, he admitted in the autumn of 1876 that he desired

[101] This account of the "understanding" reached by Democratic gentlemen and friends of Hayes is taken from an account written by Congressman Brown himself. Brown published the letters which passed. The account is found in the *New York Sun*, March 29, 1877, and *Atlanta Constitution*, April 7, 1877, both in *Brown Scrap Books*.

[102] Hill had been re-elected to the Forty-fifth Congress in November, 1876, without opposition (see Avery, p. 520). He, of course, never took his seat.

[103] *Augusta Chronicle and Sentinel*, May 15, 1875, also quoting *Albany News*.

[104] *Savannah Morning News*, December 19, 1876.

election to the Senate as an indorsement of his position in the amnesty debate with Blaine, and he warned his friends that the politicians who were representing that he could not be spared from the House were using this argument as a subterfuge to defeat him. He expressed, however, a willingness to serve wherever the people sent him.[105]

By January, 1877, the Senatorial political pot was boiling in Georgia Besides the incumbent Senator Norwood, who was in the state conducting an active canvass, Hill, Governor James M. Smith, and Hershel V. Johnson were the chief contenders.[106] The representations made by Hill's enemies regarding his course on the Electoral Commission debate, which was in process in Congress, were believed to be so false by his friends that he was prevailed on to make a flying trip to Georgia to explain his attitude before the Georgia Assembly.[107] This he did, delivering his speech the night of his arrival and returning to Washington the next day.[108]

The General Assembly balloted for three days before

[105] These views were expressed in an interview published in the *Atlanta Constitution*, November 29, 1876. In the beginning he expressed a reluctance to be interviewed on the subject.

[106] For discussion of the candidates and prospects, see *Atlanta Constitution*, December 23, 1877; *Albany News*, January 18, in *Brown Scrap Books; Augusta Constitutionalist*, December 29, 1876, and January 7, 1877.

[107] Hill, *Life of Hill*, pp. 78, 473.

[108] *Ibid.*, p. 473. The speech made on this occasion was an exhaustive review and defense of his whole political career, especially since the war. He repeated many of the arguments and explanations cited elsewhere in the course of this study. The speech is printed in his son's collection of his speeches, *ibid.*, pp. 473-93.

IN THE HOUSE—SOUTHERN CHAMPION 299

an election resulted. Norwood led for two days. The pressure of public opinion on the Assembly was so strong for Hill from the first that Norwood forces vainly endeavored to have the galleries cleared to reduce the effect of the Hill sentiment on the Assembly.[109] When the Smith following broke to Hill on the third day, he was elected, the final ballot giving him 117 to Norwood's 85.[110] The enthusiasm in the Assembly and its environs, when Hill's election was assured, is said to have been indescribable. "Men wept, hats were tossed to the ceiling, and the two Houses separated in tumult."[111] The election was characterized as a "people's victory" by Hill's friends; while his political enemies ascribed it to shrewd political management.[112]

On the twenty-sixth of January, when the Georgia Assembly reached an election, Hill was in Washington debating in favor of the Electoral Commission bill. As he began the patriotic peroration to his argument which has been quoted above,[113] a telegram was handed to him announcing his election as United States Senator.[114]

With the conclusion of the Reconstruction period, which happened to be coincidental with Hill's elevation to the United States Senate, this study ends. He had now attained national distinction and had outdistanced his politi-

[109] *Atlanta Constitution*, January 27, 1877.

[110] *Ibid.*

[111] *Ibid.* The writer in the *Constitution* was Henry W. Grady.

[112] See *Atlanta Constitution*, above date, for the favorable view; *Augusta Constitutionalist*, January 28, for the unfavorable.

[113] *Supra.*, p. 292.

[114] Cox, p. 69.

cal enemies in his own section. Being only fifty-four years of age, a long and promising political career, full of usefulness for his own people and honor for himself, seemed to await him. He lived to realize but a fraction of this promise, the fell disease of cancer causing his untimely death five years later, while still serving his first term in the United States Senate.[115]

[115] Hill died in Atlanta, August 16, 1882.

CHAPTER XIV

CONCLUSIONS

The writer has thus far in this study endeavored to present the public life and work of Ben Hill in secession and reconstruction, from the record of his own speeches and writings and the recorded testimony of his contemporaries. It may not be out of place to conclude the study with a short chapter of conclusions which may be accepted for what they are worth. It is hoped that the conclusions will have been substantiated in the previous treatment.

The primary motive and actuating ideals in Hill's life seem to have been a devotion to the Constitution of 1787, and the Union of the American States. It is a very superficial view which would challenge this assertion because of his participation in secession and the resulting war, or because of his vigorous opposition to southern acceptance of the Reconstruction Acts.

He entered public life in 1851 to oppose the agitation of the slavery question, and extreme sectional utterances on any score and from any quarter. He made the race for Congress in 1855 on this simple platform—opposition to slavery agitation and to any policies that would call in question the efficacy and desirability of the American Union.

In 1856 he conducted a vigorous canvass in behalf of Fillmore as against Buchanan, his conviction and argument being that Fillmore was the logical candidate for moderate men of all parties and sections. In this campaign he first came into almost violent collision with Alexander Stephens and Toombs, new and zealous converts to the Democratic party.

He was virtually drafted for the gubernatorial campaign against Brown in 1857. This campaign turned largely upon the alleged error of the Democratic party in having reopened the slavery question by the passage of the Kansas-Nebraska Act, which Act Hill had vigorously condemned.

In 1854, Hill, an Old Whig, had been forced by circumstances into an uncongenial association with the Know-Nothing, or American, party, whose proscriptive and ritualistic features, he condemned and did something to modify.

As the likelihood of secession increased, he entered the state senate in 1860 and acted as a moderating influence on the course of that body. At the same time he led the fight in the state for the Constitutional Union ticket headed by Bell and Everett, and before the campaign was over, vainly endeavored to consummate a fusion of the tickets opposed to Lincoln, seeing in this solution the only hope of defeating Lincoln, and the almost certain disruption of the Union that would follow his election.

Going to the state Constitutional Convention of 1861 he fought earnestly, shoulder to shoulder with old political antagonists, against the adoption of secession as a remedy for existing grievances. When, despite his every effort, the test resolution on secession was adopted, Hill saw no alternative but to bow to the will of his state, whose sovereignty he had never questioned.

He viewed the Civil War which followed, as an effort

CONCLUSIONS

to preserve outside of the old Union the principles of the Constitution of 1787 and the true and original Union of the Fathers. Hill doubted the expediency of the southern effort and deprecated the success of the southern extremists who had forced the enterprise; but he harbored no thought of disloyalty to his state and section in his mind. Indeed, he became the very prop and stay of the Confederate administration in the Confederate Senate, and he vigorously championed every measure and means to prosecute the war, and opposed every measure and means which might endanger ultimate success for the Confederacy. The end of the war found him on the stump in Georgia strenuously urging his people to continued resistance, being probably the last prominent Confederate official in the execution of such a task.

With the coming of peace, Hill retired from participation in politics until the Reconstruction Acts of 1867 were passed by the Radical Congress. Construing the features of these Acts, which contemplated a voluntary participation of the southern people in proscribing their own leaders, as requiring that the southern people consent to their own dishonor, and finding other grave objections to the Acts on the score of constitutionality and expediency, Hill assumed the leadership in a bitter fight against southern acceptance and participation. In this fight he delivered several brilliant philippics, which have been variously characterized as "magnificent" or "incendiary," according to the politics and sentiment of the commentator. Some very penetrating, exhaustive, and controversial political essays, called "Notes on the Situation," were also the result of this campaign of obstruction.

After the failure to elect Seymour and Blair on a prosouthern platform in 1868, and observing that the Reconstruction Acts and amendments were now accomplished facts, so declared and construed by all the departments of the government having jurisdiction, Hill seemed to change his course in 1870 and advocated that the South recognize the validity of the Acts and amendments and cease obstruction tactics. He was the more moved to this apparent change because from visits and conferences in the North he had become convinced that the northern Democracy, admonished by their defeat of 1868, would no longer support the South in opposition to the Reconstruction Acts and amendments, but were prepared, on the contrary, to recognize them as accomplished facts and of force, in the next presidential campaign.

By anticipating this program of the National Democratic party, and by voluntarily acting in 1870, Hill thought he saw a chance to loosen the hold of Radical state governments in the South, especially in Georgia, where Bullock possessed a precarious hold, at best, and was earnestly requesting Congressional interference to maintain himself in the state. Hill conceived that if Grant and the Radical administration could be assured that the Reconstruction Acts and amendments would be recognized by the Democrats, and the rights of negroes and Union men protected by a Democratic state government, that Bullock's designs might be defeated and Congressional interference prevented. The state would surely, then, revert to the native white Democratic control.

It was in pursuit of this policy that he advised the acceptance of Reconstruction by the South. At about the same time, December, 1870, he utilized the presence of prominent northern Republicans in Atlanta, in defeating Bullock. By attending what became the notorious "Delano banquet," and otherwise consorting with Secretary Delano, Hill secured the promise of Delano to aid in preventing further Congressional interference with Georgia. Georgia then repudiated Bullock and soon escaped from Radical misrule.

Hill's motives and agency in this work were not known at the time. Where suggested, they met suspicion, and even incredulity. Since his address advising acceptance of Reconstruction, he had been the recipient of intemperate abuse and obloquy from the Democratic press of the state. Suspicions of his integrity were increased because of his participation in December, 1870, in the lease of the state-road, the leasing company numbering, among others, the execrated Brown and H. I. Kimball, besides some northern Republicans and capitalists. In addition, the lease was awarded under circumstances which later produced a legislative investigation, which, however, did not invalidate the lease. It is the opinion of the writer, after a close study of the question, that while, under the circumstances, suspicion was quite natural, even inevitable, no evidence of fraud or collusion was ever substantiated; and that if fraud did occur somewhere back of the scenes, neither Hill nor anybody immediately associated with him was involved.

The events of December, 1870, brought about the virtual political proscription of Hill. However, he kept resolutely on his course of advising the southern people to turn their faces to the future and to new issues. In this period of proscription, 1870–75, he advocated, in speech and writing, the policies, pursuit of which in recent years has revolutionized the entire South. For the time, Hill was a prophet without honor among his own people.

In 1872 he defied the Bourbon prejudice in the South and championed the "New Departure." He saw, in this, coalition of the Liberal Democracy with the Liberal Republicans, on a basis of the recognition of Reconstruction as an accomplished fact, the only possible return to the Constitution, and to a Union of consent rather than to one pinned together by federal bayonets. The movement met defeat, and Hill had acquired more obloquy for his pains.

By the autumn of 1874 the political clouds were lifting slightly for him. His fervent and patriotic speeches, urging constructive labors in the development of a new South, and his strictures, at the same time, against Grant's course in supporting the Kellogg government in Louisiana, were regaining the confidence of the people and silencing the calumnies of the Bourbon press. The demand gradually became articulate throughout the state that he be sent to Congress to represent not only a Congressional district and the state of Georgia but the southern people.

After initial defeat and disappointment he was elected to Congress from the Ninth Georgia District. Seemingly well known when he arrived, and anticipated as a sort of southern champion, he sprang into national prominence as a result of the amnesty debate with Blaine and Garfield, in which he essayed to defend Jefferson Davis and the Confederate government against charges of brutality and inhumanity, and in which he put Radicals on notice that unfounded and gratuitous slurs against his people must stop.

There was some criticism, both North and South, as to the expediency and wisdom of Hill's course in having accepted Blaine's challenge; but the people of Georgia may be presumed to have registered their approval of it when within the year he was sent to the United States Senate.

In the meanwhile, Hill had vigorously and skilfully aided in putting through the Compromise Electoral Commission settlement of the Hayes-Tilden dispute. His action in this connection, again opposed by the Bourbon press, had been dictated by the earnest desire to prevent violence and possible civil war, and its sequel proved to be the restoration of home rule at the south.

Throughout his political career, Hill usually led minorities, and was therefore out of political office most of the time; but he always exerted a potent influence on public opinion and the course of political events. Usually, again, he could be found on the side of moderation, the only notable exception being his intemperate fight against Southern acceptance of the Reconstruction Acts, when, to his view, fundamental considerations of honor, and not mere policies, were involved.

Before the Civil War, Alexander Stephens, Toombs, and Howell Cobb were almost undisputed Georgia leaders. During the war Hill and Brown, though on opposing lines, forged to the front. After the war Hill passed the older men—Stephens, Toombs, and Cobb—in prominence and influence in the state, and shared with Brown political eminence in Georgia, although the two men were advocating very different and contrary policies. Which of the two, in these controversial years from 1867 to 1870, contributed most to the rescue of Georgia from Radical misrule will very probably remain problematical. By 1872 they had worked around to the same position, and their political hostility lessened after that time.

From Hill's entrance to Congress in 1875 to his death in 1882, it is safe to say his influence and prestige in the state was second to none. At the time of his death he had achieved national eminence, and he was usually regarded in the North as the outstanding southern figure in the Congress.

Hill was primarily an orator and close student of constitutional questions. His speeches reveal, in an extraordinary way, the powers of the logician and close reasoner, with the more popular gifts of the rhetorical phrase-maker and declamatory orator. He could both persuade the reason and arouse the passion of his auditors; the combined faculty made him one of the greatest orators in Georgia's history.

He was never a good politician in the ordinary use of that word. He gave little attention to details of political management or organization, and his tendency toward independency was always a grave concern to the organization politicians.

Hill was absolutely honest and patriotic in the opinion of this writer.[1] He was often accused of inconsistency, and indeed on occasion was inconsistent. The apparent vagaries of his course, from secession opposition to championship of the Davis administration, then from fierce resistance to Reconstruction to an earnest plea for the ac-

[1] By the courtesy of a grand daughter, Mrs. Caroline H. McConnell of Lithonia, Ga., I have read in manuscript private letters from Hill to very near relatives in which he expressed a repugnance to using his political position for securing patronage even for his own immediate family.

ceptance of Reconstruction, laid him peculiarly open to charges of inconsistency. These charges may be dismissed with the admission that he altered his policies with altered circumstances. He was also accused from time to time of lack of judgment, and even of venality.[2] A dispassionate study of his whole record does much to discredit the former charge, though it is perfectly evident that his "judgment" was far from infallible. As to the charge of venality, there is nothing upon which to support it.

As an advocate or pleader before judge or jury, Hill is said by his contemporaries to have been almost irresistible and certainly unsurpassed in his own time.[3] There is, indeed, no doubt that his legal practice, both civil and criminal, was as extensive as his time would allow, and that from it he reaped large financial returns, which however, were expended in his own lifetime upon his family, friends, and relatives or was lost in unfortunate planting ventures in southwest Georgia.[4]

There is some reason to think that Ben Hill's rôle as opponent of secession in peace, champion of the Confederacy in war, and prophet of a New South after the war, will loom larger as the historical events of this tumultuous period are clarified of passion and fall into proper perspective.

[2] Joe Brown often accused Hill of lack of judgment (accent on the "ment").

[3] Testimony of Judge George Hillyer, now living in Atlanta at an advanced age. Hill often practiced before Judge Hillyer (Conversation, July 8, 1927). Also testimony of ex-Senator Hoke Smith, who as a young man, was sometimes associated with Hill in legal practice. (Conversation, April 2, 1927.)

[4] Testimony of grand daughter, Mrs. Caroline H. McConnell to writer.

BIBLIOGRAPHY

This Bibliography makes no pretension at being exhaustive for the period covered, but merely represents those sources consulted regarding the life and work of Benjamin H. Hill.

MANUSCRIPT

Hill MMS. (Very few letters in possession of Mrs. Caroline Holt McConnell, of Lithonia, Georgia.)

Davis MMS. (Extensive collection of letters from Confederate officials to Jefferson Davis, embracing some Hill letters, in the De Renne Private Library, Wormsloe, Georgia.)

GEORGIA PUBLIC DOCUMENTS

Journal of the State Convention Held in Milledgeville, December, 1850. Milledgeville, 1850.

Journal of the Public and Secret Proceedings of the Convention of the People of Georgia Held in Milledgeville and Savanah, 1861. Together with the ordinances adopted. Milledgeville, 1861.

Journal of the Proceedings of the People of Georgia Held in Milledgeville in October and November, 1865, etc. Milledgeville, 1865.

Journal of the Proceedings of the Constitutional Convention of the People of Georgia in the City of Atlanta, in the Months of December, 1867, and January, February, and March, 1868, etc. Augusta, 1868.

Acts of the General Assembly, 1850–71.

Georgia Senate Journal, 1859–72.

Georgia House of Representatives Journal, 1851–72.

Report of the Committee to Investigate the Lease of the State Road (with Testimony). 1872.

BIBLIOGRAPHY

UNITED STATES PUBLIC DOCUMENTS

Congressional Globe, for Thirty-ninth, Fortieth, Forty-first, and Forty-second Congresses.

Congressional Record, for Forty-fourth and Forty-fifth Congresses.

Thirty-ninth Congress, First Session: *Senate Executive Documents,* Nos. 2, 25, and 26; *Reports of Committees of the House of Representatives,* Vol. II, No. 30.

Fortieth Congress, Third Session: *House Miscellaneous Documents,* No. 52.

Forty-second Congress, Second Session: *Reports of Committees of the House of Representatives,* No. 26, Pts. VI and VII ("Ku Klux Report for Georgia").

War of the Rebellion, Official Records of the Union and Confederate Armies, Series 1, 2, 3, and 4.

NEWSPAPERS

Where not otherwise indicated, the newspapers are dailies.

Atlanta:

Atlanta Constitution from June, 1868, to March, 1877.

In the Carnegie Library, Atlanta. (The *Brown Scrap Books* which were used in this study, were so filled with extracts from Atlanta newspapers that it was not deemed necessary to use other Atlanta newspaper files available.)

Augusta:

Augusta Constitutionalist from August 1868, to March, 1877.

Found in the office of the ordinary, Richmond County, Augusta. This paper was the favorite organ of Alexander Stephens and was usually hostile to Hill. It was considered a Bourbon paper during Reconstruction.

Augusta Chronicle and Sentinel from July, 1868, to March, 1877.

Found in the office of the ordinary, Richmond County, Augusta. This paper was called the Ku Klux organ by the Republican press during Reconstruction. It was usually favorably disposed toward Hill, though it deserted him between 1870 and 1875.

Augusta Press for the year 1869.

 In the office of the ordinary of Richmond county, Augusta. Called itself Independent in politics. Its editor formerly was an old-line Whig.

Augusta National Republican for the year 1868.

 In the office of the ordinary, Richmond County, Augusta. This paper was violently partisan—a hater of the Old South and all it connoted.

Charleston (South Carolina):

Charleston Daily Courier for 1862 and 1863.

 In Library of the Georgia Historical Society, Savannah.

Charleston Mercury for 1862 and 1863.

 In Library of the Georgia Historical Society, Savannah.

Columbus:

Columbus Sun from July, 1855, to March, 1877.

 In private possession of Mr. James Gilbert, Columbus. This was usually a moderate paper.

Columbus Times, occasional files.

 In private possession of Mr. James Gilbert, Columbus.

Milledgeville:

Milledgeville Federal Union from 1850 to 1861.

 In private possession in Atlanta.

Milledgeville Southern Recorder, same dates.

 In Library of the Georgia Historical Society, Savannah; also in State Library, Atlanta. Files not complete.

Richmond (Virginia):

Richmond Dispatch for the year 1862.

 In Library of the Georgia Historical Society, Savannah.

Richmond Daily Examiner for 1862 and 1863.

 In Library of the Georgia Historical Society, Savannah.

Savannah:

Savannah Daily Advertiser from June, 1868, to June, 1873.

 In Library of the Georgia Historical Society, Savannah.

Savannah Daily Republican from January, 1855, to June, 1873.

 In Library of the Georgia Historical Society, Savannah. A Democratic paper despite its name.

BIBLIOGRAPHY

Savannah Morning News from July, 1855, to March, 1877.

In the offices of the *Savannah Morning News*, excellently filed and easy of access. For the period—from April, 1866, to September, 1868—this paper was merged with the *Savannah Daily Herald* and was known as the *Savannah Daily News and Herald*.

SCRAP BOOKS

Brown Scrap Books.

A collection of twenty-six large books, made by the wife of the war governor, and covering his whole political life. They constitute much of the newspaper material for Georgia history during the period of Ben Hill's life. In the possession of Miss Sallie Eugenia Brown, the governor's daughter, Atlanta.

Hill Scrap Book.

A collection covering the latter period of Hill's life. In the possession of Mrs. Caroline H. McConnell, Lithonia, Georgia.

LETTERS, MEMOIRS, AND RECOLLECTIONS OF HILL'S CONTEMPORARIES

BLAINE, JAMES G. *Twenty Years of Congress.* 2 vols. Norwich, Connecticut, 1886.

COX, SAMUEL S. *Three Decades of Federal Legislation.* Providence, 1885.

CLEVELAND, HENRY. *Alexander H. Stephens in Public and Private, with Letters and Speeches, before and during and since the War.* Philadelphia, 1866.

This book seems properly included in this category since it is largely made up of Stephens' own letters and speeches.

DAVIS, JEFFERSON. *Rise and Fall of the Confederate Government.* 2 vols. New York, 1881.

FELTON, MRS. WILLIAM H. *My Memoirs of Georgia Politics.* Atlanta, 1911.

Highly biased and contentious.

HINSDALE, BURKE A. (ed.) *The Works of James Abram Garfield.* 2 vols. Boston, 1883.

HILL, BENAMIN H. JR. *Senator Benjamin H. Hill of Georgia. His Life, Writings and Speeches.* Atlanta, 1891.

 Chiefly valuable because of the large collection of speeches and writings. The slender biographical sketch is, as would be expected, filio-pietistical.

HILLIARD, HENRY W. *Politics and Pen Pictures.* New York, 1892.

HOAR, GEORGE F. *Autobiography of Seventy Years.* 2 vols. New York, 1903.

JOHNSTON, JOSEPH E. *Narrative of Military Operations.* New York, 1874.

JOHNSTON, RICHARD M., and BROWN, WILLIAM H. *Life of A. H. Stephens.* Philadelphia, 1883.

 Included in this category because this book is almost exclusively made up of Stephens' own letters and conversations.

JONES, JOHN B. *A Rebel War Clerks Diary at the Confederate States Capitol.* 2 vols. Philadelphia, 1866.

LONGSTREET, JAMES. *From Manassas to Appomatox.* Philadelphia, 1896.

PHILLIPS, ULRICH B. (ed.). *Correspondence of Robert Toombs, Alexander H. Stephens and Howell Cobb.* Being the *Annual Report of the American Historical Association, 1911,* Vol. II. Washington, 1913.

 This collection of letters is invaluable to students in Georgia history, and Professor Phillips is entitled to the lasting gratitude of such students for his excellent work.

REED, JOHN C. "Reminiscences of Ben Hill," *South Atlantic Quarterly,* Vol. V (April, 1906).

ROWLAND, DUNBAR. (ed.). *Jefferson Davis Constitutionalist. His Letters, Papers and Speeches.* 10 vols. Jackson, Mississippi, 1923.

SMITH, THEODORE C. *Life and Letters of James Abram Garfield.* 2 vols. New Haven, 1925.

STEPHENS, ALEXANDER H. *A Constitutional View of the Late War between the States.* 2 vols. Philadelphia, 1870.

BIBLIOGRAPHY

WORKS DEALING WITH GEORGIA HISTORY

AVERY, I. W. *History of Georgia, 1850–1881.* New York, 1881.

    The most valuable of all Georgia histories, though Colonel Avery, a newspaper man, has cited no authorities, is somewhat "gossipy" in treatment, and is an ardent admirer of Joe Brown. The book is far more useful than the designation of it by some wag, as "The History of Joe Brown's Georgia," would indicate.

BUTLER, JOHN C. *Historical Record of Macon and Central Georgia.* Macon, 1879.

HORNADAY, JOHN R. *Atlanta, Yesterday, Today and Tomorrow.* Atlanta, 1922.

HULL, A. L. *Annals of Athens, Ga., 1801–1901.* Athens, 1906.

LEE, F. D., and AGNEW, J. L. *Historical Record of the City of Savannah.* Savannah, 1869.

MARTIN, JOHN H. *History of Columbus, Georgia, 1827–1865.* Columbus, 1874.

PHILLIPS, ULRICH B. *Georgia and State Rights.* Being the *Annual Report of the American Historical Association, 1901,* Vol. II. Washington, 1902.

    This study of Professor Phillips' is a veritable *vade mecum* for the historical student of the period.

REED, WALLACE P. *History of Atlanta.* Syracuse, 1889.

THOMPSON, C. MILDRED. *Reconstruction in Georgia. Economic, Social, Political.* Being Vol. XLIV, No. 1, of the "Studies in History, Economics and Public Law," edited by the faculty of political science of Columbia University. New York, 1915.

    Miss Thompson has done a most thorough, exhaustive, and scholarly piece of work. The student in this field must remain substantially in her debt.

WOOLEY, EDWIN C. *The Reconstruction of Georgia.* Being Vol. XIII, No. 3, of the "Studies in History, Economics and Public Law," edited by the faculty of political science of Columbia University. New York, 1901.

    Less exhaustive than Miss Thompson's work, confining attention exclusively to political questions; but good.

BIOGRAPHIES OF GEORGIANS

BOYKIN, SAMUEL. *A Memorial Volume of the Hon. Howell Cobb.* Philadelphia, 1870.

BREWTON, WILLIAM W. *Life of Thomas E. Watson.* Atlanta, 1926.

FIELDER, HERBERT. *Life and Times and Speeches of Joseph E. Brown.* Springfield, Massachusetts, 1883.
    Highly eulogistic.

KNIGHT, LUCIAN LAMAR. *Reminiscences of Famous Georgians.* 2 vols. Atlanta, 1907.

PENDLETON, LOUIS. *Alexander H. Stephens* ("American Crisis Biographies"). Philadelphia, 1907.

PHILLIPS, ULRICH B. *Life of Robert Toombs.* New York, 1913.
    Scholarly, as is all of Professor Phillips' work.

SMITH, GEORGE G. *Life and Times of George F. Pierce.* Sparta, Georgia, 1888.

STOVALL, PLEASANT A. *Life of Robert Toombs.* New York, 1892.

WADDELL, JAMES D. *Biographical Sketch of Linton Stephens.* Atlanta, 1877.

OTHER BIOGRAPHIES

DODD, WILLIAM E. *Jefferson Davis* ("American Crisis Biographies"). Philadelphia, 1907.

DUBOSE, JOHN W. *Life and Times of William L. Yancey.* Birmingham, 1892.

ECKENRODE, HAMILTON J. *Jefferson Davis—President of the South.* New York, 1923.

LONGSTREET, HELEN D. *Lee and Longstreet at High Tide.* Published by the author, 1905.
    To all intents a biography.

POLLARD, EDWARD A. *Life of Jefferson Davis with a Secret History of the Southern Confederacy.* Philadelphia, 1869.
    Pollard's bias against Davis is well known.

STANWOOD, EDWARD. *Life of James G. Blaine.* Boston, 1905.
    Stanwood was a kinsman of Blaine.

WADE, JOHN DONALD. *Augustus Baldwin Longstreet.* New York, 1924.
    Of little value for the present study, but quite a contribution to southern historical studies.

GENERAL SECONDARY WORKS

ANDREWS, E. BENJAMIN. *The History of the Last Quarter Century in the United States 1870–1895.* 2 vols. New York, 1896.
    Of no great value.

ANDREWS, SIDNEY. *The South since the War.* Boston, 1866.
    First-hand account by a trained newspaper man.

BASSETT, JOHN S. *Short History of the United States* (enlarged edition). New York, 1925.
    The encyclopedic character of this book is well known.

DUNNING, WILLIAM A. *Reconstruction, Political and Economic* ("American Nation Series"). New York, 1907.
    Professor Dunning was the pioneer scholar in Reconstruction studies.

FICKLEN, JOHN R. *Reconstruction in Louisiana.* Baltimore, 1910.

GARNER, JAMES W. *Reconstruction in Mississippi.* New York, 1901.

HERBERT, HILLARY A. (ed.). *Why the Solid South.* Baltimore, 1890.

HOSMER, JAMES K. *Outcome of the Civil War* ("American Nation Series"). New York, 1907.

———. *The Appeal to Arms* ("American Nation Series"). New York, 1907.

MOORE, ALBERT B. *Conscription and Conflict within the Confederacy.* New York, 1924.
    Scholarly and suggestive.

MUZZEY, DAVID S. *The United States of America.* 2 vols. New York, 1922.
    Necessarily general and sketchy, but written in the new spirit.

OBERHOLTZER, ELLIS R. *A History of the United States since the Civil War.* 3 vols. New York, 1917.
    Mr. Oberholtzer as a historian needs no comment.

OWSLEY, FRANK L. *State Rights in the Confederacy.* Chicago, 1925.
>A real contribution to southern history. Most suggestive and useful.

REYNOLDS, JOHN S. *Reconstruction in South Carolina.* Columbia, 1905.

RHODES, JAMES F. *History of the United States from the Compromise of 1850 to the Restoration of Home Rule at the South.* 7 vols. New York, 1893–1906.
>It would be superfluous to comment on James Ford Rhodes as a historian.

SCHWAB, JOHN C. *The Confederate States of America.* New York, 1901.
>Very useful for the civil history of the Confederacy.

Studies in Southern History and Politics. Inscribed to W. A. Dunning, by his former pupils, with Preface by James W. Garner. New York, 1914.
>Containing some valuable studies.

MISCELLANEOUS COMPILATIONS

Appleton's Annual Cyclopedia, 1865.

CANDLER, ALLEN D. (ed.). *Confederate Records of the State of Georgia.* 2 vols. Atlanta, 1909.

FLEMING, WALTER L. *Documentary History of Reconstruction.* 2 vols. Cleveland, 1906.
>Most valuable for the period.

FLEMING, WALTER L. (ed.). *Documents Relating to Reconstruction.* Morgantown, West Virginia, 1904.

Memorial Addresses on the Life and Character of Benjamin Harvey Hill. Delivered in the Senate and House of Representatives of the Forty-seventh Congress, Second Session, January 25, 1883. Washington, Government Printing Office, 1883.

RICHARDSON, JAMES D. *Messages and Papers of the Confederacy.* 2 vols. Nashville, 1906.

———. *Messages and Papers of the Presidents.* New York, 1908.

Southern Historical Society Papers, Vols. XIV and XIX.

INDEX

Akin, Warren, American candidate against Brown (1859), 34; defeated, 35; supports Bell (1860), 37

Alabama, secedes, 49

Amendments; *see* War Amendments

American party, platform (1856), 12, 13; state contest in Georgia (1857), 23, 24; nominates Hill for governor, 23; platform (1857), 23; overwhelmed in 1857, 31; party practically dissolved in 1859, 34; attempts at forming new opposition party, 34, 35; supports Bell and Everett (1860), 36, 37; *see* Know-Nothing party

Amnesty, H.R. No. 214, 267; debate, 268–77

Andersonville "atrocities," literature on, 267 n.; Blaine's charges, 268; Hill's refutal, 272–76

Augusta (Georgia), center Radical clique, 182

Augusta Chronicle and Sentinel, deprecates Hill-Stephens controversy, 105 n.; prints Hill's "Notes on the Situation," 148; Hill's protest to, 236; scurrilous attack on Hill, 245; praises Hill, 259, 260

Augusta Constitutionalist, attacks Hill, 209; friend of Stephens, 210 n.; praises Hill, 257; criticizes Hill's reply to Blaine, 280

Augusta National Republican, views on Cobb, Hill, Toombs, 190

Avery, I. W., on Hill's proscription, 239

Bacon, Augustus O., quoted, 10

Barnes, Surgeon General, quoted by Hill, 274, 275

Barton, Robert M., letter to Hill, 83

Bartow, Francis S., supports Breckenridge (1860), 37; opposes amicable conventions with North, 52, 53; early death, 53 n., in Montgomery Congress, 55

Bell, John, platform (1860), 35, 38

Benning, Henry L., supports Breckenridge (1860), 37

Black Codes, opposed in Georgia, 123–26; in Mississippi, 125 n., 126 n.

Blaine, James G., opposes amnesty for Davis, 266, 267, 268; Hill's reply to, 268–77

Blair, Frank P., vice-presidential candidate, 172, 173, 174; Brodhead letter, 175; defeated, 200; Liberal Republican, 247

Blair, Montgomery, visits Richmond, 102

Blodgett, Foster, and state road, 217; bids for state road, 221, 223; at Delano banquet, 230

Bourbons, southern, oppose new departure, 245; policies decried, 253; praise Hill's jury speech, 256; on Hill's party regularity, 284, 285; on Hayes-Tilden dispute, 288, 289

Bradley, Alperia A., expelled from Assembly, 179 n.

Bradley, Justice Joseph P., in Hayes-Tilden dispute, 292 n.

Breckenridge, John C., slavery views (1860), 36; carries Georgia (1860), 37

Brodhead, James A., letter to, 175

Brown, Gratz, Liberal Republican, 247

Brown, John, effect on southern extremists, 32, 33; resolution of Georgia legislature, 33

Brown, John Y., aids electoral settlement, 296, 297
Brown, Joseph E., rivalry with Hill, 22; nominated for governor, 24, 25; stumps state against Hill, 26–29; debate at Franklin, 28, 29; at Lexington, 29–30; defeats Hill, 31; defeats Akin, 35; vigorous message to General Assembly, 41; letter of December 7 urges immediate secession, 46; orders Pulaski seized, 49; attacks conscription acts, 64–66; attacks Hill's position on acts, 75, 76; attacks Davis, 78; elected governor for fourth term, 83, 84; warfare on Davis administration, 87–92; views on peace, 94; Johnston controversy, 101; connection with Hampton Roads Conference, 102; last message to Legislature, 107; arrested, 115; relations to Johnson, 116; on 14th Amendment, 137; views on freedmen, 124–25; counsels submission, 142, 151, 152; obloquy and criticism, 152, 153; reviews Hill's "Notes," 154–55; is questioned by Hill, 154; guides Georgia Convention, 163, 164, 165; leads fight for ratification Radical constitution, 165, 166, 167, 168, 169; in Republican Convention, 174; on Negro eligibility, 188; position on Reconstruction compared with Hill's, 214, 215; and state road lease, 218–24; appointed Chief Justice, 220 n.; at Delano banquet, 230; on Hayes-Tilden dispute, 287, 288, 290, 296
Brown Company, awarded state road lease, 218, 223; organization of and personnel, 219, 220, 221; see State road
Buchanan, James, fears Know Nothings (1856), 14; indorsed by Georgia Assembly, 33
Bullock, Rufus B., elected governor, 170; inaugurated, 173; influential in Augusta, 182; on Negro expulsion, 189; on Camilla riot, 190; demands congressional interference, 201 and n., and third reconstruction, 202–4; in "prolongation scheme," 203, 232, 233; exploitation state road, 216; awards lease, 222, 223; gives Delano banquet, 230, 233; defeated by Hill, 234, 235; flees the state, 237, 238
"Bush arbor meeting," 173–74, 175–81
Butler, Benjamin F., aids Bullock, 203; defeated, 235

Cabaniss, E. G., attacked by Brown, 168
Cameron, Simon, in state road lease, 220, 221; press comments on relations to Hill, 236
Camilla riot, the, 188; charged to Conservatives, 190; Hill's views, 192
Campbell, John A., nominated assistant secretary of war, 81
Candler, Milton A., moves Negro expulsion, 188
Carpet-baggers, in Georgia Convention, 164
Centennial bill, Hill's vote, 283
Central Railroad and Banking Company, and state road lease, 222
Chappell, Absalom H., on Conservative party Committee, 162 n.
Civil Rights bill (1866), passed over veto, 128, 130; accepted by south, 196
Civil Rights bill (1874), agitates south, 258, 259
Clay, Cassius M., in debate on Supreme Court, 81
Cobb, Howell, Compromise views, 2; elected governor, 3; in Buchanan-Fillmore canvass, 14; aids Brown against Hill, 26, 27; supports Breckenridge (1860), 37; urges secession, 48; in Montgomery

INDEX

Congress, 55; elected President of Congress, 56; jibe at 13th Amendment, 119-20; inactive, 169; speaks at Atlanta, 176; abused by Radicals, 186; at the north, 191

Cobb, Thomas R. R., urges secession, 42; opposes amicable conventions with North, 52, 53; early sacrifice to secession, 53 n.; in Montgomery Congress, 55, 57

Cole, Col. E. W., on state road lease, 224 n., 226

Colfax, Schuyler, vice-presidential candidate, 174

Colquitt, Alfred H., supports Breckenridge (1860), 37

Colquitt, Walter, supports Breckenridge (1860), 37

Confederacy, organization, 55-58; inauguration Davis, 59; conflict within over state rights, 61, 62; resistance to conscription, 62-76; opposition to suspension writ of habeas corpus, 76-79; fight to establish a supreme court, 79-82; causes of friction within, enumerated, 85 n.; low morale, 87; weakened by peace movement, 95, 96, 97; Davis-Johnston controversy, 101 and n.; Hampton Roads Conference, 102-5; defeatism in Georgia, 106-12

Connecticut, compared to Georgia, 243

Conscription, adopted, 62, 63, 87; produces bitter controversy, 62-76; Brown's views on, 65, 66, 76; defended by Hill, 67-74

Conservative party, organized, 161, 162; struggle against Radicals, 165-71; the Seymour campaign, 172, 173, 175, 176, 181, 182; expulsion Negroes, 188, 189; defeat Radicals in Georgia, 234-35, 237, 238; see also Democratic party, Georgia, Elections

"Constitutional Union" party, organized in Georgia, 2, 3; disbanded, 4, 5; renewed in Georgia and nation, 35, 36, 37; nominates Bell and Everett, 36; efforts to revive, 131-35

Cooper, Mark A., on state road lease, 226

"Co-operationists," efforts to delay secession, 49-52

Cox, Albert H., considered "incendiary" by Pope, 159

Cox, Samuel S., replies to Blaine, 269

Crawford, Martin J., in Montgomery Congress, 55

Davis, David, Justice, in Hayes-Tilden dispute, 292 n., 294

Davis Hall Speech, of Hill, 143-48

Davis, Jefferson, inaugurated President, 59; praises Hill, 60; favors conscription policy, 62; attacked by Brown, 64, 65; Hill's defense of, 68, 69; is attacked for suspending writ of habeas corpus, 76-79; defeated within own lines, 90; visit to Georgia 98; hostile criticism of Macon speech, 98 and n.; Johnston controversy, 101 and n.; Hampton Roads Conference, 102-5; attacked by Blaine, 267, 268, 269; defended by Hill, 271-76

Defeatism, in Confederacy, 86; opposed by Hill, 92, 96; Brown's contribution (1865), 103; strong in Georgia (1865), 107-12

Delano, John S., in state road lease, 221; extended banquet by Bullock, 230; friendly relations with Hill, 233, 234, 235; assists Hill to defeat Radicals, 235; press comments on relations to Hill, 236

Democratic party (Georgia), divided (1851), 2, 3; reunited, 5; Augusta deadlock (1857), 24, 25; nomination Brown for governor, 25; Brown elected, 31; reorganization as Conservative party, 161, 162;

split over New Departure, 246–50; see also Conservative party, Georgia, Elections

Democratic party (national), presidential contest (1856), 14 ff.; position on Reconstruction acts (1872), 152, 161; Seymour campaign, 172, 173, 174; defeated by Grant, 200; Hill anticipates change of 1872, 232, 233; adopts "new departure," 246, 248, 250; course in Hayes-Tilden dispute, 286, 287, 288, 293, 294, 295, 296; see also Conservative party, Elections

Disfranchisement, in Johnson's Reconstruction plan (1865), 116, 117; in 14th Amendment, 136, 137; in "Military" bills, 138–39 and n.

Douglas, Stephen A., part in Kansas-Nebraska Act, 7, 8; slavery views (1860), 36, 38

Edmunds, George F., opposes "prolongation," 203 n.

Elections (Georgia), Cobb-McDonald, 3; Jenkins-Johnson, 5; Hill-Warner, 9, 10; Hill-Brown, 34; Brown's second election, 35; Brown's fourth election, 84; Toombs defeated for Senate (1863) by H. V. Johnson, 84, 85; for constitutional convention (1865), 116, 117; of Jenkins, 119; of Stephens and H. V. Johnson to Senate, 121; in Reconstruction program, 162, 165, 170, 171; Seymour carries state, 187, 200; Smith elected, 238; Greeley carries state, 250–51; Gordon's election to Senate, 255; Hill's election to Congress, 263; Hill's election to Senate, 297–99

Elections (national), Buchanan-Fillmore (1856), 21; presidential election of 1860, 36–40; congressional elections (1866), 130–35; Grant's election, 200; re-election, 250; Hayes-Tilden disputed election, 285–97

Electoral Commission, created, 291, 292; Hill's argument for, 292, 293; shows partisan spirit, 293, 294; see also Hayes-Tilden dispute

Elmira prison, the mortality at, 274

Erskine, Judge John Hill, argues before, 256

Estes, Col. J. B., 9th District congressional candidate, 262, 263,

Evans, Miss Augusta, letter from Hill, 107 and n.

Exemption laws, adopted 63, 64

Fifteenth Amendment, action of Georgia Assembly, 202, 203; Hill's interpretation, 254

Fillmore, Millard, presidential candidate, 12 ff.

Finley, J. B., candidate for Congress, 263

Florida, secedes, 49; in Hayes-Tilden dispute, 285, 286, 287, 294

Floyd, John B., resigns from Buchanan's cabinet, 48

Foster, Charles, aids electoral settlement, 296, 297

Fourteenth Amendment, passed, 128–29, 130; refusal of southern states to ratify, 135–36; reasons therefor, 136–37, 196; Hill's interpretation, 254

Freedmen, legislation on by Georgia Assembly, 123–26; views of Jenkins, 123–24, of A. H. Stephens and Brown, 124–25; of Hill, 208; see also Negroes

Freedmen's Bureau, bill of Trumbull, 127; vetoed, 128; new bill passed, 129, 130; accepted by South, 196

Furlow, Timothy, candidate for governor (1863), 84

Gainesville Convention (9th District) failure to nominate, 262, 263

Gardner, James, on Hill, 256 n.

INDEX 323

Garfield, James A., on refusal of south to ratify 14th Amendment, 135, 136; in Amnesty debate, 277, 278; in Hayes-Tilden dispute, 291

Gaskill, Varney H., in campaign of 1860, 40

Georgia, reaction to Compromise Measures, 1–3; political realignments (1851–54), 4–6; effect of Kansas-Nebraska Act on state politics, 6–8; Fillmore-Buchanan canvass, 13–21; Brown-Hill gubernatorial race, 22–31; effect of John Brown raid on, 32, 33; presidential campaign of 1860, 34–60; secession agitation, 40–49; constitutional convention at Milledgeville 49–53; secedes, 52; delegation to Montgomery, 55–57; Assembly embarrassed over conscription, 65–67; opposition to suspension writ of habeas corpus, 78, 79; gubernatorial contest (1863), 83–84; senatorial contest (1863), 84, 85; Assembly adopt Stephens' resolutions, 88, 93; defeatism, 105–12; reconstructed under Johnson plan, 115–21; ratification 13th Amendment, 119; legislation regarding freedmen, 123–26; accepts reconstruction in good faith, 125, 126; Reconstruction acts unnecessary in, 140; effect of "military bills" on, 142; fight against Acts, 142–50; organization Conservative party, 161, 162; reconstruction applied, 162–71; "omnibus bill," 172, meeting "reconstructed" assembly, 173; Bush arbor meeting, 173, 174, 176–81; goes for Seymour, 187, 200; remanded to military rule, 202; prolongation scheme, 203, 204, 232, 233; state road lease, 216–29; escape from Radicals 237–38

Georgia Platform, adopted, 1; ends disunion talk, 2, 3

Georgia Railroad, and state road lease, 219, 220; debate of directors at Augusta, 225–27; value of lease to, 226–27

Gordon, John B., on 14th Amendment, 137; defeated candidate for governor, 170; at the North, 191; senatorial candidate, 251, 252; elected, 255; aids electoral settlement, 296, 297

Grady, Henry W, quoted on Hill's "Notes," 148; quotes Hill on Delano banquet, 231

Grant, Ulysses S., letter to, from Pope, 158; reprimands Pope, 159; state university reopened, 160; presidential candidate, 174; defeats Seymour, 200; deserts Radicals on Georgia, 235; low political morality of administration, 246; and Kellogg government in Louisiana, 259; opposed exchange of prisoners, 276; in Hayes-Tilden dispute, 290

Greeley, Horace, presidential nominee, 246; praised by Hill, 249; defeated, 250; quoted by Hill, 254

Greeleyism, decried in South, 285

Guerry, Theodore, on Conservative party committee, 162 n.

Habeas corpus, writ of, suspension in Confederacy, 76, 87; arouses bitter opposition, 76–79, 87–92

Hampton Roads Conference, 102–5; terms reviewed, 109–10

Harris, A. L., on state road lease, 228 n.

Hart, John R., interview with Hill, 214

Hayes, Rutherford B., electoral vote, 285; promises to South, 296, 297; see Hayes-Tilden dispute

Hayes-Tilden dispute, electoral vote, 285; problem, 286–91; solution, 291–97; see also Hayes, Tilden

Hendricks, Thomas A., embarrassed Democrat, 250

Hill, Benjamin H., enters political life, 1; compromise views, 3, 301; in General Assembly, 3, 4; against slave trade, 4; joins "Know Nothing" party, 6, 8, 302; views on Kansas-Nebraska Act, 7, 302; opposes Warner for Congress, 9, 10; party activity, 10, 11, elector on Fillmore ticket, 13, 301; active in campaign, 14, 15; debate with Stephens, 15-18, 302; Stephens challenge to duel and reply, 18, 19; debate with Toombs, 15, 19, 20, 302; elected trustee, University of Georgia, 21; rivalry with Joe Brown, 22; nominated for governor 22, 23; views on Kansas, 23, 24; gubernatorial canvass against Brown, 26-30, 302; debate at Franklin, 28-29; at Lexington, 29-30; advocates sale state road, 30; defeated by Brown, 31; enters state senate, 32; moderates Georgia's course following John Brown raid, 32-34, 302; attempts new "opposition" party to Democrats, 34, 35; campaigns for Bell (1860), 37-39, 302; proposes fusion ticket, 39, 302; opposes secession in General Assembly (1860), pleads against secession before Georgia legislature, 43-46; fights secession in Convention, 49-52, 302; advocates amicable conventions with North, 52, 53; *not* responsible for secession, 53; his grief, 54; in Montgomery Congress, 55-57; elected Confederate States Senator, 58, 59; committee assignments in Senate, 59, 60; champions Davis administration, 62 ff., 303; defends Conscription acts, 67-74; is criticized for inconsistency, 74, 75; strives to establish a supreme court, 79-82; not slavish to Davis administration, 82; services acknowledged, 83; mentioned as opponent for governor against Brown, 84; uses influence to defeat Toombs for Confederate States Senate, 84, 85 n.; opposition to defeatism, 86; defends Davis on suspension writ of habeas corpus, 90-92; flatters Stephens, 195; opposes peace movement, 92-96; appealed to by Seddon, 97; accompanies Davis to Macon, 98; appeals to stop Sherman, 99, 100; hostile criticism of, 100; involved in Davis-Johnston controversy, 101 and n.; military adviser, 102; connection with Hampton Roads Conference, 102-5; controversy with Stephens over, 104, 105; visit to Georgia 105-6; intimacy with Davis revealed, 106; fights "defeatism" and Brown, 107-12; final plea at LaGrange for resistance, 108-12, 303; arrested after surrender, 112; political inactivity, 113-15, 303; urged for United States Senate and reply, 121, 133; forecasts course of Radicals, 122, 123; favors Philadelphia Convention, 132; desires new national party, 132-35; views on treatment of old Whigs, 134-35; assumes leadership in opposing Reconstruction acts, 142-43, 303; Davis Hall speech, 143-48; arguments against Acts, 144-47; praise of speech, 147, 148; wrote "Notes on the Situation," 148-49, 303; praise of "Notes," 150; controversy with Brown, 154, 155; with B. F. Yancey, 155-56; intercession with Johnson and Grant, 159; advice from the North, 160; organizes Conservative party in Georgia, 161, 162; leads fight against Radical constitution, 165, 166, 167, 168, 169, 170; attacked by Radicals, 169; at Democratic Convention, 175; "Bush arbor" speech, 176-81; and Toombs, 181; campaigning for Seymour, 181, 182, 183, 184, 185; strictures against, 186, 187; praise of, 187; at the North in the Seymour

INDEX

campaign, 190–99; letters to New York press, 192–95; New York speech, 195–98; press opinions, 198–200; period of inactivity, 204, 205; address of December 8, 1870, 204–8, 304; abused by Conservative press, 209, 210, 212, 213, 214; by Linton Stephens, 210, 211; and reply to Stephens, 211, 212; to other critics, 213–15; and state road lease, 216, 217, 219, 220, 221, 222, 224; champions lease at Augusta, 225–27; attends Delano banquet, 230, 234; reasons, 231–35, 304, 305; discussed for place in Grant's cabinet, 235, 236; advice to Georgia Assembly (1870), 236, 237; proscribed, 239, 305, 306; speech before University Alumni Society, 239–44; unfavorable comment, 243, 244; advocates "New Departure," 245–50, 306; senatorial candidate, 251, 252; speech before Assembly, 252–55; defeated, 255; offered chief-justiceship, 255; regains favor, 257, 258, 306; on Civil Rights bill (1874), 258–59; in campaign 1874, 259; candidate for Congress, 260, 261; defeated for nomination, 261, 262, 263; but elected, 263, 306; Atlanta address, 263, 264; press comment on election, 265, 266; early prestige in House, 266; reply to Blaine, 268–77, 306; press comment on, 279, 280, 281, 282, 306; other activity in Congress, 282; vote on Centennial bill, 283 n.; other congressional votes, 283 n.; party regularity, 284; in Hayes-Tilden dispute, 285, 288, 289, 290, 291, 292, 293, 294, 295, 296; argument for electoral commission, 292–94, 307; for acceptance decision, 294–96; elected United States Senator, 297–99; death, 300; personal qualities and estimate, 307–9

Hill, Joshua, Union candidate for governor (1863), 84; Sherman's peace messenger, 95 n.; senatorial term expires, 251

Hill, William P., mentioned for chief-justiceship, 82 n.

Hilliard, Henry W., in Fillmore-Buchanan campaign, 14, 15; praises Hill, 15

Holt, Joseph, appointed secretary of war, 48

Home rule, demanded at south, 291; secured, 296, 297

Homestead law, incorporated in Georgia constitution, 165

Hood, John B., in Georgia, 102

Hosmer, James K., on prison atrocities, 278

Irwin, David, nominated for governor, 170 n.

Iverson, Alfred, candidate for Confederate States Senate, 58, 59

Jackson, Henry R., supports Breckenridge (1860), 37

Jackson, James, candidate for Confederate States Senate, 58, 59

Jenkins, Charles J., defeated for governor, 5; in Georgia Constitutional Convention (1865), 117; elected governor, 119; inaugurated, 120; removed from office, 179 n.

Johnson, Andrew, fiery utterances, 113; reconstruction plan approved by Hill, 114, 115; relations to Brown, 116; approves Georgia reconstruction, 117; insists on repudiation of war debts, 118; opposes election of Stephens, 120; urges James Johnson, 121; Radical opposition to, 122, 126–31, 135, 137, 138; views on Radical bills, 128–29; supported by Philadelphia Convention, 131; defeated in congressional elections, 135; vetoes Reconstruction acts, 137, 138

Johnson, Hershel V., elected governor, 5; reply to Stephens' challenge, 19 n.; supports Douglas (1860), 37; opposes secession, 50, 51; elected to Confederate States Senate, 84, 85; in Georgia Constitutional Convention (1865), 117; elected Senator, 121; inactive, 169

Johnson, James, appointed provisional governor, 116; urged as senator, 121

Johnston, Joseph E., removal controversy, 101 and n.; surrender, 155

Jones, Dr., Andersonville surgeon's report, 271

Jurors, qualifications in federal courts, Hill's argument, 256

Kansas, effects on Georgia politics (1857), 23, 24, 25, 28, 29, 30

Kansas-Nebraska Act, splits Georgia Whigs, 5, 6; precipitates sectional controversy, 7, 8; in Hill-Toombs debate (1856), 20

Kelley, William D., replies to Blaine, 269

Kenan, Augustus H., in Montgomery Congress, 55, 56; suggests Hill for governor (1863), 84

Kentucky, deprived of representation, 146 n.

Kimball, H. I., in Brown Company, 219 and n., quoted before state road lease committee, 228; at Delano banquet, 230

King, John P., nominated for Confederate States Senate, 59; and state road lease, 219, 220, 223 n., 226; champions lease at Augusta, 225-27; re-elected, 227

King, William, Sherman's messenger, 95 n.

Know Nothing party, opposes Georgia Democracy, 6; character of party, 8, 9; *see* American party

Lease Act. See state road

Lewis, John W., criticized by Hill, 34 n.; appointed Confederate States Senator, 59 n.

Liberal Republicans, in "new departure," 246; praised by Hill, 247, 248; and Cincinnati Convention (1876), 285

Lincoln, Abraham, slavery views (1860), 36, 38; elected, 40; Hampton Roads Conference, 102, 105; terms offered at Hampton Roads, 109-10, 111

Lipscomb, Chancellor, protests closing University, 159

Longstreet, James B., urges acceptance Reconstruction acts, 156

Louisiana, course of Reconstruction, 253; Hill on Kellogg government, 259; in Hayes-Tilden dispute, 285, 286, 287

Loyal Leaguers, charges denied, 184

McDonald, C. J., governor, Southern Rights candidate (1851), 3; supports Breckenridge (1860), 37

McGregor, editor, accuses Hill of treachery, 212-14

McMillan, Garnett, defeats Hill for congressional nomination, 261

Macon & Western Railroad, and state road lease, 220

Mallory, Stephen D., arrested at Hill's home, 112

Massachusetts, compared to Georgia, 243

Matthews, Stanley, aids electoral settlement, 297

Meade, George G., removes Jenkins, 179 n.

Military bills, the, enacted, 137; summarized, 138-39; examined, 140-41; Rhodes on unconstitutionality of, 157; *see also* Reconstruction

INDEX

Militia, the, in Conscription debates, 73
Milligan Case, the, cited, 157
Mississippi, secedes, 49; Republican party there, 253
Missouri, lost to Grant's administration, 246
Morton, Oliver P., defeated as regards Georgia, 235

National Union Convention, at Philadelphia, 131, 135
Negroes, "eligibility" question in Georgia, 166, 167; social equality of, 167, 168; appealed to by Hill, 183, 184, 185; expulsion from Assembly, 188, 189 and n.; reseated by Terry's purge, 202; and Civil Rights bill (1874), 258; *see also* Freedmen
"New departure," the, appearance, 244; advocated by Hill, 245; explained, 246; the fight in Georgia, 246-50
New York Tribune, accused by Hill, 193
Nisbit, Eugenius A., introduces secession ordinance, 51, 52; in Montgomery Congress, 55; attacked by Brown, 168
North Carolina, peace movement in, 92
Norwood, Thomas M., senatorial candidate, 297, 289, 299
"Notes on the Situation," argument, 148, 149; praise of, 148, 150; reviewed by Brown, 154, 155

Omnibus bill, admitting Georgia, 172; attacked by Hill, 177-78

Pendleton, George F., embarrassed Democrat, 250
Phelan, Senator, in debate over Supreme Court, 81
Pierce, Franklin, inaugurates "business man's peace," 5, 6

Pope, General John, forbids Hill to speak, 144; letter to Grant about Hill, 158; closes state university, 158, 159; removal causes joy, 160; orders elections, 162
Prentice, George, quoted on Hill, 147-48
Price, W. P., 9th Congressional District candidate, 263
Prolongation scheme, advocated by Bullock, 203, 232, 233; defeated, 234, 235
Pulaski, Fort, seized, 49

Radicals, oppose Johnson plan in Congress, 122, 126-31, 135, 137, 138; pass Civil Rights bill over veto, 128, 130; pass Freedman's Bureau bill, 129, 130; pass 14th Amendment, 128-29, 130; victorious in congressional elections (1866), 135; enactment Reconstruction acts, 137-38; attacked by Hill, 146, 147, 149; Rhodes opinion of, 157; fight for reconstruction measures in Georgia, 162, 163, 164, 165, 166, 167, 168, 169; victory, 170-71; the Seymour campaign, 172, 173; Hill's attack on, 178, 179, 180, 184, 185; abuse of Hill, 185, 186; force third reconstruction on Georgia, 201-4; defeated in Georgia, 234, 235, 237, 238; "bayonet" platform (1872), 248; slander of south, 269; attempts to goad Hill, 284; *see also* Republican party, Elections, Reconstruction
Randall, Samuel J., elected speaker, 287; aids electoral settlement, 296
Reconstruction, Johnson's plan approved, 114, 115; application to Georgia, 115-21; Radicals oppose Johnson's plan, 122, 126-31, 135, 137, 138; enactment congressional reconstruction, 137-38; acts summarized, 138-40; acts examined, 140-41; fight against acts in

Georgia, 142-50; application in Georgia, 162-71; effects of, 197; Hill advises acceptance of, 204-8, 234, 236, 237; end presaged, 291; realized, 297; *see also* Georgia, Radicals

Reed, John C., on Hill-Stephens and Hill-Toombs debates (1856), 19-21

Reese, Judge Augustus, nominated for governor, 170 n.

"Relief" law, question in Georgia Convention, 164, 165; harsh criticism of, 168

Republican party, Chicago Convention, 174; defeats Seymour, 200; disaffection of Liberals, 245, 246, 247; Hill's plea to for amity, 277; course in Hayes-Tilden dispute, 286, 287, 288, 295; *see also* Radicals, Reconstruction, Elections

Rhodes, James F., on Reconstruction acts, 141, 157; on Negro expulsion in Georgia, 189

Ruger, General Thomas H., appointed governor, 179 n.

Scalawags, in Georgia Convention, 163

Schade, counsel for Wirz, 273 and n.

Schurz, Carl, dissatisfied with reconstruction, 126 and n.; opposes "prolongation," 203 n.; Liberal Republican, 247

Scott, Dunlap, introduces state road lease bill, 217

Scott, Thomas A., in state road lease, 220, 221

Seago-Blodgett Company, bid for state road lease, 221, 223, 224

Secession, propaganda following John Brown raid, 32, 33; agitation in Georgia General Assembly (1860), 40; Brown's encouragement, 41, 42; acts of Georgia Assembly, 46; memorials pro and con, 47, 48; action of Howell Cobb and Toombs, 48; South Carolina, Mississippi, Florida, Alabama secede, 49; fight in the Georgia Convention, 49-52; ordinance passed, 51, 52; repealed, 118

Seddon, James A., indorses Hill's appeal, 100

Semmes, Senator, opposes Supreme Court, 80

Seward, William H., at Hampton Roads Conference, 102, 105

Seymour, Horatio, presidential candidate, 172, 173, 174; wins Georgia, 187, 200; defeated, 200; embarrassed Democrat, 250

Sherman, William T., peace overtures in Georgia, 95, 97, 99; terms given Johnston, 155

Slavery, bill to prohibit slave trade in Georgia, 4; abolished by Georgia Convention, 118; disastrous effects of on South, 240-42; *see also* Negroes

Small, Sam, on state road lease, 223 n., 224 n.; prepares data for Hill's reply to Blaine, 270

Smith, James M., elected governor, 238; offers Hill chief-justiceship, 255; senatorial candidate, 298, 299

South, the, accepting results of war, 140, 141 and n., 196; Hill on deficiencies, resources, and problems, 239-44, 255; in Congress to stay (1876), 277; demands in Hayes-Tilden dispute, 291, 293; *see* Confederacy, Georgia, Reconstruction

South Carolina, secedes, 49; course of Reconstruction, 253; in Hayes-Tilden dispute, 285, 286, 287

"Southern Rights" party, opposes Compromise Measures, 3

Southwestern Railroad Company, and state road lease, 222

Stanberry, Henry, interpretation of Reconstruction acts, 139 n.

INDEX 329

Stanton, Edwin M., opposed exchange of prisoners, 276

State road (Georgia), in gubernatorial campaign (1857), 30; in senatorial debate (1859–60), 34 n.; conditions of the road, 216, 217; lease act, 217; award of the lease, 218–24; debate on at Georgia R.R. Convention, 225–27; legislative investigation of, 227–30; Hill's letters on, 229

Stephens, Alexander H., member "Constitutional Union" party, 2; bolts Scott ticket, 5, 6; joins Democratic party, 6, 8; campaigns for Buchanan (1856), 14, 15–18; debate with Hill, 15–18; characterization of, 16; letter from brother Linton, 16; challenges Hill, 18, 19; aids Brown against Hill, 26; supports Douglas (1860), 37; opposes secession, 42, 47, 50; in Montgomery Congress, 55, 56; opposes conscription acts, 64; attacks Davis, 78; attacks suspension writ of habeas corpus, 87–91; views on peace, 94; connection with Hampton Roads Conference, 102–5; controversy with Hill over, 104–5; elected U.S. Senator, 120, 121; on 14th Amendment, 137 n.; in gloomy retirement (1867), 142; praises Hill's "Notes," 150; and state road lease, 218, 219, 224 and n.; called Southern Bourbon, 245; opposes "new departure," 245, 246, 249; senatorial candidate 251, 252; defeated, 255

Stephens, Linton, champions Buchanan (1856), 14; letter to Alexander Stephens, 16 n.; supports Douglas (1860), 37; opposes secession, 50; opposes conscription acts, 64, 66; attacks Davis, 78, 79; introduces resolutions condemning suspension of writ of habeas corpus, 87, 88; introduces "peace resolutions," 92, 93; attacks Hill and amendments, 210, 211; opposes state road lease, 225, 226; called southern Bourbon, 245; opposes "new departure," 245, 246

Stevens, Thaddeus, drives Radicals, 122; leads opposition to Johnson, 127; quoted by Hill, 145

Sumner, Charles, opposes Johnson plan, 127

Supreme Court, efforts to establish, 79–82; championed by Hill, 80; defeated, 82; *see* Confederacy

Swayze, Judge, tries Linton Stephens, 211

Terry, General Alfred, purges legislature, 202

Test Oath, explained, 120 n.

Thirteenth Amendment, ratified in Georgia, 119, 120

Thomas, Thomas W., fears Know Nothings (1856), 14; letter to A. H. Stephens on Kansas, 24 n.

Thompson, C. Mildred, on Reconstruction Acts, 140; on state road lease, 217–18

Thompson, Jacob, resigns from Buchanan's cabinet, 48

Tilden, Samuel J., electoral vote on, 285; approves moderate course, 290; *see* Hayes-Tilden dispute

Toombs, Robert, Compromise views, 2; member "Constitutional Union" party, 3; bolts Scott ticket, 5, 6; joins Democratic party, 6, 8; champions Buchanan, 14, 19; debate with Hill, 19, 20; aids Brown against Hill, 26, 27; supports Breckenridge (1860), 37; urges secession, 42, 48; in Montgomery Congress, 55, 56; candidate for Confederate States Senate, 58, 59; refuses election, 59; opposes conscription acts, 64; attacks Davis, 78; defeated for Senate, 84, 85; in exile (1867), 142; speaks at Atlanta, 176; and Hill, 181; abused by Radicals, 185, 186; on lease of state road, 216; in Georgia Railroad Convention, 225, 226; called southern Bourbon, 245; opposes "new departure," 245, 246, 247; reconciled to Hill, 257, 258

Trumbull, Lyman, introduces Freedmen's Bureau bill, 127; Civil Rights bill, 128; opposes "prolongation," 203 n.

Turner, H. M., contributor to *Tribune*, 192

Twenty-second Joint Rule, abrogated, 286 and n.

University of Georgia, Hill a trustee, 21; closed by Pope, 158–60; Hill's speech before Alumni Society, 239–44

Usurpations, as source war amendments, 207, 210–11

Vallandigham, Clement L., in "new departure," 247 and n.

Vance, Zebulon, at the North, 191

"Visiting statesmen," in Hayes-Tilden dispute, 286

Voorhees, Daniel W., embarrassed Democrat, 250

Wade, Benjamin F., leads opposition to Johnson, 127

Walker, Robert J., in Georgia gubernatorial canvass, 24, 25, 28, 29

War Amendments, Hill's views on, 206, 207; views of Georgia Conservative press, 209, 210; of Linton Stephens, 210, 211; Hill advises acceptance, 204–8; 234, 236, 237; *see also* Thirteenth Amendment, Fourteenth Amendment, Fifteenth Amendment

War debts, Georgia's repudiated, 118

Warner, Hiram, beats Hill for Congress, 9, 10; supports Douglas (1860), 37

Warren Clipper, accuses Hill of treachery, 212, 213

Western & Atlantic Railroad. *See* State road

Whigs, favor compromise measures, 2; party embarrassment, 4, 5; bolt Scott ticket, 5, 6; treatment after war, 134–35, 161

White, Andrew J., testimony on state road lease, 228, 229

Wigfall, Senator, opposes Hill and a Supreme Court, 81

Wilson, Henry, on Bullock's government, 207 n.

Wirz, Henry, and Andersonville, 267 n.; refusal to incriminate Davis, 272, 273

Wood, Fernando, in Hayes-Tilden dispute.

Wright, Ambrose, on 14th Amendment, 137 n.

Wright, Augustus R., supports Douglas (1860), 37; in Montgomery Congress, 55, 56; Sherman's peace messenger, 95 n.; on 14th Amendment, 137 n.; attacked by Brown, 168; on state road lease, 218

Yancey, B. F., attack on Hill's views, 155, 156

Yancey, William L., opposes Confederate Supreme Court, 79–82; conflict with Hill, 79–81

Printed in the USA
CPSIA information can be obtained
at www.ICGtesting.com
LVHW020845140624
783156LV00001B/124